Yaśodā's Songs to Her Playful Son, Kṛṣṇa

Periyāḻvār's 9th Century Tamil *Tirumoḻi*

Yaśodā's Songs to Her Playful Son, Kṛṣṇa

Periyāḻvār's 9th Century Tamil *Tirumoḻi*

Translations with Notes by **Lynn Ate**

South Asian Studies Association
Woodland Hills, California
www.sasia.org

Published by SASA Books
A Project of the South Asian Studies Association
Woodland Hills, California 91367
A public benefit, non-profit corporation, EID 26-1437834
www.sasia.org

Cover photo courtesy of Micah Hanson
www.micahimages.com

ISBN 978-0-9834472-1-4 (paperback)
LCCN: 2011944693

To my husband, Dave Ackley,
and
our daughters, Brianna and Raineka.

Contents

Preface		ix
Part I: Introduction		
Periyāḻvār and his Works		3
Periyāḻvār		5
Periyāḻvār's *Tiruppallāṇṭu*		9
Periyāḻvār's *Tirumoḻi*		12
Periyāḻvār's *Tirumoḻi* in Tamil literature		19
Periyāḻvār's Relationship to God		27
Baby Kṛṣṇa – Adorable and Accessible		28
A Mother's Unconditional Love		31
Salvation in the *Tirumoḻi*		35
Mythology in Periyāḻvār's Works		39
The Kṛṣṇa Myth		39
The Rāma Myth		48
Vaiṣṇava Epithets and Episodes		50
Nārāyaṇa's Incarnations		53
Part II: Translations		
Translation Conventions		59
Tiruppallāṇṭu		63
Periyāḻvār's *Tirumoḻi*		67
I.1	Kaṇṇaṉ's birth	67
I.2	Kaṇṇaṉ from head to toe	70
I.3	A lullaby	75
I.4	Calling the moon	78
I.5	The red-leaf dance	81
I.6	Hand clapping	85
I.7	Learning to walk	88
I.8	A mother's delight	92
I.9	Hugging mother's back	95
II.1	Making scary faces	98
II.2	Calling Kaṇṇaṉ to suckle	101
II.3	Piercing Kaṇṇaṉ's ears	105
II.4	Kaṇṇaṉ's bath	110

II.5	Combing Kaṇṇaṉ's hair	113
II.6	A staff for Kaṇṇaṉ	116
II.7	Adorning Kaṇṇaṉ with flowers	119
II.8	An amulet for Kaṇṇaṉ	122
II.9	The neighbors' complaints	125
II.10	The maids' complaints	129
III.1	Yaśodā's doubts	132
III.2	Yaśodā's regrets	136
III.3	Yaśodā's relief	139
III.4	The maids see Kaṇṇaṉ	142
III.5	Govardhana, a victory umbrella	146
III.6	Kaṇṇaṉ's flute	150
III.7	Her mother's worries	154
III.8	Her mother's questions	158
III.9	The *Untipaṟa* game	162
III.10	Hanumaṉ's proof	166
IV.1	Some hints	169
IV.2	Tirumāliruncōlai Mountain I	172
IV.3	Tirumāliruncōlai Mountain II	175
IV.4	The people of Tirukkōṭṭiyūr	179
IV.5	On the edge of death	183
IV.6	The mother of a "Nāraṇa"	187
IV.7	The protected city of Kaṇṭam	190
IV.8	His city of Śrīrangam	194
IV.9	The temple in Śrīrangam	197
IV.10	Sleeper in Śrīrangam	201
V.1	The Āḻvār's entreaty	204
V.2	The guarded harbor	207
V.3	Father of Tirumāliruncōlai	210
V.4	The Lord's home	213

Notes to the Introduction 217
Notes to the Translations 225
Appendix 1 - Concordance of Vaiṣṇava references 229
Appendix 2 - Concordance of Sanskrit Vaiṣṇava terms 235
Bibliography 241
Index 247

Preface

Periyāḻvār in his 9th c. CE Tamil *Tirumoḻi* fully developed for the first time the personality of the child-god, Kṛṣṇa, today one of the most popular deities throughout India. He provided innovative and detailed images of the Divine depicted with chubby little hands, new teeth awash in baby drool, and a captivating appearance, at the same time humanly adorable and meant to be religiously adored. The poet expressed his songs predominantly in the voice of Kṛṣṇa's mother, Yaśodā, portraying maternal love without question or reward as a model for unconditional devotion to god. This gave rise to a prolific genre of devotional literature in many Indian languages, both North and South, later identified as *vātsalya bhakti*, maternal love as devotion, and gave Periyāḻvār and the *Tirumoḻi* a significant place in the history of Indian literature and religion.

The primary goal of my work with this text was to create a close translation for a broad audience, transmitting the content, tone, voice and major poetic elements of the original. As a translator, I have been as careful as possible to communicate what the text says - no more and no less - which may be different from what the text means as interpreted by a particular reader, a later commentator, or a modern scholar. Therefore, the predominant focus of this project has been to provide a trustworthy and understandable English version of the *Tirumoḻi* for the enjoyment of readers interested in comparative literature or religion and as a possible tool for further study of the development of Vaiṣṇavism. I hope that South Asian scholars in several fields may glean interesting tidbits from the *Tirumoḻi,* pursuing a variety of lines of inquiry: Is it noteworthy that Periyāḻvār mentions *bhaktas* and *bhagavas* separately, but describes them worshipping side by side in Śrīrangam (*Tirumoḻi* IV.9.6)? Was the Gopi's Song of the *Bhāgavata Purāṇa* (X.35) - with its Tamil second-syllable rhyme scheme, *tirumoḻi*-like structure, and content derived directly from Periyāḻvār – originally a separate Sanskrit translation of *Tirumoḻi* III.6 inserted into the later purāṇic material? How can the *Tirumoḻi* help characterize the South Indian figure of Piṉṉai? Was Periyāḻvār influenced by any earlier text or was he uniquely innovative when he referenced child Kṛṣṇa eating dirt (*Tirumoḻi* II.3.8), as opposed to the deity's cosmic form on the serpent couch or banyan leaf consuming the seven worlds? My hope is that students and scholars of Asian literature and religion will find interesting questions and perhaps some answers in this translation.

Like the Tamil text, the language and rhythm of the translation are uncomplicated and straightforward, reflecting the folk songs and heartfelt religion from which the original was drawn. The charming descriptions of the child god Kṛṣṇa, his darling infant antics, obnoxious pranks as an older child, and charismatic impact on the village women as a young man are presented in colloquial English, reflecting the original, and are easily enjoyed by any audience. I was always mindful of expressing the poet's voice and of transmitting the tone as well as the content of the Tamil, with careful attention to the sound harmony characteristic of that poetic tradition. In my opinion, Periyāḻvār is fun to read, and I am optimistic that the translations communicate his light-hearted joy in life and devotion.

The introductory material is written for a general audience or undergraduate students of world literature or religion and provides the information known about the poet, descriptions of the text, and how he made use of several significant literary features, including 1st person speech. A section titled "Periyāḻvār's Relationship to God" describes major religious elements found in the text, his devotional approach, and his perception of salvation. While there is much of interest in Periyāḻvār's works, I have focused on Yaśodā songs to her divine son to highlight the poet's vision of a mother's unconditional love as religious devotion.

To help clarify these and other ideas, I have written header notes for each decade of verse to introduce its special features, pointing out unique aspects or interesting references in order to prepare the reader to enjoy the verses and to avoid interruptions by frequent endnotes. Also included where appropriate are comments on decision making when translating difficult phrases. I have also included a narrative of Vaiṣṇava mythology from the 9th century as found in the text and other poetry of the period to provide background for readers who are unfamiliar with Hinduism, as well as historical information for scholars who otherwise do not have access to Tamil texts.

I am greatly indebted to the works of P. B. Aṇṇankarācāriyar whose commentaries on many South Indian devotional texts provide invaluable insights, research on earlier commentaries, and grammatical guidance. I am grateful to Prof. George L. Hart, III for first providing me a copy of the *Tirumoḻi* many years ago and for assuring me that I would be able to translate it. Prof. G. Vijayavenugopalan, currently a Senior Research Fellow with the École Française d'Extrême-Orient, Pondicherry, provided interesting insights on the *Tirumoḻi* and was a patient teacher as I first read through this and other Tamil Vaiṣṇava works. Prof. Alexander M. Dubyanskiy, Tamil scholar at the Moscow State University, also provided extremely helpful suggestions on the translation. I am profoundly grateful to the South Asian Studies Association for its interest in this manuscript, and in particular to its president, William Vanderbok, for his patient guidance through the publication process. I regret if any inaccuracies are still found; they are entirely my own. And as a translator, I am also indebted beyond words to the many dedicated scholars who painstakingly produce the dictionaries which have provided the basic nourishment as well as unanticipated treats that have sustained me.

Lynn Ate
Washington State University Asia Program
November 2011

Part I: Introduction

Periyāḻvār and his works

Periyāḻvār's *Tirumoḻi* is one of the intensely moving religious texts of the South Indian poet-saints who sang of their devotion in Tamil from the 6th to 9th centuries CE.[1] Their songs were revered and collected into two large canonical anthologies: the Vaiṣṇava *Nālāyira Divyaprabandham, 'the Four Thousand Divine Works'* (hereafter *Prabandham* or *Divine Works*) and the Śaiva *Tirumuṟai, 'The Sacred Collection.'* Kamil Zvelebil, in his classic text on Tamil literature, *The Smile of Murugan*, characterized the devotional movement of South India as

> the triumph of emotion over intellect, of the concrete over the abstract, of the acceptance of life over its ascetic denial, of something near and homely against something alien and distant, and above all, the acceptance of positive love against cold morality or intellectually colored compassion.[2]

In general, the sacred texts produced at this time deemphasized the philosophy and ritual of the Vedas and rejected the austerity, atheism and impersonal quality of Jainism and Buddhism.

Traditional accounts indicate that the Vaiṣṇava verses, devoted to Viṣṇu, also called Nārāyaṇa, and his incarnations, including Kṛṣṇa and Rāma, were collected by the 10th c. CE philosopher Nāthamuni who arranged them as they are presently found in the *Prabandham*.[3] He carefully organized the verses in his collection into groups of approximately one thousand, paying a great deal of attention to the structure and function of each text. For instance, he grouped together all of the *antātis* to be recited - memorized through their internally linked verses with the last word in one verse being the first word in the next – and collected verses to be sung into a musical section which included Periyāḻvār's and three other *Tirumoḻis*. The practice of singing and chanting these Tamil works was established as part of many Vaiṣṇava religious services. The *Divine Works* were included in a regular course of study for Nāthamuni's disciples, combining both Tamil and Sanskrit religious traditions,[4] a significant step as "through the acceptance of non-Sanskritic religious literature … Brahmanic orthodoxy was claimed for this new kind of South Indian Vaiṣṇavism."[5] The process of legitimization was then taken up in the orthodox language of Sanskrit and eventually produced the *Bhāgavata Purāṇa* as the definitive statement on the acceptance of devotionalism as a proper form of religious expression.

Periyāḻvār and the eleven other Vaiṣṇava poets of the *Divine Works* were later called Āḻvārs, 'those who are immersed,' ostensibly because of the recurring references in their poems to drowning in the love of god, being sunk in a divine flood, or diving and bathing in a pool of ecstatic joy.[6] For example, Periyāḻvār describes a maiden's infatuation with Kṛṣṇa (*Kaṇṇaṉ* in Tamil) as "being pushed into a deep stream … where she remains immersed" (*Tirumoḻi* III.7.4). And like a flood, an overwhelming sense of joy pours cheerfully from Periyāḻvār's intimate depictions of Kṛṣṇa as a baby, a naughty boy and then a handsome youth, providing the devout listener with an earthly and personal experience of god. This type of devotion was known as *bhakti,* - the devotee being a *bhakta* – from the Sanskrit root *bhaj*, meaning 'share, feel or experience.'[7] As opposed to Vedic ritual, yogic control of the senses, or austere renunciation, *bhakti* denotes a direct experience of, and a loving human relationship with, a personal god.

The works in the *Prabandham* by Periyāḻvār, entitled *Tiruppallāṇṭu* and *Tirumoḻi,* validate Zvelebil's description of this devotional movement while presenting the pastoral myths of the god Kṛṣṇa in more detail and continuity than any other text of the period. As discussed further below, Periyāḻvār captured the sense of a close relationship with the deity by presenting most of his verses in the voice of an individual within the Kṛṣṇa myth, often Kṛṣṇa's mother. For her and others within the mythology, god is a part of everyday life, is directly accessible, and has taken a human and immediate form. But even more unique to Periyāḻvār, he depicted god as adorable, i.e. easily adored as a baby. Infants are loved instinctually and unconditionally without consideration for reward. By developing maternal love as an approach to the divine, Periyāḻvār laid the foundation for a prolific genre of later Hindu poetry in many Indian languages steeped in *vātsalya bhakti* 'maternal love as devotion to god'; however, his representation of Kṛṣṇa as the picture of child-like charm is unrivalled not only in Āḻvār literature, but in any Vaiṣṇava text in Tamil or Sanskrit previous to it. It is Periyāḻvār who first created and developed this popular personality of the Vaiṣṇava deity. His verses are also the prototype for a form of Tamil poetry called *piḷḷaittamiḻ* 'child Tamil,' a genre which produced praise of the childhood of Hindu, Muslim and Christian religious figures, rulers, political leaders and even movie stars.[8] It is these unique aspects of Periyāḻvār's verses that fuel the need to present the poet and his works to English-speaking readers and students of Indian literature.

Periyāḻvār

Little historical information is available on Periyāḻvār, but the author of the *Tirumoḻi* tells something of himself in his own verses. His given name was Viṭṭucittaṉ, from Sanskrit *Viṣṇucitta,* and he was a Brahmin; he first introduces himself in *Tirumoḻi* verse I.1.10 as wearing "the shining thread" of the upper castes. He says he was born in the Vēyar caste (*Tirumoḻi* V.4.11), which the Madras Tamil Lexicon also identifies as Brahmin.[9] The origin of this caste name is obscure; however, the root *vēy* 'decorate or crown with garlands' might suggest that his family traditionally dressed the temple image or made garlands for the deity, the latter being, in fact, Periyāḻvār's service in the temple. In the *Tiruppallāṇṭu*, he indicates that his family had continuously served the deity in some capacity for many generations, including the poet's "father, his father, his father's father and grandfather" (*Tiruppallāṇṭu* #6). He calls himself a "true servant" (*Tirumoḻi* IV.9.11) who has taken a vow of worship (*Tirumoḻi* IV.2.11). He also refers to himself throughout the *Tirumoḻi* as a *paṭṭar*, Sanskrit *bhaṭṭa*, which refers to any learned man, but more specifically a poet or bard. He often adds that he is the lord of the Bhaṭṭas in the town now called Śrīvilliputtūr, referenced in the verses as Putuvai, Villiputtūr, or Puttūr.

In *Tirumoḻi* IV.2.7, the poet mentions a contemporary Pāṇṭiyaṉ king in Madurai, Neṭumāṟaṉ. In-depth studies by several 20th century scholars have led to debate on the historical identity of this ruler[10] as either Jaṭila Parāntaka Neṭuncaṭaiyaṉ, ruling the Pāṇṭiyaṉ kingdom from 756 to 815 CE or Śrīmāṟa Śrīvallabha, who reigned after him until 862 CE.[11] Regardless, it is safe to place Periyāḻvār in approximately the first half of the 9th c. CE, a date which coincides with Friedhelm Hardy's chronology based on geographic distribution of temples mentioned in Āḻvār texts.[12]

Besides the information on Viṭṭucittaṉ which can be gleaned from the poetry itself, traditional hagiographies of the Āḻvārs offer fantastic stories and miraculous achievements which tell more about the Āḻvārs' place in cultural history than about the poets themselves. P. B. Aṇṇankarācāriyar, commentator on the Āḻvārs' *Divine Works*, provides one story from Periyāḻvār's life as written in the traditional histories, which is summarized here from the Tamil.[13]

> The Pāṇṭiyaṉ king ruling the Tamils during Periyāḻvār's life at one point called together an assembly of theologians to discuss the divine nature of God, a debate for which the most learned scholar would receive a sack of gold. Many scholars gathered from throughout the kingdom and elsewhere from various religious backgrounds. The god Nārāyaṇa came to Viṭṭucittaṉ in a dream and revealed to him the meaning of the Vedas, then directed Viṭṭucittaṉ to join the assembly of scholars in Madurai and establish Nārāyaṇa as the highest truth. Viṭṭucittaṉ pointed out to God that he did not have even a rudimentary knowledge of the Vedic texts. The Lord replied that it was not a problem for Viṭṭucittaṉ to concern himself with; it was the Lord's responsibility to assure that the truth was established. Full of wonder, Viṭṭucittaṉ awoke and started for Madurai. When he arrived, the Pāṇṭiyaṉ king and his court immediately perceived him as a person to be venerated and placed him in a position of honor, bowing respectfully to him. The other assembled attendees were insulted, wondering why someone without adequate education should be honored more highly than those who had studied the Vedas at length. The king's advisor responded that because Viṭṭucittaṉ, whose name in Sanskrit means 'Viṣṇu-minded,' maintained his thoughts on God, Viṭṭucittaṉ grasped the full meaning of the

Vedas naturally like a fully matured fruit. Then Viṭṭucittaṉ explained the entire body of religious knowledge, histories, laws, mythologies, and scriptural wisdom, expounding on all the tenets of various religions in an unbiased manner, and ultimately provided testimony of the supremacy of Nārāyaṇa. All of the scholars who had at first been envious of him dropped their jaws in awe and joined their hands in reverence to him. The king and his advisor stretched out in full prostration before Viṭṭucittaṉ, and the sack of gold also fell of its own accord at his feet. The assembly conferred upon Viṭṭucittaṉ the title "Lord of the Bhaṭṭas," and the king took him in procession through the town, riding high on an elephant. Nārāyaṇa also appeared in the crowd to see his devotee so celebrated. When Viṭṭucittaṉ saw him, he became overwhelmed with tenderness and love, as well as anxiety for the Lord's safety in the hubbub. Lost in a sense of personal intimacy, then and there he created the *Tiruppallāṇṭu*, the "Many Years" benediction, in a blessing of the Lord, singing it to the beat of the elephant bells.

The legends of the Āḻvārs' lives were written no earlier than the 12th c. CE, several hundred years after Periyāḻvār's death.[14] These traditional views of the Brahmin poet demonstrate a shift away from Vedic philosophy to personal religious devotion, showing Periyāḻvār's absolute faith elevating him above the Vedic scholars at the royal assembly. The Āḻvār's story points to god's grace, rather than Vedic scholarship, leading to Periyāḻvār's understanding of the nature of the divine. But Periyāḻvār himself says that he has "reaped the fruits of the Vedas" (*Tirumoḻi* II.8.10) and daily "reveres the Ṛg, Sāma and Yajur Vedas" (*Tirumoḻi* V.1.6). Hardy, in his in-depth study of the Āḻvārs published in *Viraha-bhakti,* points to evidence within the *Tirumoḻi* that demonstrates that Periyāḻvār had direct knowledge of the earlier Sanskrit Vaiṣṇava text, the *Harivamśa.*[15] Periyāḻvār's verses also demonstrate a strong continuity with classical Tamil literature with which he clearly was familiar. The attempt of the later Śrī Vaiṣṇava hagiographies to depict Viṭṭucittaṉ as a naïve gardener and a man of simple faith is just not convincing in the face of other facts which demonstrate he was a well-educated, literate scholar, deserving of the title Bhaṭṭa Pirāṉ, 'lord of the learned.'

A discussion of Periyāḻvār's life must include mention of the poetess Āṇṭāḷ, the only woman among the Āḻvārs. In her *Nācciyār Tirumoḻi* 'The Maiden's Tirumoḻi' she describes herself again and again as Kōtai of Viṭṭucittaṉ, king of Villiputuvai, Lord of the Bhaṭṭas.[16] She was Periyāḻvār's adopted daughter, as described in a continuation of the above story[17]:

> One day while weeding the holy *tulasī* bushes, Periyāḻvār found an infant girl abandoned in the garden. He took her as his daughter and named her Kōtai 'Garland.' She grew up with an intense devotional longing for God, and she perceived herself as his beloved. Secretly, she would take the garlands her father had prepared for the deity and wear them herself, then put them back carefully before her father adorned the deity. When he caught her in the act, he scolded her for defiling the deity's garlands; he did not take them to the temple that day. On the following day, he brought freshly strung garlands, untouched by his daughter. The deity appeared and ordered Periyāḻvār not to bring garlands that had not been worn by his daughter first, as only those had the greatest fragrance.

The legends indicate that Kōtai then became known as *cūṭikkoṭutta nācciyār* 'the girl who wore then gave,' and she poured her devotion into poetry, like her father. As she considered herself the bride of God, by the age of sixteen, it is said that she had her father take her in a marriage procession to the great Vaiṣṇava temple at Śrīrangam where she is said to have entered the sanctum and immediately become absorbed into the temple image.[18] Her *Nācciyār Tirumoḻi* and *Tiruppāvai* earned her the title Āṇṭāḷ 'she who rules' by which she is most well known, and her verses are included with Periyāḻvār's *Tirumoḻi* in the Śrī Vaiṣṇava canon.

According to Ma. Pe. Cīṉivācaṉ in his Tamil monograph, *Periyāḻvār*, the poet ultimately retired from his temple garden and retreated to the sanctuary of Tirumāliruncōlai, so frequently praised in his verses.[19] He died there at the age of 85. His popularity which has lasted into the present day in South Indian homes[20] seems to be based in its folk roots, and as Hardy notes of the *Tirumoḻi's* author, although he was Brahmin, "In language and idiom, Periyāḻvār comes closer to ordinary people than any other Āḻvār."[21] Perhaps it was in recognition of Viṭṭucittaṉ as a people's poet that he is called Periyāḻvār 'The Great Āḻvār' and that Nāthamuni, the 10th c. CE compiler of the Śrī Vaiṣṇava canon,[22] chose this poet's works to begin the collection of Āḻvār verses, *The Four Thousand Divine Works.*

Periyāḻvār's *Tiruppallāṇṭu*

Pallāṇtu pallāṇṭu pallāyirattāṇṭu palakōṭi nūṟāyiram
Mallāṇṭa tiṇṭōḷ maṇivaṇṇā uṉ cēvaṭi cevvi tirukkāppu

Many years of many years and many thousands of years,
many hundreds of thousands of millions,
Jewel-hued Lord whose strong shoulders threw the wrestlers,
may the beauty of your feet be protected.[23]

So begins the *Four Thousand Divine Works* with Periyāḻvār's *Tiruppallāṇṭu* 'Many Years' and according to the modern temple guide in Śrīvilliputtūr, no other song can be sung without it being sung first;[24] *Tiruppallāṇṭu* is the first song of the daily prayer cycle recited by devotees at home.[25] While only twelve verses long, it is an important text within the Tamil Śrī Vaiṣṇava canon and is variously considered either an introductory benediction to Periyāḻvār's major text, *Tirumoḻi*, or a separate text on its own.[26] To some devotees, it stands, like AUM, as the sacred invocation to the Tamil Vedas.[27]

In the verses of *Tiruppallāṇṭu*, the poet speaks in his own voice directly to the listener, promoting the faith that is his life and encouraging others to "join quickly without any delay" (#4). He points out that he and his family have been in devotional service to the temple for generations and describes the hereditary benefits he has gained from his position in the temple (#8). At a time when Buddhism, Jainism and several branches of Hinduism were practiced side by side, but not harmoniously,[28] he encourages the listeners to leave their previous traditions and join the family of devotees to the god Nārāyaṇa: "Chanting his one thousand names, leave behind your old clan and come sing with us, 'Many years, many thousands of years!'"(#5).

While the hagiographies describe *Tiruppallāṇṭu* as a heartfelt outpouring of devotion, the focus of the text suggests that Viṭṭucittaṉ was also interested in propounding the Vaiṣṇava faith in an atmosphere of philosophical rivalry. It was the competition with other religious scholars of all backgrounds at the royal Pāṇṭiyaṉ court that purportedly occasioned *Tiruppallāṇṭu,* that debate fitting Nilakantha Sastri's description of the times: "... worshippers of Śiva and Vishnu felt the call to stem the rising tide of heresy [of Buddhism and Jainism]...Challenges to public debate, competition in the performance of miracles, tests of the truth of doctrines by means of ordeal, became the order of the day."[29] Some Āḻvārs displayed blatant sectarian hostility, as in Maḻicaipirāṉ's *Nāṉmukaṉ Tiruvantāti* #6.[30]

> The Jains never knew; the Buddhists, they forgot.
> The Śiva bhakta's speech is low. – And those
> Who don't praise the names Māyaṉ, Mālavaṉ, Mādhava
> Are therefore outcastes forever.

Periyāḻvār also slipped into antagonism on occasion, as in *Tirumoḻi* IV.4 in which he wonders why Nārāyaṇa created people who do not worship him (IV.4.1). They are described as being "born only to cause great pain to the bellies of their mothers who bore them" (IV.4.2), and he says, "Remove the food from their mouths as they eat and simply shove in grass!" (IV.4.5). Predominantly, however, he favored affirmations of his own religious convictions, as in *Tiruppallāṇṭu,* rather than rants against rival religions. Through the *Tiruppallāṇṭu,* Periyāḻvār establishes his hereditary credentials in the field of religious debate and identifies the spiritual and material benefits of belonging to his sect.

Periyāḻvār particularly extols the efficacy of the specific Sanskrit mantra, *Namo Nārāyaṇa*, in bringing blessings; it is the best way "to spread afar" (#11) the name of the Vaiṣṇava deity. Vasudha Narayanan documented 13 references in the *Four Thousand Divine Works* to this important mantra of the Āḻvārs, with only eight direct quotes of *Namo Nārāyaṇa*.[31] Five of these occur in Periyāḻvār's verses, with three in *Tiruppallāṇṭu,* showing Periyāḻvār as a particular adherent to this form of devotion. The Śrī Vaiṣṇava sect, in its formative stages at the time of the Āḻvārs, specifically uses this mantra in worship.[32] This sect was also distinguished by its practice of branding religious symbols on the limbs,[33] in *Tiruppallāṇṭu* #7 this being "the brilliant holy disc, a shining red-hot fiery circle." It is clear that this text is important in documenting the development of Vaiṣṇava practices during the period of the later Āḻvārs.

Disagreement on the translation of the final phrase of the first verse of the *Tiruppallāṇṭu* leads to varying presentations of its mood. A word-for-word translation of the original *uṉ cēvaṭi cevvi tirukkāppu* is 'your-fine-feet-beauty-divine-protection.' Vidya Dehejia in her book *Slaves of the Lord* renders this "To your gracious lotus feet I surrender!"[34] which ignores the difficult use of the term *kāppu*, 'protection.' The word has its root in the verb *kā* 'protect, guard, defend' and, as a noun, can refer to an amulet.[35] Periyavāccāṉ Piḷḷai, the 13th c. commentator on Āḻvār texts, pointed to this verse as highlighting Periyāḻvār's difference from other Āḻvārs. Periyavāccāṉ Piḷḷai explained that other Āḻvārs considered their Lord a protector, they being protected. However, he says, only Periyāḻvār considered himself a protector <u>of</u> the Lord. Fearing that harm would come to the Lord, he sang a benediction of protection.[36] The commentator continued specifically stating that Periyāḻvār sang the *Tiruppallāṇṭu* to allay any fear that harm may come to the Lord.[37] Modern commentator Aṇṇankarācāriyar declares that the phrase *tirukkāppu* is a blessing to provide protection against harm and that *uṉ cēvaṭi cevvi* specifically means 'for the beauty of your feet'; taken together, the line indicates that protection is <u>for</u> the deity.[38] Internal evidence in *Tirumoḻi* II.8 supports this meaning; there Periyāḻvār sings in the voice of Kṛṣṇa's mother, "Don't stand in the crossroad at nightfall! (II.8.2); I'm scared when you stay out there. (II.8.6)," with a repeated refrain by the worried mother *kāpp(u)iṭa vārāy* 'Come let me put this amulet on you.' In verse II.3.1, Yaśodā also voices her concern, saying "Your hard-working father stays out late; there's no one to protect you" (*kāpp(u)ārumillai*). Rather than a mood of surrender and awe, it seems that the *Tiruppallāṇṭu* begins with a more tender-hearted and solicitous sentiment.

Periyāḻvār's *Tiruppallāṇṭu* must have gained success during the Great Āḻvār's own lifetime, as a Śaiva text was modeled after it only 100 years later in Chidambaram.[39] This later Śaiva *Tiruppallāṇṭu* by Cēntaṉār does not focus on the concept of protection for the deity, but is filled with praises of Lord Śiva and encouragement to his devotees to sing "Many Years" to him,[40] demonstrating that the *pallāṇṭu,* of which later titles are examples, became recognized as a subgenre of devotional literature.[41] Periyāḻvār himself provides evidence of his own text's standing: *Tirumoḻi* III.3.9 describes ladies singing *Tiruppallāṇṭu* as part of the South Indian Ōṇam festival celebrating Kṛṣṇa's birth, and *Tirumoḻi* IV.2.3 indicates that the hymn had been established as a regular feature in worship at the temple at Tirumāliruncōlai near Madurai. According to traditional histories, the success of *Tiruppallāṇṭu* led to the poet Viṭṭucittaṉ then becoming known as *Periyāḻvār* 'the Great Āḻvār.'

Periyāḻvār's *Tirumoḻi*

The *Tirumoḻi,* Periyāḻvār's major work, is unique in several ways and yet, at the same time, it maintains continuity with earlier Tamil literary conventions. To understand its place in the history of literature and religion of India, the reader should first have a general picture of the text itself. The *Tirumoḻi* consists of 473 four-line verses organized at the first level into five supra-sections called Tens: First Ten, Second Ten, etc. Each Ten is further divided into approximately ten units, each labeled *tirumoḻi,*[42] literally 'sacred words,' and each consisting of approximately ten individual verses. (The use of lower case in the word *tirumoḻi* will refer to a specific set of linked verses, to be distinguished from the title of the text, *Tirumoḻi* which is capitalized.) The verses of each *tirumoḻi* are linked by theme, speaker, and repeated phrases, generally with the final line acting as a refrain. The final stanza in each *tirumoḻi* acts as a signature verse in which the listener is provided the name and town of the poet, the subject of the *tirumoḻi* unit, often the speaker in whose voice the poet has written and to whom s/he is speaking, and finally the spiritual or material benefits of singing the song. Each *tirumoḻi* generally has ten or eleven verses; however, *Tirumoḻi* I.2 has 21 verses describing Kṛṣṇa from his toes to his head, and *Tirumoḻi* II.3 consists of 13 verses, the first 12 linked by the use of Nārāyaṇa's twelve names.[43] A review of the table of contents for the translation will provide a brief overview of the overall structure and themes.

Three other *Tirumoḻis* by other authors are found in the *Divine Works* and grouped together as pieces to be sung. All of them have a similar structure as described above, and the authors of these texts are approximate contemporaries of Periyāḻvār, one being his daughter, Āṇṭāḷ, already mentioned. The term *tirumoḻi* clearly means more than just 'sacred words' as it is used to describe a definable literary structure, even though the term is not discussed in any grammars prior to the structure's appearance in literature.[44] That many *tirumoḻi* verses are written in 1st person as monologues also suggests that the term be translated 'divine speeches.' The fact that the *tirumoḻi* suddenly appears in fully developed form in Tamil texts of several authors of a similar period suggests an origin in a previously unwritten tradition. I have also shown elsewhere that the *tirumoḻi* disregarded both traditional Tamil meters and any borrowed Sanskrit meters in favor of emphatic, rhythmic beats delineated, primarily, by alliteration and word boundaries and, secondarily, by syllabic stress from consonant conjuncts and long vowels.[45] These factors suggest an origin for the *tirumoḻi* in the folk traditions of South India.

The folk character of Periyāḻvār's *Tirumoḻi* is apparent in its content as well. One can find in the verses so many details which reflect the simple village life of the times: a mother caring for, coddling and enjoying her baby, ladies going about their daily chores, scenes related to cattle herding, children at play and teasing each other, women gossiping and grousing about the neighbors, and mothers trying to deal with difficult children. The examples below show the poet's use of ordinary domestic situations to bring the divine into a comprehensible realm. Here, Yaśodā is described giving her baby a bath:

> Straightening his hands and feet,
> his mother gently bathed him,
> In a copper pot of cool water,
> with cotton daubed in turmeric. (I.1.6)

Yaśodā tries to control her playful child:

> If you catch black ants to put in the ears
> of the calves to make them run,
> You'll scatter the herd and ruin the milk. (II.4.2)
> I neglected all the cows
> which were bellowing to enter the calf shed
> And came out here to call you (II.8.2)

The listener can easily picture the busy dairy village when Yaśodā complains about Kṛṣṇa eating butter:

> You gulped down the butter and curds I'd collected
> from all three churnings of the day.
> Then you toppled and drank the pots which were carried
> on poles 'cross the herders' shoulders. (III.1.5)

Some phrases are so ordinary, they seem clichéd. The village women complain that Kṛṣṇa's unending pranks are "Like squirting tamarind juice in a wound" (II.9.1), and Yaśodā, sick of hearing complaints, says, "I've heard enough talk behind your back, … it would fill a book" (III.1.4). Even the verses in the Fourth Ten and Fifth Ten, which are outside the narrative of Kṛṣṇa's life in the cowherd village, present archetypal scenes in homespun vocabulary, as in this description of the deathbed:

Your throat will close; porridge poured at your lips
will drip out again down the sides of your chin. (IV.5.5)

Outside of the specific devotional content, much of the background comes from basic human experiences to which any listener can relate. Not only did the *Tirumoḻi's* use of a folk structure make it accessible and enjoyable to all levels of society, the rustic content and colloquial language of Periyāḻvār's text were unique in the *Prabandham* and enhanced its broad appeal.

The word *prabandha* in Sanskrit basically means 'bound together,'[46] a unique feature of Āḻvār verses when compared to earlier Tamil anthologies consisting of individual verses by various authors.[47] For example, the verses of the Āḻvār *antātis,* mentioned above, are structurally linked or bound together by the repetition of the last syllable, word or phrase in one verse as the beginning of the next verse, a mnemonic device which aided in recitation of these pieces. Even Nammāḻvār's *Tiruvāymoḻi* links all 1102 verses in this manner,[48] although there is otherwise a lack of "logical arrangement"[49] of content. As discussed above, a *tirumoḻi* is identified as a cohesive unit bound in part by thematic continuity within each of its verses. While this is true of the *Tirumoḻis* of Kulacēkaraṉ, Āṇṭāḷ and Mankaiyāḻvār, they show no thematic movement <u>between</u> *tirumoḻis,* and while Periyāḻvār's *Tirumoḻi* is similar in literary structure to those works, the Great Āḻvār's text has an additional feature of cohesion not found in the others. Within the first three-quarters of the text, Periyāḻvār's *Tirumoḻi* exhibits such a level of thematic continuity and dramatic movement from one *tirumoḻi* to the next that it can be called nothing less than a storyline, each *tirumoḻi* monologue somewhat like an act in a play, opera or dance-drama.[50]

The story opens with the birth of Kṛṣṇa and the rejoicing of the cowherd community (I.1) and continues with sections related to his infancy, including a lullaby and pointing to the moon. *Tirumoḻis* I.5 through I.9 describe Kṛṣṇa as a toddler, learning to crawl, walk and clap, then running to grab his mother while she works. Although still young enough in traditional village terms to be fed mother's milk (II.2), he reaches a naughty age, when he teases little girls (II.1), talks back to his mother (II.3) and has to be continually coaxed for his bath (II.4) and brushing (II.5). *Tirumoḻi* II.6 represents a turning point in the story when Kṛṣṇa is no longer under the constant watchful eye of his mother. He is sent out to tend the calf herd, but only after his mother has prepared him for the public eye, having adorned him (II.7) and tied him with protective amulets to ward off evil (II.8) that may harm him when he is away from her. Soon the complaints from neighboring women come pouring in about Kṛṣṇa's mischievous behavior (II.9 and 10), and his mother is forced to realize that her son is no longer a baby (III.1). From *tirumoḻi* III.4 to III.8, Kṛṣṇa is described as a maturing youth whose beauty and charm allure the maidens. As a handsome young man in III.8, he runs off to Mathurā with his favorite girlfriend in tow. Periyāḻvār ends the story of Kṛṣṇa's life with the girl's mother searching for her, keeping the narrative setting within the cowherd village and not beyond. The remainder of the *Tirumoḻi* is on various subjects, much of it however still charming in its rustic tone. The continuity of movement which Periyāḻvār maintained through the majority of the first three Tens is an important development in Tamil literature, as prior to the Āḻvārs, only a few texts (*Cilappatikāram* and *Maṇimēkalai,* for instance) could boast a storyline.

As the story proceeds, the *Tirumoḻi* develops Kṛṣṇa's childhood personality which previously had not been shown. Hardy points out that Periyāḻvār was clearly familiar with the earlier Sanskrit accounts of Kṛṣṇa's life, *Harivamśa* and *Mahābhārata,* which contain significant narrative material.[51] In those earlier texts which provided the mythological backdrop for the *Tirumoḻi*, Kṛṣṇa's human incarnation is predominantly presented as a king, a warrior, advisor, and even philosopher. The myths are filled with victories over evil beings, human and demonic, and heroic, superhuman feats. References to his childhood are meant to inspire awe at the thought of his divine power being apparent even as a child. His parents are not depicted with tender affection, but are struck with wonder and fear. This continued to be the major trend even in the earliest Āḻvārs, with few passing references to Kṛṣṇa's childhood.

Periyāḻvār's full attention in the first three-quarters of the *Tirumoḻi* is directed toward the child. Through Yaśodā's voice and responses to her son, the Great Āḻvār lets the listener get to know the human child, Kṛṣṇa, for the first time. His character is developed with images of the baby bouncing on his mother's hip, drooling, prattling, and tottering as he learns to walk. And of course, he is smeared with butter and dust. He has a little pot belly, chubby hands and feet, and new teeth showing when he smiles. His mother nurses him in her arms as he coos; she begs kisses and hugs from him. As he ages, she learns that he is not an easy child to raise: he's uncooperative and uncontrollable, and full of spunk and mischief. Periyāḻvār has painted such a clear picture of the god as human, that the listener, like Yaśodā, becomes lost in that illusion of a fully fleshed-out human child, a person, with whom the devotee can have a very personal relationship. With the popularity of this image pervasive throughout all of modern India on god posters, advertisements and calendars, it is hard to imagine that culture without baby Kṛṣṇa. This picture of childlike charm is Periyāḻvār's most enduring gift to Indian literature and religion.

Aside from images of baby handclapping and teasing the herder maids, this text contains numerous references to Kṛṣṇa's divine deeds and heroic feats as well, as documented later in the section on mythology. However, while liberally peppering the verses with allusions to Nārāyaṇa's divine majesty, Periyāḻvār uses the refrains to maintain focus on Kṛṣṇa's human form, his boyhood personality and growth. In the first three Tens, the refrains predominantly consist of phrases repeated in each fourth line in each verse that are related to Kṛṣṇa as a baby, child or handsome youth. What is more, the Great Āḻvār bolstered this feature, and at the same time created a novel version of the *tirumoḻi* structure, by often repeating the refrain twice within the fourth line, thereby doubling its length. *Tirumoḻi* II.1, with a refrain "He's making scary faces," and *Tirumoḻi* I.9, with repetition of "he hugs my back," both provide good examples of this structure (with contrastive episodal content respectively referring to Nārāyaṇa's salvation of the elephant king and his dwarf incarnation):

That bull elephant, when caught
    in the fierce crocodile's mouth,
Raised its trunk in prayer, crying, "Kaṇṇaṉ, my Kaṇṇaṉ,"
Who came riding a bird and there ended its pain.
That Mighty One is making scary faces.
    Eeek! He's making scary faces. (II.1.9)

As a lone brahmācarya bearing an umbrella,
From him who stood near the northern altar,
While warriors watched, he took all the land.
That embodiment of blessings hugs my back;
    He who measured the earth hugs my back. (I.9.6)

The poet contrasts the majestic character of the god with the familiar description of an adorable child making faces and scampering up behind his mother, but keeps the focus on the charm of the youngster through the verse structure by extending the fourth line through repetition of the refrain. It is clear in the original Tamil verse that the extended phrases do not constitute fifth lines because they do not fit the rhyme schemes, and alliteration marks a *caesura* in the middle of the single long line. Neither Kulacēkaraṉ nor Āṇṭāḷ used this structure in their *Tirumoḻis*, and Mankaiyāḻvār used it only once out of 108 *tirumoḻis*, significantly in a "hand clapping" song. As with Periyāḻvār's verses in *Tirumoḻi* I.6, the phrase "please clap" is doubled in the fourth line of each verse of Mankaiyāḻvār's *Periya Tirumoḻi* X.4. This set of facts suggests that Mankaiyāḻvār directly borrowed the concept from Periyāḻvār's *Tirumoḻi* where the innovative lengthened fourth line is well developed. Zvelebil's dating of Mankaiyāḻvār in the late 9th c. CE after Periyāḻvār would support this postulation; however, several other scholars place Mankaiyāḻvār 25 to 30 years earlier than Periyāḻvār.[52] The above analysis of extended fourth lines with doubled refrains suggests that the active years of the two poets overlapped to the extent that Mankaiyāḻvār was familiar with Periyāḻvār's innovation on the *tirumoḻi* structure and used the "hand clapping" verse as a model for his own to highlight the contrast between Kṛṣṇa's majesty and his infant charm.

The structure, focus and language of the *Tirumoḻi* exhibit significant impact from oral tradition and the commonplace activities and lifestyles of the time. Periyāḻvār seemed keenly sensitive to the details of life all around him and was able to bring that imagery and tone into the recognized literature. His unique blending of the formal with the informal resulted in songs that appealed to all strata of society and won the Great Āḻvār a place in the hearts of South Indians and the history of Tamil literature.

Periyāḻvār's *Tirumoḻi* in Tamil Literature

George Hart points out that the poets of classical Tamil secular literature, the Pulavaṉs, "took their conventions and subject matter almost entirely from the oral bards."[53] Written expression of an oral tradition is just one mark of the continuity between classical Tamil literature and Periyāḻvār's *Tirumoḻi*. Several features of the devotional texts, including the Great Āḻvār's, are directly developed or adapted from earlier secular poetry.[54] Excellent monographs on classical Tamil secular poetry are available for detailed information on that period and translations from the classical anthologies.[55] For the purposes of this discussion, readers should be familiar with some basic characteristics, discussed below.

A bright line divides the two major themes found in classical Tamil poetry with love poems on one side and heroic poems of praise and glory on the other, known respectively as *akam* 'inner' and *puṟam* 'outer' verses. Inner poetry is intimate and emotional, focusing on relationships, exploring love in all of its aspects: ardor, fidelity, unfaithfulness, longing, and separation. The characters who populate these verses are universalized *personae* with no names given: the heroine, the hero, the confidante, the watchful nanny, and sometimes even the mistress. Each verse, presented as a speech in the voice of one of these characters, portrays a momentary glimpse of a scene from the universal story of love. Norman Cutler noted that the full storyline is only maintained in the minds of the poet and the listener.[56] A complex system of metaphors, rich references to the natural world which suggest inner emotions and relationships, assists the listener to grasp the full meaning of the verses.

Natural description evokes enhanced meaning in outer poetry as well; however, its content, in contrast to inner poetry, often focuses on specific kings, warriors, kingdoms or cities. The poet may speak in his or her own voice, glorifying battle scenes, beneficence of a king, great cities, or the prosperity of a kingdom. Rather than intimate, the heroic scenes are dynamic, expansive, and in the open public arena.

One might argue that devotional poetry is best seen as a development within the *puṟam* genre of outer verse of praise and glorification, and this is the case with the early Tamil devotional texts: the 5th c. CE *Paripāṭal*, exalting various deities, and the earlier *Tirumurukāṟṟupaṭai* which praises the Tamil god Murukaṉ.[57] In the *Tirumoḻi*, verses of heroic praise often include references to Nārāyaṇa's incarnation as the warrior-king Rāma or to Kṛṣṇa's role in the Great Bhārata War, as well as to his defeat of the many demons that populate the mythology. In *Tirumoḻi* IV.8, Nārāyaṇa is described, for example, as "the protector of this world who fought and destroyed in battle Rāvaṇa, full of faults, who had gained great powers" (IV.8.5), "the destroyer of underworld demons who blocked their rise from below, By discharging his discus to destroy even their unborn in the womb" (IV.8.6), and "Perumāṉ who reduced to corpses the evil demon horde, So that their thickly flowing blood swelled, foaming in floods" (IV.8.7). These types of gruesome, martial images reflect the heroic poems of the classical period which describe the carnage of the battle field in glorification of war.[58]

Like other Āḻvārs, Periyāḻvār included heroic poems in tribute to Nārāyaṇa's power and glory, especially those that describe and eulogize temple cities; these verses reflect the conventions of secular heroic poetry in praise of a king and his kingdom. Francis X. Clooney described this development in devotional poetry as a shift in "focus of praise from palace to temple."[59] Poems in praise of specific shrines and images in sacred cities are a central feature of devotional literature, in both the Vaiṣṇava and Śaiva traditions.[60] They appear to be a direct reflection of the heroic *āṟṟuppaṭai* or 'guide' poems where, in Zvelebil's words, "bards are directed by their fellow professionals to famous heroes who are patrons of the arts."[61] One of the earliest Tamil devotional texts, *Tirumurukāṟṟupaṭai,* is styled as a guide poem "which directs the devotees to various shrines of the god," Murukaṉ.[62] Indira Peterson proposes that these songs of devotion to specific shrines and the images of the deity residing there constitute a mental pilgrimage.[63] Through the poems, the devotee maintains a mental image of the deity as well as of the sacred city, thereby gaining the benefits of pilgrimage as if s/he has actually made the journey. While several hagiographies indicate that some devotional poets did, ostensibly, make pilgrimage to the cities which they praised,[64] there is no suggestion of Periyāḻvār traveling from temple to temple. That being said, the Great Āḻvār praised or at least mentioned a total of 18 shrines in his works.[65] It is unlikely that he traveled to locations in the Himalayas, such as Kaṇṭankaṭinakar or Badarī, or even to northern sacred sites, such as Ayodha, Mathurā, or Dvāraka. Legend indicates that he took his daughter, Āṇṭāḷ, to Śrīrangam which he praised in 36 verses. One can assume he also had been to Tirumāliruncōlai, near the Pāṇṭiyaṉ court at Madurai, a sacred site to which he dedicated 33 songs and where he is said to have retired and died. His descriptive verses, based on either his own experiences or his imagination describing sacred cities and shrines, reflect the classical tradition of *puṟam* poetry, as well as developments from "guide" verses.

Āḻvār literature reflects influences from classical *akam* 'inner' poetry even more, with its attention to the full scope of relationships, but with a shift from secular love to sacred love. In the 8th c. CE,[66] Nammāḻvār wrote several hundred verses which featured a heroine longing for her beloved,[67] but in that case, the hero was Nārāyaṇa, often represented in his Kṛṣṇa incarnation. Some of these songs reflect the classical theme of patiently waiting for the beloved, but others are more heart rending and desperate in their expression of separation from god, as in the description by the mother of a suffering maiden:

> She reels and faints, her long eyes fixed and glazed;
> She pours sweat; tears quaver in her eyes;
> her breath is hot, and her body withers.
> So altered! "Kṛṣṇa," she calls

and cries out, "Come to me, Lord!"
This passion of great love besets my girl.
What can a wretch like me do?
Tiruvāymoḻi IV.4.10[68]

The mood is different in Periyāḻvār's *Tirumoḻi*, where the village girls are predominantly depicted in full enjoyment of Kṛṣṇa's presence, reflecting the classical theme of love in union or fulfillment. In early Tamil secular poetry, lover's union is often associated through literary convention with the *kuṟinci* flower which grows in mountainous areas, a setting fit for trysts. Periyāḻvār directly links Gopāla Kṛṣṇa to this classical theme in a description of the mountain temple at Māliruncōlai "where throng crowds of girls of the hill tribes dancing and singing *kuṟinci* songs of our Gopāla Govinda" (IV.3.4). Periyāḻvār's maidens are joyful in expression of their first romance. Below, one girl prepares for a tryst with Kṛṣṇa:

Adorning herself with a golden neckband,
she looks in the mirror,
jingling the bangles on her hand.
Arranging her raiment, she's weak with excitement
and reddens her *kovvai* fruit lips.
She calms herself with thoughts of his godliness
and babbles his one-thousand names.
She's gone mad for him whose hue
is of an immutable dark jewel.
Tirumoḻi III.7.8

Girls thrill as he walks down the street (III.4.3) and contrive ways to get closer to him (III.4.6). One girl titters, "I can't stop my young breasts from rising under my dress" (III.4.4), and, in a highly suggestive verse, even a worried mother can't help but notice "His clothes as fine as a creeper's new leaf fold on his flawless hips, Where a dagger bulges in a wide waistband, clinging as tightly as a lizard on a wall" (III.4.2). Kṛṣṇa's own mother is disturbed about the time he spends with the village girls, saying:

Embracing their shoulders and sporting with them,
    you've done unspeakable things! (III.1.8)
Their mothers go out to sell buttermilk;
    their fathers go out behind the herd.
The young virgins of the herder hamlet,
    you carry off at your leisure. (III.1.9)
Taking one maiden, her hair bunched in blossoms,
    you enter the dense forest grove.
Her pearl-laden breasts, you embraced all the night,
    and emerged only after eight hours! (III.1.10)

Periyāḻvār's maidens do not waste time longing to be with Kṛṣṇa, but are presented as fully engaged with him to the point of creating gossip about their behavior. To be certain that there is no misunderstanding about the girls' emotions, Periyāḻvār specifically states that their feelings are of *kāma,* 'love' or 'lust' (III.4.10). Mothers and hormones rage in Periyāḻvār's cowherd village, all in keeping with the conventions of the classical Tamil *akam* theme of lover's union.

Another feature of classical *akam* poetry which is reflected in the *Tirumoḻi* is the poet's presentation of dramatic monologues, each *tirumoḻi* in the voice of a character from the core storyline. While the scenes and speakers in the classical poems are from the universal love story, Periyāḻvār's verses are staged on a backdrop of Kṛṣṇa mythology, the main speaking role going to his mother, Yaśodā. Just as the speeches of the classical heroine provide a glimpse of her emotions and relationship with her lover, in Periyāḻvār's songs, one can hear in Yaśodā's voice the ardor of affection she has for her child, as well as her conflicted emotions and confusion about her son and his unfathomable behavior. More will be said about Yaśodā's feelings in the discussion of devotion in the *Tirumoḻi.* The main point here is that the verses are structured as dramatic speeches which allows the listener to take on the fictive role of Yaśodā and thereby better imagine him or herself in a relationship with the deity;[69] this feature is linked by a straight line back to conventions in classical Tamil love poetry wherein the reader directly experiences universal emotions, feelings and moods expressed in the poem. Friedhelm Hardy has also shown an indirect link, via succession of gurus, between Āḻvār *bhakti,* specifically of those Āḻvārs who wrote in the voice of an infatuated maiden, and 16th c. Bengal Vaiṣṇavism, featuring its emotional identification with, and acting out of, characters from the Kṛṣṇa myth. This suggests that the use of 1st person speech which the Āḻvārs drew from a standard Tamil literary device influenced the development of the later religious role-playing practices of the Bengal Vaiṣṇavas.[70]

Inner *akam* verses and outer *puṟam* verses were anthologized in distinctly separate collections of classical Tamil poetry, but their effects are both felt in later devotional literature, including Periyāḻvār's *Tirumoḻi.* Ramanujan and Cutler point out that "Bhakti poets are direct inheritors of this erotic/heroic ambience and its poetic genre" in part due to the fact that the main focus of the early devotional text, *Tirumurukāṟṟupaṭai*, is Murukaṉ, who is both a warrior and a lover.[71] Devotional expression in Tamil from its earliest beginnings mixed classical conventions from both inner and outer poetry. And completely new models were developed as well.

While standing squarely on a foundation of classical Tamil poetry, the *Tirumoḻi* presented the formative stages of a new genre of literature which has inspired poets up to the present. Periyāḻvār's sweet portrayal of the god Kṛṣṇa as a baby led to imitation and to the development of *piḷḷaittamiḻ* 'child -Tamil.' While Zvelebil considered Periyāḻvār the first poet to develop literature of this character, Paula Richman in her detailed study of *piḷḷaittamiḻ*, *Extraordinary Child,* places the *Tirumoḻi* in "the prehistory of the *piḷḷaittamiḻ* genre."[72] She describes the fully developed and conventionalized *piḷḷaittamiḻ* as being first presented in Pakaḻikkuttar's *Tiruccentūr Piḷḷaittamiḻ*, a text devoted to the Tamil god Murukaṉ from approximately the beginning of the 15th c. CE.[73] The composition of a formalized *piḷḷaittamiḻ* includes the following ten topics, each with a full *paruvam,* a *tirumoḻi* -like structure of approximately 10 verses, devoted to each theme: 1) protection, 2) the red-leaf dance, 3) lullaby, 4) clapping, 5) kissing, 6) calling the child to come, and 7) calling the moon; additional *paruvams* for boys are 8) don't destroy the sand houses, 9) little drum and 10) little chariot, and *paruvams* for girls are 8) playing jacks/marbles, 9) bathing and 10) swinging.[74] In each verse of the protection or *kāppu paruvam*, a deity is asked to protect the divine baby. This first section seems to combine the intent of Periyāḻvār's *Tiruppallāṇṭu,* a benedictory verse devoted to the protection of the deity, and the content of *Periyāḻvār Tirumoḻi* I.3, each verse of which describes a baby gift brought by a deity who has come to honor the child. Periyāḻvār's *Tirumoḻi* also includes *piḷḷaittamiḻ* themes of the red-leaf dance (I.5), lullaby (I.3), clapping (I.6), and calling the moon (I.4). There are three *tirumoḻis* with a refrain of "Come here": come to be bathed (II.4), come to be adorned with flowers (II.7), and come for an amulet to be tied (II.8). Periyāḻvār's *Tirumoḻi* II.4 also is similar to the girl's *paruvam* asking the deity to bathe. Out of the ten standard *paruvams* of the later conventionalized *piḷḷaittamiḻ,* the *Tirumoḻi* includes seven themes.

The structure of the later *piḷḷaittamiḻs* into *tirumoḻi*-like units with a refrain focused on the child is also material to this discussion. The refrain, which Richman notes keeps "the poetry anchored to that theme,"[75] is repeated twice in the fourth line of each *piḷḷaittamiḻ* verse, and as discussed in the previous section, among the devotional texts this feature is developed only in Periyāḻvār's *Tirumoḻi,* a fact which further suggests Periyāḻvār's text as the direct prototype for the *piḷḷaittamiḻ.* The *piḷḷaittamiḻs* from the medieval period to the present reflect significant features of Periyāḻvār's *Tirumoḻi,* giving it an important place in the history of this Tamil genre.

Periyāḻvār inherited a rich literary tradition from the classical Tamil poets, and he clearly was adept in applying the practices and principles of their works. As with other devotional Tamil texts, features of both the inner *akam* and outer *puṟam* verses can be seen reflected in the *Tirumoḻi.* The classical use of dramatic speech as developed by Periyāḻvār, with Kṛṣṇa's mother being the predominant voice, is unique among the Āḻvār texts up to that time in the degree of its theatrical continuity. This text not only played an important part in the development of the literary genre of the *piḷḷaittamiḻ*, Tamil to a child, but also in the appearance in Vaiṣṇava religion of *vātsalya bhakti*, maternal love of a child as devotion, expounded in the continued discussion.

Periyāḻvār's Relationship to God

As the earliest full development of Kṛṣṇa's childhood personality and of *vātsalya bhakti* 'maternal love as devotion to god' Periyāḻvār's *Tirumoḻi* has a noteworthy place in the history of the devotional Vaiṣṇava religion in India. A study of the *Tirumoḻi's* role in the devotional movement must begin with an understanding of how the poet depicts god. While the majority of his verses are devoted to the Kṛṣṇa incarnation, the Āḻvār believed in a supreme form of the deity named Nārāyaṇa. The poet refers to him as the "highest form" (*paramamūrtti*, IV.10.5) and the "highest being" (*paramapuruṣa*, V.4.2), as well as the "primal one" (*ātiyāṉ* IV.4.11) and the "cause" (*kāraṇa* V.1.1). In many verses, Periyāḻvār describes his archetypal form lying in the Sea of Milk on a serpent bed, as in the following:

> Manifest Supreme asleep on the Milky Sea
> with the hooded serpent for a couch,
> Wanting to create and sustain the world,
> you produced from your navel four-faced Brahma.
> (IV.10.5)

Creation comes not directly from Nārāyaṇa, who is in a state of yogic sleep (*uyōku tuyil I.5.1)*, but through the god Brahma who arose from a lotus in Nārāyaṇa's navel, whereby Periyāḻvār interestingly calls Nārāyaṇa "mother [*aṉai*] to the four-faced one" (I.5.2), while other Āḻvārs refer to him as father to Brahma.

Nārāyaṇa's heaven is Vaikuṇṭha (Tamil *vaikuntam),* a "realm of fiery rays dispelling darkness" (IV.9.3). There he is surrounded by heavenly immortals and celestials singing his praises and bringing him offerings of flowers. At his chest is his consort, Tiru (*Śrī* in Sanskrit), who has limited importance to the Āḻvārs when compared to her prominent position in later Śrī Vaiṣṇaism.[76] Whereas some later Śrī Vaiṣṇavas ascribe to the goddess "uniquely salvic powers,"[77] Periyāḻvār sees her with special access to Nārāyaṇa, but without powers of her own. In verse IV.9.2, the poet insinuates that the goddess may get jealous of god's attention to his devotees, and that she may make complaints about them; Periyāḻvār writes that Nārāyaṇa will ignore her protests and say "My servants wouldn't do that; if they did, they did it for good." She is inseparable from god, and when Nārāyaṇa takes form in the Āḻvār's heart, he brings the Milky Sea, his serpent couch and the goddess with him (V.2.10). The poet provides a picture of heaven with distinct sights, smells and sounds surrounding the heavenly ruler, Nārāyaṇa. To Periyāḻvār, the divine is not an abstraction or illusion, but a reality with form that piques the senses.

Periyāḻvār gives an equally detailed description of his vision of hell, which he generally calls by its Sanskrit name, *naraka,* but also *pātāla*. It is ruled by Yama with his legion of demons, their "tongues curled with rage [who] inflict endless torture" (IV.10.2). They poke people with tridents, torture them with snakes, and send hell-dogs to snap at their legs (IV.5.6). Overall, listeners get a very clear picture of their potential options in the afterlife and are urged to become devotees in order to reach heaven and avoid the tortures of hell.

Periyāḻvār's perception of the divine also affirmed the message in the *Bhagavadgīta* about god's descents to earth: *Dharma samsthāpanārthāya sambhavāmi yuge yuge,* "For the sake of firmly establishing righteousness, I am born from age to age"[78]. Throughout the *Tirumoḻi*, the poet refers to the salvic deeds of Nārāyaṇa in his various incarnations on earth, each of whose purpose was protecting the good and reestablishing virtue and order. Early in his *Tirumoḻi*, the poet explains that Kṛṣṇa was "begotten by Devakī … to protect the whole world" (I.2.17) and that he took a "human form when he came as the cowherd king" (I.6.11). The poet specifically addresses the purpose of the Kṛṣṇa *avatāra* in verse II.1.4, saying "He was born at midnight to end the fears of the simple cowherd folk and to overthrow and kill the cruel demon, Kaṃsa." The detailed images in *Tirumoḻi* III.5 of Kṛṣṇa holding up Mount Govardhana to shelter the cowherd village from Indra's vicious storm epitomize his role as a savior.

Baby Kṛṣṇa – Adorable and Accessible

To Periyāḻvār, the deity's descents were related not just to his divine nature as a savior, but to his graciousness in taking an approachable and comprehensible form. The Tamil language of the Āḻvārs' *Divine Works* made the religion of devotion familiar to a broad spectrum of South Indian society, and sculpted images specifically described by the Āḻvārs as sitting, standing or reclining in religious sites throughout the Tamil area allowed the devotees to approach and gaze directly upon the deity. But Periyāḻvār brought god even closer, into everyday home life. Devotion became accessible to the common man - - - and woman and child. Devotional songs with themes such as lullabies, baby hand clapping and calling the moon seem specifically written for mothers to sing to their children, incorporating devotional religion into both of their lives in a casual and easy manner. Periyāḻvār apparently saw god's descents to earth as an opportunity to express religion in a down-to-earth manner, making religious worship as simple as singing folk songs around the house while doing chores, bathing the children, combing their hair, or getting them dressed. As pointed out by Hawley in *Krishna, the Butter Thief, Bhāgavata Purāṇa* X.9.2 specifically refers to Yaśodā singing songs about Kṛṣṇa while doing her housework, perhaps indicating the influence of Āḻvār literature on the *Purāṇa*.[79] Periyāḻvār also points out that chanting god's names - to him the best way to reach Nārāyaṇa (often 'Nāraṇa' in Tamil) - becomes effortless if the parents give their children names of god; he seems baffled that there are people who have not figured this out. Even nagging the children can lead a mother to salvation!

> If you who are born as humans give to your human babes
> The names of other humans,
>   there's no chance for your salvation.
> If she calls her child, "Govinda,
>   my Mādhava, Ruler of heaven,"
> The mother of a "Nāraṇa" will never go to hell.
>   (IV.6.4)

Periyāḻvār's message is similar to that of *Bhagavadgīta* XVIII.56: "Though ever performing all actions, taking refuge in Me, by My grace he obtaineth the eternal indestructible abode."[80] Just as Yaśodā's mind was fixed on Kṛṣṇa through her routine day as his mother, devotees who sing in her voice these *Tirumoḻi* songs meant to accompany daily activities easily incorporate devotion into their work-a-day lives without the hardship of ascetic renunciation or a scholarly career.

Through his expression of Yaśodā's sweet affection for her delightful child, Periyāḻvār demonstrates a relationship to god that is joyful in its intimacy, a desire to be close to god, always by his side, but not merged into the godhead. The poet addresses god directly with, "My Lord, bless me daily with the fortune to exalt and be near you" (V.1.8). A mother who has resigned herself to her daughter's love of Kṛṣṇa says, "Place her at the side of him who once measured the earth" (III.7.10). And the Great Āḻvār plays with the concept of god's imminence in verse IV.5.9:

> As pain swells at the sides of their mouths
> and their eyes flutter, sunken and rheumy,
> As on one side is Mother, one side is Father,
> and on one side weeps the wife,
> Before the fires catch at their sides,
> those who keep red-eyed Māl
> At their side as their closest relation
> will escape the torture of snakes.

Periyāḻvār's last message to his listeners in the final phrase of the *Tirumoḻi* is "Those who can sing of the celestials' King, … [will] be as near to the Lord as his shadow" (V.4.11). While Nammāḻvār and others sang laments in anguish at being separated from god, Periyāḻvār imparts a more positive message that a devotee can keep god close by his or her side through joyful remembrance of him in daily life, just as Yaśodā did.

The later Śrī Vaiṣṇava philosopher Kūrattāḻvāṉ propounded that god's nature as approachable and easy to be near was a sign of his divine love and more important than his majesty in his supreme form.[81] In the *Bhagavadgīta* XI.50, since Arjuna was terrified and overwhelmed when Kṛṣṇa revealed his cosmic nature, "Vāsudeva … consoled the terrified one; the Mahātman again assumed a gentle form."[82] Periyāḻvār fully expresses this concept as he depicts god as not only approachable in his earthly descent, but exceptionally 'adore-able,' i.e. easily able to be adored as a charming infant. If the deity in a human incarnation is less intimidating than his cosmic presence, appearance as a helpless infant allows devotees to be eminently more comfortable and free from anxiety. The devotee's relationship with Kṛṣṇa as a baby is intimate and instinctually human, surging directly from the basic gut-level responses of a parent, but elevating deep, maternal affection to the level of devotion to god. Gauḍīya Vaiṣṇavas of later Bengal, after analyzing the devotional stances of individuals in the stories of the *Bhāgavata Purāṇa,* concluded that those whose relationship with god was characterized by sweetness had the closest bond with Kṛṣṇa.[83] As the listener to the *Tirumoḻi* verses hears Yaśodā's own words describing her darling son or speaking directly to him, how easy it is for the devotee to identify with the role of the mother[84] and experience that delightful intimacy with a personal deity.

In order to sustain the effects of this sweet maternal devotion called *vātsalya bhakti*, the poet had to maintain a careful balance of attention. If he focused only on the human baby, the work would cease to be devotional; if Kṛṣṇa's majesty overshadowed his infant charms, the verse would lose its sweetness and intimacy. By centering the cohesion of the storyline on the child, Periyāḻvār evoked innate feelings of tenderness and maternal love, and through his liberal use of side references to god's supremacy, he raised the level of those natural, tender feelings to religious devotion.

A Mother's Unconditional Love

Periyāḻvār was the earliest poet, in either the Tamil or Sanskrit written traditions, to use the sustained sentiment of parental affection to evoke a devotional mood. The contemporary poet Kulacēkaraṉ wrote several *tirumoḻis* in the voice of a parent: *Perumāḷ Tirumoḻi* VII, the lament of Kṛṣṇa's birth mother after her son was taken from her to be raised by Yaśodā, and *Perumāḷ Tirumoḻi* IX, the lament of Rāma's father when his son went into exile, are songs of desperate longing in separation from god and do not share in the sweet, joyful union experienced by Yaśodā. Kulacekaraṉ sang in his own voice *Perumāḷ*

Tirumoḻi VIII, a lullaby to the warrior-king Rāma, exalting his majesty in that incarnation and in his supreme form; again, these verses do not approach the tender, maternal delight found in Periyāḻvār's *Tirumoḻi.*

Later non-Sanskritic works, Sanskrit texts from South India, oral literature and sculpture attest to the subsequent popularity of Periyāḻvār's baby Kṛṣṇa figure.[85] Migration of this theme onto the North Indian landscape occurred via the Sanskrit *Bhāgavata Purāṇa* from the 10th c. CE onward. Friedhelm Hardy has carefully demonstrated that the material in the *Bhāgavata Purāṇa* about the milkmaids' love of Kṛṣṇa (that was not derived from the *Viṣṇu Purāṇa*) came from the Āḻvārs, and that the associated emotional sentiment expressed by the Āḻvār texts also influenced the *Bhāgavata Purāṇa.* [86] The episodes in that text about baby Kṛṣṇa eating dirt, stealing butter, and killing a heron also are first expressed in Āḻvār texts, as is discussed in the section on the mythology of the *Tirumoḻi.* But it is Yaśodā's affection and her expression of emotions as well as a focus on her daily motherly duties that are the strongest indicators of specific influences by Periyāḻvār on the *Bhāgavata Purāṇa's* attention to the child Kṛṣṇa. While that *purāṇa* generally contains third-person narration, the single long speech by Yaśodā appears to have been derived from the monologues of the *Tirumoḻi*, as excerpted here from the *Bhāgavata Purāṇa* Book X, Discourse 11, lines 14 - 19:

> Yaśodā repeatedly shouted for Śrī Kṛṣṇa, who had been playing …, her breasts overflowing from affection for her son: "Kṛṣṇa, Kṛṣṇa, O darling with lotus-like eyes, come suck my breasts! You are emaciated from hunger and fatigued with sport, O dear son! … You had your breakfast early in the morning. Hence you ought to dine (now). The lord of Vraja (your father) is waiting for you … in order to take his meals… Take your bath, my boy, - you whose person is soiled with dust. The star presiding over your birth is in the ascendant today… Lo! Look at your playmates who have been washed and well-adorned by their mothers. Resume you your play after you have bathed and finished your meals and are well adorned."[87]

Compare this speech to the following lines from the *Tirumoḻi*:

> Bull of the cowherds who sleeps on a serpent,
> wake up now to suck my breast.
> You went to sleep without eating last night
> and now it's nearly noon, is it not?
> I don't see you coming; your tummy must be grumbling.
> Drops of milk trickle from my breast.
> Come cling close to me, kicking up your feet
> and drink, sucking with your blessed lips. (II.2.1)
> Just look at you - covered with calf dust,
> Groom of peahen-like Piṉṉai.
> I got your bath all ready; wash yourself up and come eat.
> Your father has not eaten yet;
> he will eat now with you. (III.3.3)
> … Ōṇam, the star of your birth
> Is today, so you should bathe;
> Our Lord, don't run away. (II.4.2)

It is clear that many of the specific elements found in the Great Āḻvār's earlier monologues find their way into Yaśodā's speech in the *Bhāgavata Purāṇa.*

The *Bhāgavata Purāṇa* also affirmed that *vātsalya bhakti* was accepted by the 10th c. CE in orthodox religious terms as shown by excerpts from Book X.6:

> … Pūtanā [the demon nurse] … attained the destiny of saints! How much more then should one deserve such a state who offers… devotion to Lord Śrī Kṛṣṇa, the Supreme Spirit, as did his affectionate mothers and cows full of motherly affection … the said ogress, whose breasts the Lord sucked covering her body with His feet … ascended heaven, a destiny worthy of his mothers! Rebirth … could never be possible … in the case of those that incessantly look upon Śrī Kṛṣṇa as their son.[88]
>
> *Bhāgavata Purāṇa* X.6, lines 35-40.

As the *Tirumoḻi* was apparently a direct source of episodes and sentiments found in the *Bhāgavata Purāṇa,* Periyāḻvār must be accorded a position of significant importance in the later development of baby Kṛṣṇa poetry and of maternal devotion centered around the Vaiṣṇava deity in that darling form.

In the course of Periyāḻvār's story of Kṛṣṇa's childhood, Yaśodā's maternal feelings are not always tender. As the mother of an extremely active child, she goes through a multitude of feelings and emotions. She is bewildered by her son's victories over a slew of demons ("I don't know what's going on!" II.8.7) and, of course, feels extremely anxious ("What can I do? You make my stomach whirl! You have no fear of anything!" III.3.6). She finds being his mother daunting and demoralizing ("My Prince, I don't have your strength. Please don't run away" II.4.8; "Maybe raising you is too hard for me" III.3.8), and, at times, she simply bemoans her fate ("I have no fortune, my Lord, but the misfortune of getting you" III.1.7). As his naughty behavior gets worse and worse, she anguishes over her own reputation in the village ("The cowherd clansmen won't stand for this conduct; I'm ruined! I have no life" III.1.8). Her neighbors complain about one prank after the other and say again and again, "Please call your son" (II.9), but Yaśodā cannot control Kṛṣṇa. She makes excuses for him ("You're just a kid full of tricks, aren't you" II.9.6) and is incapable of scolding or getting angry (II.8.3). Although she feels bewildered, overwhelmed, and frustrated and finds her son hard to comprehend (II.3.2), she loves her child unconditionally.

David R. Kinsley points out that even in the early Sanskrit *Harivamśa* 62.12, Kṛṣṇa's cowherd foster-father could not control him.[89] For Periyāḻvār, Yaśodā provides the model for the devotee to maintain a personal and unconditional loving relationship with god even when life proves difficult and incomprehensible. The poet's down-to-earth verses, directed at a folk audience, help listeners understand Kingsley's thesis that, like a child, "the nature of the divine [is] unconditioned…He behaves spontaneously, impetuously, without regard to 'musts' and 'oughts,'" and he moves with " energetic, aimless, erratic activity that is pointless yet significant,… imaginative and rich, and therefore creative."[90] This is the Hindu concept of *līlā* 'divine play.' Kinsley explains that since Kṛṣṇa is complete in himself, he desires nothing, so his actions are aimless and have no objective, but "proceed from a fullness, an overflowing of abundance. And so they are properly called play."[91] Periyāḻvār does not use the Sanskrit term *līlā* to describe Kṛṣṇa's antics in the *Tirumoḻi*. The Tamil words placed in the speeches of Yaśodā and the villagers to describe Kṛṣṇa's pranks are more serious. To them, they are crimes (*kuṟṟam* III.1.4), evilness (*tīmai* III.2.2), deceit (*kiṟi* III.8.2), and mischief (*kaḻakaṇṭu II.4.6).* Yaśodā and the villagers do not understand god's actions, but the poet makes it clear in the signature verse to *Tirumoḻi* II.9 that this behavior is an amusement to god, using the Sanskrit term *krīdā*, (Tamil *kirītai,* II.9.11), meaning 'play, sport,'[92] just plain fun. One of the poet's messages seems to be that, although devotees may not understand the ups-and-downs of life, they should still take delight in the world around them, as Kṛṣṇa is present in everything - in everyday, routine existence - and he finds joy in it.

Salvation in the *Tirumoḻi*

For Periyāḻvār, a devotee's aim should be to keep god near in daily life on earth so that s/he can live near god in heaven in the afterlife. Such is his message in a number of the signature verses at the end of *tirumoḻis*. He also assures devotees who sing god's praises that they will not suffer hardships in their current lives (I.3.10), experience misfortune (II.5.10), or have sorrows (III.9.10). Religious practices and purpose voiced by the poet are often oriented toward this world and focus on benefits of devotion to be gained by the living. For Periyāḻvār, this especially means begetting children, possibly as a means to enhance a devotee's ability to directly partake of Yaśodā's unconditional love of her divine child. He says,

> Those who can recite this fine verse of Viṭṭucittaṉ … will have children who will worship the jewel-hued feet of Māyaṉ. (I.7.11)
>
> Those who can recite these …Tamil verses joyfully given by Viṭṭucittaṉ … will rejoice in begetting good children. (I.9.10)

> Those who can master this Tamil Ten … [will] beget good children and live happily in this world. (II.6.10)

Religion is presented as a simple and straightforward practice of chanting god's names or singing songs and remaining mindful of god throughout the day; it leads directly to a happy family life, well-being, and bliss in this life and the next. But does Periyāḻvār see such devotion as a guarantee of salvation? Is this all that is necessary?

Periyāḻvār's concept of religion and of who is responsible for salvation is not that straightforward. Later commentators on Āḻvār literature saw two paths to salvation: *bhakti yoga,* a type of mental discipline of the senses directed toward god, and *prapatti*, complete surrender to god's grace.[93] Periyāḻvār commends those devotees whose senses are purified (IV.4.6), but says it is through god that his senses are controlled (V.2.3) and desires are restrained (V.2.7). He clearly says that god raises his devotees to heaven "though his grace" (IV.9.3). These statements might lead to a conclusion that salvation is the dominion of god to whom the devotee helplessly surrenders, following the later analogy of the mother cat who carries her dependent kitten in her mouth.[94] Yet Periyāḻvār also asserts the importance of service, religious duties and devotional practices, following the analogy of the baby monkey who must make an effort to cling to its mother's back.

The poet's own efforts include reading the Vedas daily and making flower offerings (V.1.6); he is a strong advocate of the practice of chanting the Sanskrit mantra, "Namo Nārāyaṇa" (V.1.3); he marks his body with a religious brand (V.4.1); and he has donated his property and belongings to the deity, suggesting that he has gone into ascetic retirement (V.1.5). He even insinuates that his active service to the temple and his good *karma* built on his good works in some way give him the power to impact Nārāyaṇa's status: "I have gained power in service to you. If I now go to someone else and serve him at his front gate, it will damage your reputation" (V.3.3). Who is in control of a devotee's fate? Like some other Āḻvārs, Periyāḻvār seems to anticipate a later Vaṭakalai Śrī Vaiṣṇava concept that salvation is dependent on god's grace, but not wholly, because grace is granted based in part on both a devotee's past *karma* and current actions.[95] Patricia Mumme states in her study of karma and grace in Nammā̲lvār's works that "though the Lord's innate and 'uncaused' grace or compassion is the primary cause of salvation, the pretext of an *upāya* [disciplined method], which is conditioned by the soul's karma, can be legitimately considered as an auxiliary cause."[96] It is in *Tirumoḻi* IV.10 that Periyā̲lvār makes the clearest statement of this idea: he says he is dependent on god to save him at the time of death because he will be too weak and confused then to make any effort of his own. But he says he is "speaking up right now in advance" (IV.10.1), so although his salvation is ultimately dependent on god, he does see that some effort is required during his life. He points out in several verses that he wants karmic credit for those efforts: "Whenever I could speak, I said all of your names; take note of me for that. Don't let me suffer. You must protect me" (IV.10.3) and "When I could think, I thought all of your names; take note of me for that. My Lord, you must protect me" (IV.10.6). This suggests that, for Periyā̲lvār, although god's mercy is causeless, the granting of mercy is occasioned by the devotee simply coming to god's attention through the devotee's religious efforts.

In order for Nārāyaṇa, the protector and savior, to "take note" of a devotee, Periyā̲lvār counsels his listeners: Be happy; delight in your family and your life. Serve god, sing songs in his praise, and keep him near you in joyful remembrance throughout your busy day. And fill your heart with unconditional, sweet love of god, just as Yaśodā adored her divine darling. Periyā̲lvār's songs were uplifting and world affirming, leading to a long-lasting appeal that permanently influenced the future of the Vaiṣṇava religion.

Mythology in Periyāl̲vār's works

Periyāl̲vār's *Tirumol̲i* presents the pastoral Kṛṣṇa legend in more detail and imagery than any of the other Āl̲vār texts and has been shown to be a source for the Sanskrit *Bhāgavata Purāṇa.*[97] The *Tirumol̲i's* storyline focuses on the birth of baby Kṛṣṇa and his development into a naughty child and handsome youth; however, the contrastive mythological episodes are presented without logical arrangement, unlike the continuous narratives of the earlier Sanskrit purānic texts, the 4th c. CE *Harivamśa* and 5th to 6th c. *Viṣṇu Purāṇa.*[98] References to mythological episodes are liberally scattered throughout Periyāl̲vār's verses in contrast and comparison to his focus on the personality and charm of the child Kṛṣṇa. Therefore, readers who are unfamiliar with the Kṛṣṇa legend and other Vaiṣṇava myths and references may have difficulty in understanding some imagery or poetic symbolism found in the verses. A review of episodic content found in this and other Āl̲vār texts may also inform studies of the development of Vaiṣṇavism in South India upto the 9th c. CE. Therefore, a summary of the myths as they seem to have been known to Periyāl̲vār is presented here with at least one related verse noted for each episode, with additional citations found in the concordance in the appendices.[99]

The Kṛṣṇa Myth

References in the *Tirumol̲i* to Kṛṣṇa's birth are fairly consistent with earlier Sanskrit texts. Noble Vasudeva and his wife, Devakī, were held in captivity by Devakī's cruel brother, Kaṃsa, who feared a prophecy that he would be destroyed by a male issue of their union. He, therefore, slew each of her first six children at their births by dashing them on a stone (V.3.1). Her seventh embryo was divinely transferred to one of Vasudeva's other wives and resulted in the birth of Kṛṣṇa's older brother, Baladeva (I.7.5). Nārāyaṇa, as foretold in the prophesy, descended in his eighth incarnation as Kṛṣṇa and was born to Devakī for the purpose of destroying Kaṃsa (II.1.4). The very night of his birth, he was whisked away to safety to a cowherd village (II.1.6) and given to the herder, Nanda, and his wife, Yaśodā, to raise and love as their own son (II.1.7).

Even as a tiny baby, Kṛṣṇa's miraculous abilities were apparent. Once Yaśodā lay him down to nap under the family cart, not knowing that it was a demon in disguise. Kṛṣṇa kicked out his little feet and tipped the cart over, destroying the demon (I.2.11). A bird demoness, Pūtanā, (I.2.5) also entered the village disguised as a herdess. She gave Kṛṣṇa her poisoned breasts to suck, but he sucked out her life and destroyed her (II.10.6).

When he was slightly older, Yaśodā tied him to a mortar to restrain him. This episode occurs in both early Sanskrit and Tamil variations. In the Tamil verses, being tied down is a punishment for stealing butter (II.1.5), while the early Sanskrit texts have no references at all to butter theft, one of the most popular themes of the later Kṛṣṇa legend. One of the earliest Āḻvārs, Poykai (6th c. CE) says in *Mutal Tiruvantāti* #22, "You ate the butter, with a heady fragrance, churned by soft bamboo-like shoulders, and bear the bruise where she bound you with a rope."[100] The full story is told by a contemporary of Periyāḻvār, Mankaiyāḻvār (9th c. CE) in his *Ciṟiya Tirumaṭal*, also included in the Vaiṣṇava canon, the *Four Thousand Divine Works*:

> ...One day in the cowherd village,
> The firm-breasted lady with the leathern girdle
>   and a beautiful garment,
> Lovely waist and feet, and red coral lips,
> Taking up the churning rod 'til it strained her waist,
> Oh, how long did she churn the curds to collect butter!
> That naïve lady with sweat at her brow put it in another pot,
> And lifting it into the twine nets, left it firmly fixed there.
> When that simple lady with wide spear-like eyes had gone out,
> From a false sleep rose he,
>   who was sleeping like an innocent fellow,
> And stretching his hand
>   the full length of his garlanded shoulder,
> He gulped down the butter, but it wasn't enough!
> He tipped the nearby buttermilk pot, then returned to his spot,

And lay there sleeping like an innocent fellow,
where then she saw him.
But she didn't see what she had stored away, untouched,
and beat her belly in despair,
"Who has been in here, but this herder boy?
It was you who did this!"
So saying, she took a long rope and, so all the city could see,
That angry woman tied him to a mortar
And beat him 'til his full stomach couldn't bear it.
(*Ciṟiya Tirumaṭal*, lines 55 – 73)[101]

But there is more to the story! Mankaiyāḻvār in *Periya Tirumoḻi* XI.4.9 also says,

By the full-breasted herdess, he was tied to a mortar,
after he touched the butter.
He ran away, still tied, and broke the twin laurel trees
so they fell. Thus, he learned to walk.[102]

Periyāḻvār adds more information when he calls the trees "demons who became magic laurels" (III.1.3) and insinuates in I.5.5 that those spirits were released when the trees fell: "You of great strength pushed out with your hands and thighs those who rose from the twin laurel trees joined together." By piecing together several readings, the episode as known to Periyāḻvār and his Tamil contemporaries becomes clear. Naughty Kṛṣṇa was caught stealing butter and was restrained with ropes tied to a mortar. But this didn't stop him, and he dragged the mortar between entwined laurel trees, knocking them down and releasing the magic spirits dwelling there.

Kṛṣṇa's childhood wanderings in the woods near the herder village are marked by other attacks on trees. In the Tamil *Cilappatikāram*, 5th to 6th c. CE,[103] Kṛṣṇa is described as, "Māyavaṉ who broke the wild lime tree in the grove on the lovely hillside."[104] This episode crops up throughout the *Divine Works*, including *Tirumoḻi* IV.4.7, but his breaking down of the wild lime does not appear in any Sanskrit texts. In the same portion of the *Cilappatikāram*, Kṛṣṇa is also described as having "made fruit to fall using a calf for a club."[105] This episode occurs throughout the *Divine Works*, with the tree being identified as a woodapple (Tamil *viḻāmpaḻam).* Periyāḻvār also says that the calf was a demon in disguise (III.3.7), suggesting that Kṛṣṇa was cleverly able to both destroy a demon and harvest a snack in one fell swoop. In verse III.3.7, the Great Āḻvār also insinuates that the calf was thrown by the deity in his white-hued Baladeva incarnation, when he says, "You whose hue is of the Milky Sea, You caught with your hands a demon disguised as a calf grazing in the field, And then, it seems, you threw it to fell fruit from a woodapple tree." This episode of the calf demon does not appear in earlier Sanskrit texts, but is told in the later Sanskrit *Bhāgavata Purāṇa*, written at the end of the Tamil devotional period.

Bakāsura, a heron demon of the later *Bhāgavata Purāṇa*, also first appears in Tamil, rather than early Sanskrit texts. The Āḻvārs often refer to Kṛṣṇa splitting a bird's mouth. Periyāḻvār provides a few more details in II.5.4, saying, "When he saw a cunning demon disguised as bird fishing in a waterhole, he thought, 'It's only a bird,' and quickly split its mouth." Dhenuka is an ass demon slain in both early Sanskrit texts and the *Bhāgavata Purāṇa*; however, in those episodes, the demon is killed by Kṛṣṇa's brother, Baladeva. Throughout the *Divine Works*, the episode is ascribed to Kṛṣṇa himself. Specifically noting the demon's name, *teṉukaṉ*, Periyāḻvār says that he "once tossed Dhenuka up onto a palm fruit so that its breathing ceased" (II.10.4), a somewhat similar scenario to the calf demon story. Early and late Sanskrit texts also ascribe the destruction of Pralamba, a demon disguised as a herder, to Baladeva, while Periyāḻvār mentions the demon by name (Tamil *pilampaṉ*) as one destroyed by Kṛṣṇa (IV.9.3). Āḻvār literature also presents the story of Kṛṣṇa slaying the horse demon which Periyāḻvār mentions only once in his text (IV.9.3).

Kṛṣṇa continued to grow up in the cowherd village, playing with his brother and the other herder boys. In the *Bhāgavata Purāṇa,* Book X, discourse 8, there is an episode in which Kṛṣṇa was caught eating dirt. There, he escaped punishment when he stunned his mother by revealing the universe when she looked in his mouth.[106] Although there are numerous references in the *Divine Works* to Nārāyaṇa consuming the whole earth to protect it, the earliest mention of Kṛṣṇa eating dirt as a child occurs in Periyāḻvār's verse II.3.8, which is part of a heated dialogue between the boy Kṛṣṇa and his beleaguered mother. He says, "When I ate dirt one day, what a loving look you had when you caught me and beat me for everyone to see." In this version, Kṛṣṇa did not escape punishment. There are separate verses (I.1.6 & 7) in which Yaśodā saw the "seven worlds" in his mouth when she was bathing him as a baby and cleaning his tongue.

The story of the black serpent, Kāliya, is given at length and in detail in both early Sanskrit Vaiṣṇava texts, the *Harivaṃśa* (chap. 66-67) and *Viṣṇu Purāṇa* (book V, chap. 7). Periyāḻvār's *Tirumoḻi* shows that this story was well known by direct reference to the serpent's name (Tamil *kāliyaṉ*, I.5.6) and specific features of the story, i.e. that Kṛṣṇa climbed a *kadamba* tree and jumped into a pool (II.1.3), then climbed onto the serpent's five hooded heads and danced (II.10.3). In addition, while the earlier Sanskrit texts end the story with Kṛṣṇa banishing the serpent and his clan from the pool near the herder village, Periyāḻvār indicates that the serpent was blessed by the grace of god's feet: "He jumped in and churned up Kāliya's pond and danced on his five hooded high heads to mete out his grace and redeem that snake" (III.9.7), providing a retelling of the episode more in keeping with the devotional movement of the times.

Another popular part of the Kṛṣṇa legend from early Sanskrit that is found throughout Āḻvār texts is the story of Kṛṣṇa lifting Govardhana Mountain. Periyāḻvār devotes a complete *tirumoḻi* to this theme (III.5), providing extensive details of the episode: to stop the herders from worshipping Indra, king of celestials and god of rain (IV.2.4), Kṛṣṇa devoured the offerings (III.3.8) which enraged Indra, who sent torrents pouring on the village "for seven days" (III.5.2). At the entreaty of both the herders and the cows (III.5.3), Kṛṣṇa plucked up Govardhana Mountain (III.5.4) and lifted it like an umbrella over the herders and herd, "with the five fingers of his lotus-like hand as the ribs and his long jeweled arm as the handle" (III.5.6). Holding that mountain like a shield, he "faced in open battle a multitude of massive clouds roaring, pouring rain arrows from all sides" (III.5.8), protecting the herd and the village and defeating Indra.

Kṛṣṇa grew into a handsome youth, infatuating the girls of the herder village. In many verses of the *Four Thousand Divine Works*, an Āḻvār takes the voice of a girl passionately longing for a divine lover and languishing in separation from him. This theme is the focus of a detailed study by Friedhelm Hardy, titled *Viraha-bhakti,* in which he traced the development of the milkmaid motif in both Sanskrit and Tamil Vaiṣṇava literature and characterized its presentation in the Āḻvār texts as an integration of early Tamil secular love poetry and developing devotionalism.[107] The milkmaids became a symbol for the human soul longing for god. Periyāḻvār devotes one full *tirumoḻi* (II.10) to the milkmaids, but they are not lamenting in separation; they are complaining, "We are at our end," because he has stolen their clothes and bangles. The episode of his stealing clothes and bangles appears early in Tamil literature as a milkmaids' song in the 5th c. CE *Cilappatikāram:*

> Shall we tell of him who hid the clothes
> so she crouched, bending her waist as if broken?
> Shall we tell of her sweet face, quickly tired of the teasing
> of him who hid the clothes?
>
> Shall we tell of the chastity of the Lady Heart-Stealer
> who bathed in that Swindler's Toḻunai River?
> Shall we tell of him who swindled the bangles and
> the chastity of the Lady Heart-Stealer?
>
> Shall we tell of her face which she hid in her hands,
> having lost her clothes and her bangles?
> Shall we tell of him, suffering and confused when he saw
> her face which she hid in her hands?[108]

This episode is a favorite in the *Tirumoḻi* (II.10.2) and in later Kṛṣṇa literature, but not found in early Sanskrit texts or in many of the other Āḻvārs' verses.[109] Periyāḻvār also mentions Kṛṣṇa tearing the women's saris (II.7.3) and stealing fruit from them (II.9.10).

Besides tormenting the milkmaids, Kṛṣṇa also danced in Periyāḻvār's text both for and with them, but these dances are specific to Tamil literature. The dance most like the *rasa līlā* of the later *Bhāgavata Purāṇa* is called a *kuravai* (II.3.6), which is described in great detail in the earlier Tamil *Cilappatikāram* as a dance-drama in which milkmaids enact the roles of Kṛṣṇa, Baladeva and Piṉṉai and join hands and dance in a circle.[110] More frequently in Āḻvār literature, Kṛṣṇa danced *solo* with pots on his head (II.7.7), for the amusement and pleasure of the herder women. The modern South Indian acrobatic dance called *karakāṭṭam* 'pot dance' seems to be similar. The *Tirumoḻi* also mentions Kṛṣṇa playing the flute and its infatuating affect on the milkmaids (III.6). The Great Āḻvār treats the milkmaid theme fairly lightly in many of his verses, characterizing Kṛṣṇa's relationship with the women and girls of the village as playful and mischievous, even capricious.

As Kṛṣṇa matured, his affairs with the milkmaids became more intimate, as he crept into their houses when their parents were gone (III.1.9). He singled out one girl in particular and spent the whole night in the forest with her (III.1.10). In the *Divine Works*, Kṛṣṇa's favorite is called *Piṉṉai* 'young girl' or *Nappiṉṉai* 'our young girl.' She is Kṛṣṇa's cross-cousin (III.8.5), his mother's brother's daughter,[111] and therefore he is designated at an early age by South Indian kinship practices as her appropriate bridegroom (II.5.1). In order to marry her, he must demonstrate his herding skills by controlling bulls (IV.1.4), an episode unique to South Indian Kṛṣṇa mythology and a favorite among the Āḻvārs.[112] Influence of this episode is, however, found later in the *Bhāgavata Purāṇa* as one of Kṛṣṇa's wives, Nagnajitī, is described as being won by Kṛṣṇa conquering seven bulls.[113]

At this stage in the story, the reader hears from the girls' mothers who rail against his outrageous behavior toward their daughters (II.9), as well as his unrelenting pilfering of butter and ghee. These indiscretions concern Yaśodā; she's worried about the gossip, complaints, and her own reputation in the village, saying, "I'm ruined!" (III.1.8) and "I have no fortune but the misfortune of getting you" (III.1.7). Yaśodā is at her wit's end with worry about how to control her impetuous son. Periyāḻvār concludes his pastoral Kṛṣṇa verses with

Tirumoḻi III.8, written in the voice of a distraught mother looking for her daughter who has left the herder village to go with Kṛṣṇa to the city of Mathurā. Although she disapproves of Kṛṣṇa's behavior and worries about how he will treat her daughter, the poet points out that even the anxious and angry mother is "following the path of Māyavaṉ" (III.8.10).

A central underlying theme in the Kṛṣṇa myth is that he was born on earth to destroy all demons (I.2.16) and to overthrow his evil uncle, Kaṃsa (II.1.4). Kaṃsa invited Kṛṣṇa and Kṛṣṇa's brother to a bow festival in Mathurā in order to lure them to destruction. But Kṛṣṇa overcame all obstacles in Mathurā: he broke the tusk of a raging elephant and destroyed it (V.1.5) as well as the elephant driver (IV.7.7); he and his brother killed several wrestlers who were sent to oppose him (II.7.6); he broke the festival bow (IV.7.7); and finally he kicked and destroyed Kaṃsa (III.2.1) and freed his birth father from captivity (V.1.4). He also cured a hunch-backed girl who gave him unguents (I.8.4).

References in the *Tirumoḻi* to episodes from Kṛṣṇa's adult life are intermittent and not a central focus for Periyāḻvār; however, it is clear from the text that the poet was familiar with the mythology. Elements of this chapter in the Kṛṣṇa cycle first appear in Tamil in the late classical *Kalittokai* verses and include his slaying of the elephant and wrestlers.[114] In summary, after killing Kaṃsa, Kṛṣṇa took his place in the Yādava clan of his birth. He and his brother were sent to study leadership and the Vedas with their instructor, Sāndīpani. They paid their instructor's fee by freeing his son from an ocean demon, Pancajana (IV.8.1). At the same time, Kṛṣṇa acquired the conch battle horn, Pāncajanya (III.3.5). As the new clan leader, Kṛṣṇa moved the whole community of Mathurā to a new city, Dvāraka, (IV.7.8) to protect them from war with encroaching enemies.

Kṛṣṇa began his own family in the Yādava community when he fell in love with a princess, Rukmiṇī, from a neighboring kingdom, but she was unhappily betrothed to Śiśupāla. Kṛṣṇa saved her from this marriage by whisking her away in his chariot, then defeated both Śiśupāla (IV.3.5) and her brother, Rukmin, who came after her (IV.3.1), and shaved Rukmin's head (III.9.3). Satyabhāmā was another one of his multiple wives; Kṛṣṇa stole the heavenly *kaṟpaka* tree and planted it in Satyabhāmā's garden (I.9.9). Ultimately, Kṛṣṇa married eight major wives, but when he defeated the demon Naraka (IV.3.3) and freed sixteen thousand and one hundred captive virgins, he brought them all to Dvāraka and married them, also (IV.9.4).

After many years, Kṛṣṇa's oldest son bore him a beautiful grandson who was the incarnation of the love god, Kāma (I.7.6). The grandson fell in love with the daughter of the demon Bāṇa, but Bāṇa found the lovers together and imprisoned the grandson. When Kṛṣṇa came to the rescue, he defeated Bāṇa and cut off his one-thousand arms (IV.3.4), and his grandson was able to marry his beloved.

Regarding the source of Kṛṣṇa mythology in the *Tirumoḻi*, Friedhelm Hardy noted that Periyāḻvār paraphrased the 4th c. CE Sanskrit *Harivaṃśa* in his verse III.5.1 describing the offerings to Indra that Kṛṣṇa himself ate.[115] Further analysis of episodal content supports the *Harivaṃśa*, rather than the *Viṣṇu Purāṇa*, as the basis for Periyāḻvār's references. Verses I.5.7 and IV.8.2 refer to Kṛṣṇa returning four children to life after they had each died at birth. This episode occurs in Chapter CCLX of the *Harivaṃśa*,[116] but does not occur in the *Viṣṇu Purāṇa*. Vasudha Narayanan also documented references to this episode in Mankaiyāḻvār's *Periya Tirumoḻi* and Nammāḻvār's *Tiruvāymoḻi*,[117] indicating that Periyāḻvār's contemporaries were also familiar with the *Harivaṃśa*.

Periyālvār also knew of the Sanskrit epic *Mahābhārata*, to which the *Harivaṃśa* is considered a supplement, and of Kṛṣṇa's role in that saga. At the heart of this epic is a struggle for empire between the five Pāṇḍava brothers, known in the *Tirumoḻi* as the Five, and their numerous cousins, the Kauravas, known as the One Hundred (I.6.6) and led by the eldest, Duryodhana (I.8.5). The Pāṇḍavas are also Kṛṣṇa's cousins, his paternal aunt's sons, as well as his in-laws (V.3.8), because Kṛṣṇa's sister married one of the brothers, Arjuna. The Pāṇḍavas lost their share of the kingdom in a gambling match (II.1.1), and therefore, they and their common wife, Draupadī - also known as Pāncālī (IV.3.6) - became exiled. After they returned from their period of exile, they requested a fair portion of the kingdom. Kṛṣṇa participated in the negotiations of their return by acting as a messenger and ambassador for the Pāṇḍavas (III.9.5). Duryodhana, however, would not give up even the smallest portion of land; thus the factions entered into all-encompassing combat (II.6.5). Kṛṣṇa joined the fray as a charioteer for Arjuna (I.6.6). Periyāḻvār devotes a number of verses to Kṛṣṇa's relationship with and assistance to Arjuna, who is known in this text by the names Pārtha (II.1.2), Vijaya (I.8.6) and Dhananjaya (I.9.4) and who is described as having white horses and a monkey banner (IV.1.7). Ultimately, after eighteen days of battle and many deaths, the Pāṇḍavas were victorious and established as rulers (V.3.8), with Arjuna's grandson Parikṣit (by his son's wife Uttarā) being crowned king (IV.3.6).

The epic *Mahābhārata* is a massive text of about 215,000 lines,[118] but with only a few specific events mentioned in Periyāḻvār's verses. The poet briefly reminds the listener that Duryodhana went against his father's advice in his enmity toward the Pāṇḍavas (I.6.6) and that, in the midst of battle, Kṛṣṇa accessed an underground pool to provide water for Arjuna's horses (IV.2.7). It is interesting to note that the incident described in the most detail in the *Tirumoḻi* seems to present Kṛṣṇa as devious and dishonest. The event took place on the day that Arjuna made a vow that he would have himself put to death if he did not slay the enemy king, Jayadratha, before sunset, the time when both armies withdrew from the battle field. The fighting was fierce that day, with numerous Kaurava warriors protecting Jayadratha from attack. Kṛṣṇa felt that there was no reasonable way that Arjuna could fulfill his vow and avoid death, so Kṛṣṇa used his divine powers to hide the sun with his discus. The Kaurava army, thinking the sun had set and Jayadratha was safe, put down their weapons, whereupon Kṛṣṇa urged Arjuna to strike and behead Jayadratha (IV.1.8). While the Great Āḻvār may have presented this episode to demonstrate god's love and protection of his devotee, the behavior is also reminiscent of the poet's depiction of Kṛṣṇa as a capricious trickster.

The Rāma Myth

While Periyāḻvār looked to the pastoral and heroic Kṛṣṇa legends as the foundation for most of the episodal content in the

Tirumoḻi, he clearly considered Rāma of the epic *Rāmāyaṇa* an equal, full incarnation of the Supreme Deity, Nārāyaṇa. For example, *Tirumoḻi* III.9 is presented in the voice of village girls playing a game of tag and singing a folk song about the god who is both Kṛṣṇa and Rāma. The poet variously refers to the Rāma incarnation by using his name directly (IV.1.1), as Dāśarathi, Daśaratha's son (III.9.2), as Kākutstha, Kakutstha's descendent (II.9.2), as Sītā's groom (III.3.5), and as the King of Ayodhya (III.10.4). Rāma is described as the bearer of the Śārnga bow (I.6.7), the Nandaka sword (V.2.9), the club, conch and discus (IV.1.2).

In the epic, as the boy Rāma matured into a capable leader, his father wanted to name him as the heir apparent; however at the instigation of his father's scheming wife, Kaikeyī (III.10.3), and her hunch-backed servant (IV.8.4), Rāma was exiled to the Daṇḍaka Forest (III.9.8) on Citrakūṭa Mountain (II.6.7). His brothers, Lakṣmaṇa (III.10.7) and Bharata (II.1.8), are both mentioned by name, noting that Lakṣmaṇa accompanied him into exile (III.10.7), while Rāma gave the loyal, young regent, Bharata, his sandals as a symbol of his rule in his absence (III.9.6).

Periyāḻvār presents several characters from the period of exile: Guha (III.10.4) who housed the family and helped them on their way, and Śūrpanakhā (III.9.8), demoness and sister of Rāvaṇa, whose nose Rāma severed when she attacked Rāma's wife, Sītā. Rāma also pierced the eye of a demon crow which pecked Sītā's breast (III.10.6). Of Sītā's capture by Rāvaṇa, the poet says little, but he does have one reference to the demon deer (III.10.7) which tricked Rāma and Lakṣmaṇa into leaving Sītā alone so that Rāvaṇa could kidnap her.

The brothers then pursued Rāvaṇa to rescue Sītā, and along the way, met a clan of monkeys. When their king questioned Rāma's abilities, Rāma shot seven fig trees with one arrow (IV.1.3). Ultimately, the monkey Hanumaṉ became loyal to Rāma and went ahead to Śrī Lanka to find Sītā imprisoned there. Periyāḻvār devoted *Tirumoḻi* III.10 to Hanumaṉ's speech to Sītā in which he provides testimony of his fealty to Rāma and presents Rāma's ring as proof.

Once Rāma knew the location of Sītā's imprisonment, he was ready to lead his army into Śrī Lanka to save her, but they had no means to cross the ocean. Rāma requested the sea to give way to his army, but when it failed to do so, he shot arrows into the water until the spirit of the ocean begged him to stop (I.6.7). The ocean spirit suggested instead a bridge, which was then built with the help of the monkey troop (I.6.8). Rāma's forces fought a great battle, with Rāma bombarding the city with fiery arrows (IV.3.8). In the final combat, Rāma cut off Rāvaṇa's ten heads (II.6.8), then gave the kingdom to Rāvaṇa's brother, Vibhīṣaṇa, who had supported Rāma (II.6.9). Of the later episodes in the final version of the Sanskrit *Rāmāyaṇa*, in which Rāma questioned Sītā's faithfulness, Periyāḻvār makes no mention. Other episodes in the Rāma story which occur in the *Tirumoḻi* are the slaying of the demoness, Tāḍakā (III.9.2), destroying the powers of Paraśurāma (III.9.2) and breaking the bow in King Janaka's court in order to win Sītā's hand in marriage (IV.1.2).

Vaiṣṇava Epithets and Episodes

The predominant epithet of the Vaiṣṇava deity used in Periyāḻvār's *Tirumoḻi* is *Kaṇṇaṉ,* the Tamil form of the Prakrit, *Kaṇha*, from Sanskrit, *Kṛṣṇa*, and is used throughout the verses 23 times. The supreme form of this Vaiṣṇava deity - lying in yogic repose on the serpent, Ananta, (I.7.2) in the midst of the Milky Sea (III.3.7), dark (I.5.4) and jewel-hued (I.2.2) like collyrium (I.3.10) or rainclouds (I.5.6), with golden raiments (III.4.3) and a jewel on his chest (I.2.10) - is known in the text as Nārāyaṇa, or the Tamil form *Nāraṇa,* occurring in total 17 times. From his navel blooms a lotus from which Brahma, the creator, arose (II.5.8), and at his chest lies the Goddess Śrī, or *Tiru* in Tamil (I.7.4.) In some citations in the *Tirumoḻi* as well as in the *Tiruppallāṇṭu*, the name occurs in the sacred Sanskirt mantra, "*Namo Nārāyaṇa*." The earlier Tamil epithets for this deity, *Māl*, *Māyōṉ*, *Māyaṉ*, and *Māyavaṉ*, all derived from the Tamil root *mā* 'dark,' are more frequent, occurring all together 35 times, sometimes in conjunction with the phrases "red eyed" (I.7.10) or "tall" (IV.8.9). He is the god with the conch and discus (I.2.12) who rides the Garuḍa bird (III.2.6) and bears the Garuḍa banner (II.3.8). In *Tirumoḻi* II.3, Periyāḻvār lists one epithet for the deity in each of 12 verses, using names associated with the twelve months:[119] Keśava, Nārāyaṇa, Mādhava, Govinda, Viṣṇu, Madhusūdana, Trīvikrama, Vāmana, Śrīdara, Hṛṣīkeśa, Padmanābha, and Dāmodara. Here is the only occurrence of the name Viṣṇu (II.3.5) in this Vaiṣṇava text by the Āḻvār whose given name was from the Sanskrit, Viṣṇucitta.

The sleeper on the serpent in the midst of the sea took a unique form in South India that is of particular interest in the study of the *Tirumoḻi*. Tamil verses from the earliest Āḻvārs of the 6th c. CE onward also present the deity as a baby sleeping on a banyan leaf in the sea; for example, "In the form of a child, he slept on a banyan leaf, having eaten the universe" (*Mutal Tiruvantāti* 69)[120] and "As a child, he compressed the world inside himself and slept quietly on a banyan in the midst of a roaring wavy flood" (*Mūṉṟān Tiruvantāti* 93).[121] Periyāḻvār says of the deity, "You devoured the world you created and protect it in your jeweled stomach, Supreme Lord. From age to age in a yogic sleep, you lie calmly on a banyan leaf" (I.5.1) and "Nārāyaṇa … sleeps on a banyan leaf, after devouring the entire earth" (III.7.11). The composite image given by the Āḻvārs is of a baby sleeping in a cosmic flood on a floating banyan leaf, having consumed the world in order to protect it. The origins of this divine aspect may be the Vanaparvan of the *Mahābhārata* in which the deity speaks to the sage Markaṇḍeya who had entered his body, saying,

> I am called Nārāyaṇa and I … who am the Universal Soul, sleep, overwhelming all creatures in insensibility. And, … I stay here thus for all time, in the form of a boy though I am old… I showed thee the universe (within my stomach). And while thou wert within my body, beholding the entire universe, thou wert filled with wonder."[122]

While the divine aspect of the baby on a banyan leaf seems to find no place of any importance in later Sanskrit Vaiṣnava literature, it developed into one of the most popular images in the Āḻvār texts and can still be seen on calendars and god posters today. However, Periyāḻvār directly identifies the banyan-leaf baby with baby Kṛṣṇa, as shown in his verse of Yaśodā calling the moon to play with her son:

"Don't be insulting and think, 'He's just an infant.' This is the babe of long ago whose abode was a banyan leaf." (I.4.7) One might conjecture that South India's fascination with the banyan-leaf baby image may have led to an increased appeal of Periyāḻvār's verses on baby Kṛṣṇa, or the alternative, that the popularity of the *Tirumoḻi* may have affected the development of the banyan leaf baby myth.

Along with the numerous references to the Kṛṣṇa legend found in the *Tirumoḻi*, Periyāḻvār alludes to merciful acts taken by the deity in his supreme form. A particular favorite is the story of Nārāyaṇa saving the elephant king: an elephant was picking blossoms by a pond to offer to Nārāyaṇa, when a crocodile leaped out and grabbed its leg. Nārāyaṇa, perceiving the elephant's devotion, cast his discus at the crocodile and saved the elephant (II.10.8). Periyāḻvār often presents this story of Gajendra Mokṣa, salvation of the elephant king, as proof of god's mercy, as well as a reminder to god of his salvic responsibility.

In verse I.6.10 and others, the poet tells the story of the creation of the nectar of the immortals. Nārāyaṇa upturned Mount Mandara and placed it in the cosmic sea as a churning rod, then wrapped the celestial serpent, Vāsuki, around it as a churning rope and churned the ocean to create ambrosia for the immortals.

The tale of Nārāyaṇa relieving Śiva of a curse is provided in some detail in I.8.9: according to the commentator Aṇṇankarācāriyar, once Brahma had five heads, but Śiva chopped one off. As this constituted the sin of slaying a Brahmin, Śiva was cursed with the skull sticking to his hand; it would only come off when he had used it as a begging bowl and garnered enough offerings to fill it up. But it seemed to be bottomless! Only when he entreated Nārāyaṇa to remove the curse did the bowl drop from his hands.[123] Periyāḻvār's contemporaries provide even more information as seen from this compilation from several texts of the *Prabandham*:[124] Nārāyaṇa "ended the harsh curse put on Hara [Śiva] by Aja [Brahma]" (*Periya Tirumoḻi* I.4.8) which caused Śiva to "wander all the worlds" (*Periya Tirumoḻi* V.9.4) "wandering to other's houses" (*Tirukkuṟantāṇṭakam* 19) "bearing a gory head" (*Periya Tirumoḻi* V.9.4), "that stinking pot which was Brahma's head" (*Tiruviruttam* 86). Śiva "begged for alms" (*Periya Tirumoḻi* VI.7.9) from Nārāyaṇa who "filled that unfillable skull"

(*Periya Tirumoli* III.9.3), "giving pure water" (*Periya Tirumoli* V.9.4), "fragrant water which was on your [Nārāyaṇa's] chest" (*Tiruccantaviruttam* 113), "the shining nectar-like water which was on your blessed chest" (*Periya Tirumoli* I.5.8). In these verses from the *Divine Works,* the Āḻvārs reveal their sectarian perspective in describing the means of ending Śiva's curse: Nārāyaṇa's sweat!

Nārāyaṇa's Incarnations

In the 1st c. CE[125] *Bhagavadgīta* IV.8, Kṛṣṇa explains his divine descents to the earthly world:

For the protection of the good,
 for the destruction of evil-doers,
For the sake of firmly establishing righteousness,
 I am born from age to age.[126]

The character of Nārāyaṇa as a savior and his divine ability to descend into the world again and again in various incarnations or *avatāras* is known in Tamil literature from the earliest devotional texts. The late classical Vaiṣṇava songs of the *Paripāṭal* refer to the boar, dwarf, man-lion and swan incarnations; the boar, dwarf and man-lion themes are found in the three earliest Āḻvārs, who also include the Rāma and Kṛṣṇa incarnations. Throughout the *Divine Works*, the Āḻvārs use the stories of various incarnations as the basis for their songs of devotion, each generally including five to eight *avatāras*. Maḻicaipirāṉ mentions that there are ten incarnations, calling the deity "the one great truth with ten births" (*Tiruccantaviruttam* 79), but does not list them. Periyāḻvār's verse IV.9.9 provides one of the earliest lists of ten incarnations as they are generally recognized today, when he describes the deity as he "who was a divine fish and turtle, a boar, a lion and a dwarf, who became three Rāmas [Paraśurāma, Dāśarathi Rāma and Balarāma] and Kaṇṇaṉ, and who will conclude with Kalki." Nārāyaṇa made each descent to protect the world and rid it of evil.

In his fish incarnation, the deity saved Manu from a destructive flood by having Manu make a boat which the fish then pulled; Periyāḻvār provides no details of this *avatāra,* but merely mentions it in various lists of incarnations, including I.5.11. The poet treats the tortoise incarnation in a similar manner (III.3.7), without providing any details of Nārāyaṇa's role in his tortoise form as the base for the churning rod when the sea was churned for nectar. On the other hand, the boar incarnation is an early favorite in the *Divine Works*, and Periyāḻvār mentions it eight times, including some details in II.10.9 and IV.1.9, explaining how Nārāyaṇa dug up the earth from under the primeval waters and held it aloft on his tusks to protect it; he also married the Earth goddess.

While the Sanskrit names for the first three incarnations are not found in the *Tirumoḻi*, Periyāḻvār uses both Tamil *ari* 'lion' (I.5.2) and Sanskrit-derived *narasinkaṉ* 'man-lion' (IV.4.6) in his references to the next *avatāra*. The man-lion descended when the demon Hiraṇya, *Iraṇiyaṉ* in Tamil (I.2.5), tormented the three worlds, oppressing even his own son, a devotee of Nārāyaṇa (I.5.2). When Hiraṇya struck a pillar (I.6.9), Nārāyaṇa burst from the stone column as a man-lion "who roared, mouth wide, when he seized proud Hiraṇya's chest and pierced it with pointed claws, crushing his crown 'til his eyes bulged" (IV.9.8). The late classical *Paripāṭal* presents a particularly vivid retelling of the man-lion incarnation, ending with the following lines:

> Then, on the mountain-like chest of him
>   who fixed himself as the one,
> Up you sprang upon him, to destroy his maddened power,
> As the thundering drums resounded, foretelling evil omens,
> As the heavy pillar burst, shattering,
>   when he beat it with a club,
> O You whose extended claws
>   sliced through the bits of flesh.[127]

This horrific form of Nārāyaṇa continued to be popular and inspire powerful poetic expressions throughout the devotional period.

The next demon to oppress the earth was Māvali (I.4.8), Sanskrit *Mahābali*. When Māvali was conducting a ceremony of offering, Nārāyaṇa came to the altar in the form of a Brahmin dwarf named Vāmana and requested a gift of the amount of land he could cover in three steps (II.10.7). Māvali's advisor counseled him against granting the boon (I.8.7), but Māvali agreed to the request, and Nārāyaṇa expanded into a huge heavenly form (IV.7.2). With three steps, he measured the world (I.5.3) and beyond and sent Māvali to Hell (IV.9.7). When Māvali's son, Namuci, complained, Nārāyaṇa hurled him into space (I.8.8). Kalpana Desai in *Iconography of Viṣṇu* begins her discussion of the dwarf incarnation with the statement that "It is an established fact that the Vāmana myth has its germ in the 'three steps' of Viṣṇu in the *Rig-veda*."[128] Periyāḻvār used both Sanskrit epithets *Trīvikrama* 'three stepper' and *Vāmana* 'dwarf' in his references to this incarnation; however the majority of his 29 verses covering this subject either use the Tamil word for dwarf or describe measuring the universe.

Periyāḻvār has only a few brief references to the sixth incarnation of Nārāyaṇa - Paraśurāma or Rāma with the axe – who Desai believes might have been an historical figure.[129] He was a Brahmin who took an oath to destroy the warrior race which was harassing Brahmin hermitages. Thus the poet refers to him as "Prince Rāma who on his right bears the king-conquering axe" (V.4.6). In an interesting twist, Dāśarathi Rāma, the seventh incarnation of Nārāyaṇa, is said to have destroyed the power and bow of Paraśurāma (III.10.1), the previous incarnation of the same deity.

The seventh and eighth incarnations in the list of Nārāyaṇa's *avatāras* are Rāma and Kṛṣṇa, who are described in detail in separate sections above.

The ninth incarnation has varied depending on the text, but for Periyāḻvār, it is Kṛṣṇa's brother, *Baladeva* (also *Balarāma*), whose white hue contrasts with Kṛṣṇa's dark body (I.7.5). Not only is this Rāma included in the *avatāra* list in verse IV.9.9, but Baladeva's traditional weapons, the plough and the pestle, are listed in Nārāyaṇa's arsenal (IV.7.5). This treatment of Baladeva demonstrates continuity with the late classical Tamil text, the *Paripāṭal,* which describes the white god with the plough as a divine emanation equal to Māyōṉ, the dark one who sleeps in the Milky Sea.[130]

The tenth and final incarnation is the *avatāra* of the future, Kalki, who is simply referenced by name in Periyāḻvār's list of ten incarnations (IV.9.9), with no other references occurring in the text.

Nārāyaṇa will ride a white horse in this descent in order to destroy the wicked.

While Periyāḻvār provided an early list of the ten incarnations of Nārāyaṇa in his verse IV.9.9, in other places in his text, an additional descent is described: the swan. This form, though minor, occurs in some detail in the late classical Tamil *Paripāṭal* which states that the deity "as a male swan dried with his wings the waters that flowed from heaven."[131] The *Tirumoḻi* clarifies that

> When the world was wrapped up in a great thick darkness
> Completely concealing the four eternal Mysteries,
> He removed that darkness which enveloped the world.
> When he was a swan … Oh, my! Oh, my!
> He returned the rare Mysteries … Oh, my! Oh, my!
> (*Tirumoḻi* I.8.10).

This descent then seems to have been for the purpose of saving the four Vedas from the primeval flood at the dissolution of the universe.

The above summaries and discussions should provide the reader with an understanding of the stage of development of Vaiṣṇava mythology at the time Periyāḻvār wrote the *Tirumoḻi* and will prepare the reader to enjoy the verses with an appreciation of the imagery and figurative language used by the poet. I have provided further highlights in header notes at the beginning of each set of verses, with a concordance of Vaiṣṇava episodes in the appendices.

Part II: Translations

Translation Conventions

In translating Periyāl̲vār's *Tirumol̲i,*[132] I have maintained the overall structure of the text which is based on a Tamil literary unit called a *tirumol̲i,* generally consisting of ten individual verses as discussed in the Introduction. As with the original, the translation presents the *tirumol̲is* in groups of ten – First Ten, Second Ten, etc.- resulting in each Ten consisting of approximately 100 verses. The verses are maintained as individual units, numbered consecutively within each *tirumol̲i.* In keeping with the original, each verse of the translation has four lines, most often divided into two measures, as with the Tamil.

In that the original verses are meant to be sung with a rhythmic beat that takes the place of classical literary meter, I have tried to maintain this character by consistently using a rhythmic beat in the translation. In general, the English lines, as with the Tamil, have a *caesura,* a natural break or pause, in approximately the middle of each line. For the most part, the translated verses are meant to be read with two to four stress-beats per half line.

The English version of the poetry does not include a traditional Western rhyme scheme. The rhyme of the Tamil text follows a highly structured, but typical, scheme of initial second syllable rhyme for each four lines of a verse. Verse I.2.3 provides a good example, as its four lines begin respectively with these four words: *paṇaittōḷ, aṇaittār, iṇaikkāl and kaṇaikkāl.* The four-line verse is bound as a unit by the repetition of the second syllable of each line, *-ṇai-*. In this case, the first two lines are further bound by the extension of the syllable to *-ṇaitt-* in both lines, while the third and fourth lines rhyme with the syllable *-ṇaikk-* as the second of each line. The English language is not the least suited to a second syllable rhyme scheme, nor is the Western ear attuned to it, and so I did not attempt this poetic device in the translation.

How can the translation reflect the resonance of the original? The Āl̲vār poets also used both assonance, repetition of vowel sounds, and consonance, repetition of consonants, within each line and across lines to enhance the flow of the verse. On a very regular basis,

Periyāḻvār marked a *caesura* with repetition of the first sound of the line, alliterating the consonant or vowel occurring at the beginning of the line. In fact, the poets of this period used this type of repetition of sounds to a degree that might be considered quite heavy to the English-speaking listener. I have attempted to use a fair amount of vowel and consonant harmony and alliteration to enhance the translation in order to give the reader a sense of the original, but hopefully have avoided the verses sounding ponderous.

Periyāḻvār wrote in the colloquial Brahmin Tamil of his time and avoided a highly literary or scholarly style. The *Tirumoḻi*, as it presents simple scenes from Kṛṣṇa's childhood in the herder village, used spoken phrases, idioms and proverbs to suit not only the content of the verses, but also the poet's audience. The translation attempts to convey this same character through the use of comparable colloquial expressions, simple phrases in English or a conversational tone. In that the development of the devotional mood of the poetry is closely tied to the text's ability to convey the human feelings of the speakers in the verses, I have tried to present an English translation that communicates these same passionate emotions to the Western audience. Overall, I have greatly concerned myself with creating a translation that is true to the voice of the poet, as well as the content of the original text.

The episodal content of Periyāḻvār's texts includes many references to various elements of Vaiṣṇava mythology. To avoid the need for numerous contextual notes interrupting the verses, I have utilized three strategies to assist the reader to understand and appreciate Periyāḻvār's works: 1) I have provided a summary of the mythological stories as they were known to the poet at the time, 2) I have written header notes at the beginning of each *tirumoḻi* to highlight specific elements and features of that song or to discuss the translation of problematic words, and 3) I have provided endnotes where necessary. I suggest that the reader become familiar with the mythology by skimming through the brief summaries provided and by looking through each header note prior to reading a *tirumoḻi*, so that the reader can fully understand and appreciate Periyāḻvār's images and monologues.

Some words have not been translated, particularly proper names of people, plants and places. When the word is a borrowing into Tamil from Sanskrit, I have used standard Sanskrit transliteration, while I have used the accepted Tamil transliteration for Tamil words.[133] Therefore, Kṛṣṇa's mother's name appears in its standard Sanskrit form *Yaśodā*, rather than a transliteration of the Tamil *Acōtai*. Where a name or term in Sanskrit occurs in the original, I have used that word, as in *Vedas*, but where its Tamil rewording is used, I have translated that phrase, as in 'Mysteries' for Tamil *maṟai,* the term used commonly by the Āḻvārs to refer to the Vedas. A chart showing Sanskrit Vaiṣṇava terms with their Tamil transliterations and textual citations can be found in the appendices. The exceptions to the practice described above are few: the Tamil form of *Kṛṣṇa, Kaṇṇaṉ*, has been used throughout to reflect the thorough 'tamilization' of the theme, and the poet's given name *Viṭṭucittaṉ* has remained in his own language, rather than in its Sanskrit form *Viṣṇucitta*. Where possible, I have used English equivalents for trees and plants. Some plants indigenous to India, however, cannot be translated; these have been transliterated, or at times I have provided a descriptive phrase to reflect a poetic image. Tamil *tuḻāy* is provided in its familiar Sanskrit form, *tulasī*, the fragrant basil plant sacred to the Vaiṣṇava sect,[134] and the *kalpataru*, the magic tree in Indra's heaven, is left in its Tamil form, *kaṟpaka* tree.

Readers who are unfamiliar with the Tamil language should not let themselves become bogged down with concern for proper pronunciation to the detriment of enjoying the verses. However, for those readers who are interested in the sound of the original proper names, a few hints may be helpful. Both Tamil and Sanskrit distinguish separate letters for short and long vowels: a (s*u*pper), ā (s*o*p), i (s*i*p), ī (s*ee*p), u (s*oo*t), ū (s*ou*p), e (s*e*t), ē (s*a*ve), ai (s*i*gh), o (s*oa*p), ō (s*o*ld), au (s*ou*th). Tamil consonants are pronounced variously depending on where they occur in the word; they are unvoiced in the beginning or if doubled, but voiced or softened if they occur medially or with a nasal. Examples in that order are as follows: k (*k*id, bla*ck c*at, a*h*ead, hunger), c (*s*o, hat*ch ch*icks, a*s*ide, un*j*ust), ṭ (ca*tt*ail, A*d*am, grin*d*er, pronounced with the tongue bent back), t (*t*o, ho*t t*oddy, brea*th*ing, Hin*d*i, pronounced with the tongue on the teeth), and p (*p*eas, sou*p p*ot, ba*b*y, am*b*er). The nasal n is pronounced with the tongue on the teeth, while the nasal ṉ is similar to English and ṇ is pronounced with the tongue bent back. Velar and palatal nasals occur as n prior to k or g and c or j respectively and approximate English pronunciation. The semivowels – y,r,l,v – are familiar to English speakers, but Tamil has additional semivowels that do not occur in English: ḷ is pronounced with the tongue bent back slightly, while ḻ requires the tongue to bend more and is pronounced with a slight *zh* sound. The consonant ṟ when doubled (ṟṟ) is pronounced as in ci*tr*us, while in combination with ṉ (ṉṟ) sounds like su*ndr*ied.

Sanskrit includes separate letters for aspirated consonants - consonants pronounced by exploding more air - which are transliterated by adding an h: for example, k (*k*ite) and kh (*c*ough). The Sanskrit vowel ṛ as in Kṛṣṇa occurs in a growl (*grrrrr*!) or the word b*ir*d. Sanskrit also has sibilants not found in Tamil: s (*s*ee), ś (*sh*eep) and ṣ (u*sh*er pronounced with the tongue bent back).

Tiruppallāṇṭu

Periyāḻvār is said to have proclaimed the twelve verses of *Tiruppallāṇṭu* when he prevailed in a religious debate held at the traditionally Śaiva Pāṇṭiyaṉ court where he also converted its ruler to the Vaiṣṇava sect. The predominant intent of the text is to declare the worship of Nārāyaṇa - through chanting his names and his mantra - as the unsurpassed means of religious salvation, as established through generations of devotees. The introductory material on the poet's life and texts provides further details. Verse #11 uses the word *celvaṉ* when describing the king of Tirukkōṭṭiyūr as a Vaiṣṇava devotee. While the word can be used as a given name, it means 'wealthy or happy man, king, or god.'[135] As there is inadequate evidence of this verse referring to a specific historical figure,[136] I have translated it as 'noble.'

1

Many years of many years and many thousands of years,
many hundreds of thousands of millions,
Jewel-hued Lord whose strong shoulders threw the wrestlers,
may the beauty of your feet be protected.

2

Many thousands of years to you and your servants, inseparable;
Many years to the Lady who dwells on your finely formed chest;
Many years to the bright disc which shines at your right;
Many years to Pāncanjanya, the conch which roars in battle!

3.

Those who remain devoted in life,
let them bring sandal paste and scent;
We will not admit to our company those devoted only to wealth.
For seven generations, we've been reproach less,
and so we proclaim, "Many years"
To him who in battle laid waste to demon-dwelling Lanka.

4

Before putting yourself at fault, enter into our company.
Those of suitable mind, join quickly without any delay.
Those servants with a mind to sing, "Namo Nārāyaṇa,"
Known to bring goodness to city and countryside,
come proclaim, "Many years!"

5

You in the clan of devotees to Hṛṣīkeśa,
sovereign of the clan of heaven
Who removed the clan of ogres and demons,
come worship at his blessed feet.
Chanting his one thousand names, leave behind your old clan
And come sing with us, "Many years, many thousands of years!"

6

My father, his father, his father's father
and grandfather, from seven generations ago,
All have continuously served him, the One
who during the Ōṇam festival
Destroyed his enemy at dusk, in the form of a lion.
To break our bonds, let us sing,
"Many years, many thousands of years!"

7

We have served generation after generation,
each stamped with the temple mark
Of the brilliant holy disc, a shining red-hot fiery circle.
For him able to spin that disc at Bāṇa,
with magic battle weapons,
To severe his thousand arms, copious blood flowing,
we proclaim, "Many years!"

8

Self-restraint and royal service, rice mixed with fine ghee,
Handsful of betel nut, jewels 'round my neck
and rings for my ears,
And sandal paste for my skin: all these he has granted
and made my life pure.
To the Bearer of the banner with the hooded serpent's foe,
we proclaim, "Many years!"

9

We, his servants, who wear his cast off yellow clothes,
Who crown ourselves with discarded *tulasī*
and eat what was made for him,
We correct our actions which have gone off track.
To him who sleeps on the hooded serpent couch,
Throughout the holy Ōṇam festival, we proclaim, "Many years!"

10

On whatever day it was written
that we are your servants, great Lord,
On that day we in your family of servants
gained salvation and were saved, you know,
One fine day, you appeared in Mathurā
to break the bow, my Lord,
And to leap on the serpent's five hooded heads;
to you we proclaim," Many years!"

11

Like the king, the honored noble, of jeweled Kōṭṭiyūr
Where injustice is never known, Tirumāl ,
I also am your enduring slave.
I spread afar your name in the best way,
saying, "Namo Nārāyaṇa."
To you who are pure in so many ways, I proclaim, "Many years!"

12

"Many years!" - these heartfelt words said to the pure Lord,
Supreme Being, Ruler with the Śārnga bow,
words by Viṭṭucittaṉ of Villiputtūr,-
Those who repeat them with practice in all years,
saying, "Namo Nārāyaṇa,"
Will dwell for many years near the Supreme soul,
praising him with "Many years!"

Periyāḻvār's *Tirumoḻi*

First Ten, 1st tirumoḻi – Kaṇṇaṉ's birth

Periyāḻvār, in the voice of a storyteller, begins his song of Kṛṣṇa with the god's arrival in the cowherd village as a newborn baby. The Āḻvār tells the reader in the first verse that this child, called Kaṇṇaṉ in Tamil (*Kṛṣṇa* in Sanskrit), is a clan noble, a prince, and identifies him with the god Nārāyaṇa. In verse 7, an early Tamil name for Nārāyaṇa, *Māyaṉ*, is also introduced. Periyāḻvār describes a scene of simple rejoicing and amazement in the village, with the herders demonstrating all of the behaviors associated with ecstatic *bhakti*, i.e. devotional worship: dancing, singing, and drumming as they lose themselves in joy. The Āḻvār presents just a few allusions to Kṛṣṇa's majesty and miracles: his stomach containing the universe (verses 6 and 7), lifting Govardhana mountain (verse 8), and kicking the demon cart (verse 9). Toward the end of the *tirumoḻi*, the poet has shifted from third person narration to first person monologue, the predominant voice maintained throughout the text, as we first hear mother Yaśodā's sighs as she realizes the weight, figuratively and literally, that she must bear in raising this divine child. By the final signature verse, Periyāḻvār leaves no doubt that he is telling the story of the Supreme Lord.

I.1.1

When Prince Keśava, Kaṇṇaṉ, was born
In Tirukkōṭṭiyūr with magnificent mansions,
They sprinkled each other with turmeric and oil,
That mixed in a mire in Kaṇṇaṉ's courtyard.

I.1.2

They run and tumble as they shout with joy;
"Where is our Lord?" they anxiously ask.
And the many drums beat in abandon
As they sing and dance in the herder hamlet.

I.1.3

When he was born – this cherished noble child –
Those who came to see him, when entering, would say,
"What being can be like him! He has no equal. See!
He of the Ōṇam star will surely rule the earth."

I.1.4

They dance, spinning pots in the courtyard;
They freely sprinkle milk, sweet ghee and curds.
Their thick soft hair falls loose; they're exhausted.
The herders of the village lose their thoughts in joy.

I.1.5

Those with hanging pots, and these with axes,
Those with herding staffs, and these who make palm mats,
And these with teeth like just-blown jasmine buds -
The cow herders come in crowds to bathe themselves in oil.

I.1.6

Straightening his hands and feet, his mother gently bathed him,
In a copper pot of cool water, with cotton daubed in turmeric.
When she opened up his mouth to scrap clean his tiny tongue,
She saw the seven worlds inside that child's mouth.

I.1.7

Then said that simple lady, who saw the worlds in his mouth,
"This isn't a herder's son; he's an amazing god.
A boy of eminence, of fine quality and character."
That lady said in rapture, "He is surely Māyaṉ!"

I.1.8

On the second day after the first ten,
They placed victory sticks in all eight directions.
The villagers were joyful at the "bringing out" festival
For the boy who supported the huge wild mountain.

I.1.9

When lying in the cradle, he kicked it into bits.
When I lift him to my hip, my sides are overstrained.
When I clutch him close to me, he bounces on my belly.
My strength is failing, Ladies; I am wasting away.

I.1.10

There will be no suffering for those who can sing
These praises composed by Viṭṭucittaṉ,
who wears the shining string,
About eternal Lord Nārāṇa's birth in Tirukkōṭṭiyūr,
The blessed city surrounded by fields of fertile rice.

First Ten, 2nd tirumoḻi – Kaṇṇaṉ from head to toe

Tirumoḻi I.2 is unique in its length as it is composed of 21 verses, as opposed to the approximate decade structure (ten or eleven verses) of most *tirumoḻis*. The additional verses are needed by the poet to completely describe baby Kṛṣṇa in a format known in Sanksrit as *nakha śikha*, 'toenail to hairtuft.'[137] The repeated end phrase, "come and see," is spoken to invite the village ladies to visit the new infant and, according to the final signature verse, is spoken by mother Yaśodā, although she is referred to in third person in several verses. In singing or hearing this song, a devotee creates a mental image of baby Kṛṣṇa, and thereby is blessed with *darśana*, 'seeing the divine,' by visualizing the god in detail. The poet uses the descriptive theme to weave in numerous episodes from Kṛṣṇa mythology. In particular, verses 1 and 6 make it clear that, while Periyāḻvār depicts Yaśodā as Kṛṣṇa's mother, the prevailing myth at the time of the *Tirumoḻi* included that it was Devakī who gave birth to him, while Yaśodā was his foster mother in the cowherd village. Both Kṛṣṇa's birth father, Vasudeva, and his foster father, Nanda, are also mentioned in this song, completing the readers understanding of Kṛṣṇa's parentage. In I.2.5, Periyāḻvār refers to the episode of Kṛṣṇa destroying the demoness, Pūtanā. For poetic enhancement and imagery, I have translated the original *pēycci* 'demoness' here and at times elsewhere as 'harpy,' the Greek bird monster with a woman's head, based on information from other Vaiṣṇava texts. The *Harivamśa*, an earlier Sanskrit text, makes it clear that Pūtanā in her undisguised form was a bird,[138] and Periyāḻvār's contemporary, Mankaiyāḻvār, also affirms that Kṛṣṇa was born on earth "to kill Pūtanā who came at midnight in the form of a bird" (*Periya Tirumoḻi* X.9.1).

I.2.1

See the lotus feet which the sweet babe grabs and sucks.
He was sent by Devakī, like nectar from the cool sea,
To Yaśodā whose hair is bound with fresh flower blossoms.
Coral-lipped ladies, come and see.

I.2.2

See on the feet of the Jewel-hued One,
Ten tiny toes, lined up like rows
Of alternately set jewels, pearls, diamonds and gold.
You with shining foreheads, come and see.

I.2.3

See the ankles shining with silver chains
Of this child who lies sucking the milk-flowing breasts
Of the young milkmaid with bamboo-like lithe arms.
Graceful young girls, come and see.

I.2.4

See his knees on which he crawled in fear
when chased with a churning rope,
Pulled from the churning rod in anger by her who lost
Her only pot of fragrant ghee, for which she toiled, but he ate.
You with budding breasts, come and see.

I.2.5

See the thighs of this child who now lies sleeping,
As he slept after he sucked the breast of that huge harpy,
He, who long ago, split the chest of vile Hiraṇya.
You with rounded breasts, come and see.

I.2.6

See the penis of Acyuta, of him who appeared
On the tenth day of the Hasta star from the womb of Devakī,
Who is never abandoned by the mind
of Vasudeva, a rutting elephant.
You with budding smiles, come and see.

I.2.7

See the waist where fine chains are tied with coral and pearls
Of the Supreme who from the rutting bull elephant
Tore out the tusk and chased the driver.
You with shining foreheads, come and see.

I.2.8

See the perfect navel of the son of Nanda,
Who played alone like a tusked bull elephant,
Proving his strength to the group of boys who followed.
Lustrous-jeweled ladies, come and see.

I.2.9

See his belly which was bound with an old rope,
By the herdess who fed him from her sweet breasts
And fearlessly schemed to catch him, the hue of the roaring sea.
You with shining bracelets, come and see.

I.2.10

See this chest on which shines a heavy swaying jewel,
Of this child who snapped apart two enormous trees
When he was tied tightly to a huge mortar.
Finely jeweled ladies, come and see.

I.2.11

See the shoulders of him who, when four or five month old,
Snatched the life of the demon with sharp and curling teeth,
When he kicked his foot out straight, toppling the cart.
Curly-haired girls, come and see.

I.2.12

See the palms of his hands, the hue of blue field-lilies,
Where are etched the conch and the blood-edged disc,
On the small babe raised by Yaśodā, wide eyes lined in kohl.
Girls with golden earrings, come and see.

I.2.13

See the throat which gulped and contained heaven and earth
Of this little herder who was raised as the son
Of the dairy woman, her hair with bee-laden blossoms.
Graceful young girls, come and see.

I.2.14

See his mouth, as red as caper fruit, kissed by caper fruit lips
Of the maids who thirst for his caper-mouth nectar,
Saying, "Come, Lion of the caper-red lips."
Red-jeweled ladies, come and see.

I.2.15

See the eyes and the nose, the mouth, teeth and lips
And this Prince's tongue which is scraped
As he is bathed with finely ground turmeric paste
by careful Yaśodā.
Ladies with bee-swarming hair, come and see.

I.2.16

See the eyes of the son of Vasudeva with vast lands
Who was raised to wipe out the strong demons
And remove the pain of the heavenly immortals.
Thick-bangled maidens, come and see.

I.2.17

See the eyebrows of him, like a shining black jewel,
Begotten by Devakī, Lady Tiru in beauty,
To protect the whole world before reaching his full age.
Jewel-breasted ladies, come and see.

I.2.18

See the thick *makara* earrings of beautiful color
Of this child who, eating contently, revealed what he ate:
The seven worlds, their seas, mountains and the lands.
Finely-jeweled ladies, come and see.

I.2.19

See the forehead of the Supreme Lord
Who ran and grabbed the girls when playing with their toys:
A winnowing fan, pots and little houses,
    and a mynah on the forearm.
Ladies with strung jewels, come and see.

I.2.20

See the curls of him who watches the calf herd,
His hand with an ornamented staff of fine gold
And little bells on his ankles, jingling as he wanders.
Round-breasted ladies, come and see.

I.2.21

Those who repeat these twenty-one songs
    describing him from his toes to his top,
Composed in devotion by the Bhaṭṭa
    dwelling in southern Putuvai,
As first spoken by Yaśodā, whose hair swarms with bees,
They will be united in heavenly Vaikuṇṭha.

First Ten, 3rd tirumoḻi - A lullaby

In this sweet song, the Āḻvār assumes the voice of mother Yaśodā singing a lullaby, with each verse ending in the twice-repeated lulling sounds, '*tā lē lō*.' Through this repetition, the final line in each verse is doubled in length, creating a structure unique to Periyāḻvār's *Tirumoḻi* among devotional texts of this period and lending to the verse the flavor of a folksong. The verse depicts the baby being showered with divine gifts from the gods, including Brahma, Śiva (here, Īśa), Indra, Kubera Vaiśravaṇa, Varuṇa, and three goddesses: Śrī (Tamil *Tiru*), the Earth, and Durgā who rides the stag. In this way, the poet promotes the Vaiṣṇava god as supreme with all other deities doing homage to him. Some verses celebrate particular pilgrimage sites, but the poet has cleverly chosen shrines in which the image of Nārāyaṇa is in a reclining position as he sleeps on his serpent couch; Yaśodā, like any weary mother of an infant, is hoping her darling will also sleep. Verse 5 provides a reference to Nārāyaṇa-Viṣṇu's five weapons: the discus, conch, mace, sword and bow.

I.3.1

Brahma, to honor you, sent a colorful cradle
Made completely of the finest gold
And alternately tied with diamonds and rubies.
Brahmācharya dwarf, tā lē lō; Spanner of the universe, tā lē lō.

I.3.2

Īśa-with-a-Skull who rides on the bull
Sent a girdle of gold beads strung with pomegranate buds
And a bright charm the shape of a dagger for your waist.
Don't cry; you can have them, tā lē lō; Spanner of the universe, tā lē lō.

I.3.3

Indra gave sandalwood for our Lord's blessed chest
And for his lovely lotus-like feet,
There are beautiful tinkling ankle bells.
He stands nearby, tā lē lō; Lotus-eyed Kaṇṇaṉ, tā lē lō.

I.3.4

The immortals in the vast heaven have sent
A right-whorled conch, sacred thread and chained waistband,
Bangles fit only for your hands and ankle bells for your perfect feet.
Red-eyed dark cloud, tā lē lō; Lion of Devakī, tā lē lō.

I.3.5

Lord Vaiśravana, faultless and liberal, brings
A necklace strung with charms shaped like your five weapons
Saying, "Only these befit his beautiful blessed chest."
He stands in adoration, tā lē lō; Pure-hued Jewel, tā lē lō.

I.3.6

Varuṇa brought fitting gifts from the roaring sea:
A necklace of splendid pearls, the best of ocean corals
And an elegant bracelet from a conch shell.
Heavenly light is your crown, tā lē lō;
Handsome are your shoulders, tā lē lō.

I.3.7.

Lady Tiru who dwells on the nectar-laden lotus
Sent a chaplet, handmade from the fragrant forest *tulasī*,
And a garland of *kaṟpaka* buds from the green groves of heaven.
Little king, don't cry, tā lē lō; You sleep in Kuṭantai, tā lē lō.

I.3.8

Goddess Earth sent for Acyuta a belt with a gold dagger,
A bamboo-shaped bracelet, a jeweled charm for his forehead,
And a row of gold flowers on a shining bough.
You sucked the poison breast, tā lē lō; Don't cry, Nārāyaṇa, tā lē lō.

I.3.9

Our lady who rides the wild stag stands by
Bearing vermillion and, for your bright wide eyes, collyrium,
And turmeric with perfumed powders to sooth your soft skin.
Master, don't cry, tā lē lō; You sleep in Śrīrangam, tā lē lō.

I.3.10

There will never be hardships for those who master without error
These words of the Bhaṭṭa of Putuvai, abode of Mysteries,
The sweet verses of the herdess while lulling
        the collyrium-colored One
Who sucked the breast of the deceitful demoness.

First Ten, 4th tirumoḻi – Calling the moon

Kṛṣṇa's mother now calls to the moon to attract her son's attention so that he will calm down and sleep. She uses various approaches from a simple invitation to guilt, insults and overt threats to make the moon appear. Periyāḻvār includes a particularly clever ploy in I.4.8 by referring to Nārāyaṇa's dwarf incarnation. Yaśodā reminds the moon that Nārāyaṇa once appeared in the court of the demon king, Māvali, as a dwarf who requested to be given as much land as he could cover in three steps. Thinking this would be a very small offering, Māvali agreed, whereupon Nārāyaṇa took his supreme form and covered the earth, the heavens and beyond. In this veiled threat, the moon is encouraged to recognize the baby's divinity and attend to him.

I.4.1

A diadem dances on his brow as he crawls;
Gold trinkets on his ankles tinkle in the dust.
Lovely young moon, if the eyes in your face are real,
Come watch the frolicking of my son, Govinda.

I.4.2

My little fellow, as sweet as nectar to me,
My Lord waves his little hands, point to you and calls.
If you want to play with him – dark-hued as collyrium-
Don't cower in the dark clouds, Moon. Come cheerfully; be quick!

I.4.3

Though your haloed sphere spreads light everywhere,
Whatever you do, you can't compare to my son's face.
The sage of Vēnkaṭa Mountain claps and calls you, Moon.
Don't let his hands hurt. Hurry! Come here!

I.4.4

This Discus-bearer with bud-like eyes blossoming wide
Now sits on my hip and points to you. See!
Don't persist in this stubbornness, Moon, if you know what's best.
Without kids of your own, Old man, you should come and see him.

I.4.5

Drooling nectar from his sweet lips,
Prattling unclear with infant lisps, he coos.
Though called by baby Śrīdara, you just keep on going.
Are your ears hollow holes, Glorious Moon?

I.4.6

The club, discus and Śārnga bow he bears in his wide hands
Which rub his heavy eyes as he sleepily yawns.
If he doesn't sleep, you know, the just-sucked milk will not digest.
Don't nestle in the bosom of the clouds.
Hurry, lovely Moon. Come here!

I.4.7

Don't be insulting and think, "He's just an infant."
This is the babe of long ago whose abode was a banyan leaf.
If you displease him, he'll jump up and seize you.
Don't disregard Lord Māl, Moon. Come cheerfully; be quick!

I.4.8

Don't slight my young Lion by thinking that he's little;
Go ask Māvali for an inkling of how little he is.
And if you still belittle him, you deserve what you'll get.
Tall Māl calls you, so hurry, Full Moon.

I.4.9

He gulped by the handful butter from the pot;
Our pot-bellied Lord now calls you, you know.
He'll hurl his disc at you; have no doubt, Lovely Moon.
If you'd like to keep living, come cheerfully; be quick!

I.4.10

For those who are able to master all of these
Tamil songs set forth by Vittuciṭṭaṉ, renown in famed Puttūr,
These words said to soothe the son of Yaśodā,
Her wide eyes lined with kohl, for them there will be no suffering.

First Ten, 5th tirumoḻi – The red-leaf dance

The term *cenkīrai*, which appears in the refrain of this song, literally means 'red spinach,' but its attributes are what lend to the imagery of the verse. It is most likely a type of *Amaranthus*, an agricultural plant used in the Asian tropics from ancient times which is very tall and produces large edible red leaves.[139] In this verse, the imagery is of a toddler just learning to stand on his own, swaying on unsteady feet, just as the *cenkīrai* reaches up and sways in the field breezes. The poet writes in the voice of mother Yaśodā singing to Kṛṣṇa as she encourages him to stand up. In the course of the verses, she reminds the deity of his many divine exploits, suggesting that the "feat" of learning to stand as a toddler will be easy for him. Also mentioned in verse 8 are several Vaiṣṇava sites important for pilgrimage at the time.

I.5.1

You devoured the world you created and protect it
in your jeweled stomach, Supreme Lord.
From age to age in a yogic sleep, you lie calmly on a banyan leaf,
you of long lotus eyes and kohl form.
Remember your broad chest is the refuge for the Red Lady.
As your costly *makara* earring shimmer and shine
Lord, just once for me, do the red-leaf dance;
Battle bull of the herders, dance; please dance.

I.5.2

In the form of a lion, you slit asunder the demon's chest
sinking your sharp claws into the rising flood of blood,
Intent on revealing the truth to the son and rescuing him.
When the Lord of the celestials came filled with rage,
Filling the sky with darkness and black clouds pouring stones,
you protected the cattle with a mountain as an umbrella.
My Ruler, just once for me, do the red-leaf dance;
Battle bull of the herders, dance; please dance.

I.5.3

Our Leader, Meaning of the Mysteries, Mother
to the four-faced Lord born of your lotus navel,
You expanded over the whole earth,
touching the world beyond the stars and still further.
You are the one who conquered the elephant
and the seven bulls when they charged.
Darling, just once for me, do the red-leaf dance;
Battle bull of the herders, dance; please dance.

I.5.4

You who drank poisoned milk from the breast of the demoness,
you toppled the mighty cart, to the joy of the celestials.
Intending to knock down woodapples in the grove,
you grabbed a calf and threw it, my little calf.
You fought 'til the battlefield shook when you slew the demons
named Dhenuka, Mura and strong, cruel Naraka.
Little elephant, just once for me, do the red-leaf dance;
Battle bull of the herders, dance; please dance.

I.5.5

By the handful, you gulped the ghee
stored by the simple herdess with long hair,
as well as the curds heaped as high as the churning rod.
You of great strength pushed out with your hands and thighs
those who rose from the twin laurel trees twined together.
So your lovely thick hair sways on your face
with its tiny pearl-like teeth, not matured yet,
Like that, just once for me, do the red-leaf dance;
Battle bull of the herders, dance; please dance.

I.5.6

You, the blue of the *kāyā* flower, you like a dark cloud, my beauty,
You destroyed, one after the other, the wrestlers skilled at fighting;
You plucked out the tusk of the tall rutting bull elephant.
You practiced your dance on Kāliya's head in the forest pond.
You had two feet for dancing then!
Little herder, just once for me, do the red-leaf dance;
Battle bull of the herders, dance; please dance.

I.5.7

Without swerving from the words of the wise herders,
once long ago by destroying seven strong bulls,
You became the Lord of Nappiṉṉai,
her pure black hair like feathers of a peacock.
You alone drove the chariot into the great light
to reunite the lost children with their mother.
My father, just once for me, do the red-leaf dance;
Battle bull of the herders, dance; please dance.

I.5.8

The maids put you on their hips and return to their houses
where they each enjoy you and fulfill their desires,
As those who look on satisfy their eyes
and the scholars mutter continuous praises.
Be gracious to me, your own, Lord of Kurunkuṭi and Veḷḷaṟai
King of well-walled Cōlaimalai, Nectar of Kaṇṇapuram
Destroyer of my distress, do the red-leaf dance;
you containing the seven worlds, dance; please, dance.

I.5.9

Filled with the fragrance of milk, ghee and curds,
sandalwood and camphor, lotus and magnolia flowers,
As your few teeth, like new white shoots,
glisten between your fragrant red coral lips,
Nectar from your sweet mouth drops and falls,
running among the blue amulets of your five weapons.
Meaning of the Mysteries, do the red-leaf dance;
you containing the seven worlds, dance; please, dance

I.5.10

Bright bells are on your red lotus feet
and rings on your petal-like fingers.
On your waist is a gold chain hung with gold pomegranate buds;
finger rings, coral bangles and armbands,
Five weapon-shaped charms for good luck,
a forehead jewel, earbobs and *makara* earrings will all glitter,
King of our clan, if you do the red-leaf dance.
You containing the seven worlds, dance; please, dance

I.5.11

"Leader of the cowherd who became a swan,
a fish, man-lion, dwarf and tortoise,
Destroyer of my distress, do the red-leaf dance;
you containing the seven worlds, dance; please, dance."
Those who master these joyful words of Yaśodā with a swan's gait,
the garland of ten in this sweet Tamil song
Of the Bhaṭṭa of famed Putuvai, will gain joy
famed in the eight directions of the world.

First Ten, 6th tirumoḻi – Hand clapping

In *Tirumoḻi* I.6, the Great Āḻvār presents rich descriptive passages providing a detailed picture of the deity as a baby learning to clap his hands. *Darśana,* 'seeing' the image of god, is an important expression of devotion in Hinduism, whether the deity is seen as a statue in a temple or home shrine, an illustration, or a mental image, as provided here. In several verses, the poet uses repetition of a complete word at the beginning of each line, instead of just the second syllable as is standard in Tamil rhyme, thereby weaving the content of the stanza around several uses of one word. Verse 6 refers to the great epic, the *Mahābhārata*, while verses 7 and 8 draw on episodes from the *Rāmāyaṇa*, juxtaposing Kṛṣṇa's sweet infant play with his majestic divine feats.

I.6.1

As ruby-jeweled anklets jingle, on your waist above
Are perfect gold bells made with the best of ore.
Your pearl-like teeth set in the coral of your lips shine.
Clap your hands that once took the lands of Māvali;
Little dark-haired boy, please clap your hands.

I.6.2

A golden hip chain glitters strung with ruby-jeweled bells,
As your hips sway with the swaying of a single gem on your brow.
From my hip, slip down and go to the king of the cow herders.
Sit on his hip and clap your hands;
Māyavaṉ, please clap your hands.

I.6.3

Like jeweled pearls set midst fine coral
From your jeweled lips glisten pearl-like teeth.
My jewel-hued child with gold leaf earrings
On the jeweled hips of your mother, clap your hands;
My discus bearer, please clap your hands.

I.6.4

Go to the moonlit courtyard and call the moon to play;
"Moon, heavenly orb, Chandra, do come here!"
He will shine with joy, the king of the cowherds who adores you.
Go to him and clap your hands;
You who lies in Kuṭantai, clap your hands.

I.6.5

With your chubby body covered in dust and mud
You entered the house, unseen, smearing mud everywhere,
And ate up the butter from the mud pots and a whole jar of curds.
Little calf of the cattlefold, please clap your hands.
Padmanābha, please come clap your hands.

I.6.6

The resolute One Hundred without heeding their father's word
Entered full force into a fight to rule the land.
The day those stalwart kings were killed,
you drove the chariot of the Five.
With those hands that held the reins, please clap;
Lion of Devakī, please clap your hands.

I.6.7

You shot an arrow to agitate the sea which refused to grant your wish,
Making high waves crash above the entreating hands
Of the King of the Sea, ever vast and deep.
Your hands bear the Śārnga bow; please clap;
With those very hands, please clap.

I.6.8

With a legion of monkeys, you assailed the roaring sea,
And building a bridge across the wide waters,
You assaulted Lanka, annihilating the ogre clan.
With your hands that shot the arrow, please clap;
Discus bearer, please come clap your hands.

I.6.9

When he viciously kicked the pillar which he'd built,
You burst from that spot as a sharp-clawed lion,
And then split Hiraṇya's glittering broad chest.
With those hands that dug out his entrails, please clap;
    You who drank from the demoness' breast, please clap.

I.6.10

For the imploring immortals, you pushed back the deep sea
And there fixed Mount Mandara as a churning rod.
For a rope, you wrapped around it the serpent, Vāsuki.
With your hands that churned the sea, please clap;
    Black cloud, please come and clap your hands.

I.6.11

For those who say with longing the twice-five handclapping verses
Written with longing by the Bhaṭṭa of Villiputtūr,
    with fragrant gardens blooming daily,
Describing the Lord's human form when he came as the cowherd king,
All evil fate for them will surely disappear.

First Ten, 7th tirumoḻi – Learning to walk

In this song, Periyāḻvār focuses on Kṛṣṇa's infant charm, presenting the deity in an utterly adorable form - a toddler learning to walk. References to divine feats are minimal, the verses being filled with descriptions of his chubby feet, new baby teeth, and hesitant steps as he drools. However, the mention in I.7.9 of Trīvikrama (Tamil *tirivikkiramaṉ*) 'three stepper,' a reference to Nārāyaṇa's dwarf incarnation in which he grew and covered the universe in three strides, sharply contrasts with the deity's toddling pace, to the amazement of his mother who is worried that he will fall. She is immersed in the gracious illusion of Kṛṣṇa as her baby son. The poet introduces Kṛṣṇa's older half-brother, Baladeva (Tamil *palatēvaṉ*) in verse 5 whose white complexion contrasts with Kṛṣṇa's dark hue. Like most little kids, Kṛṣṇa is intent on trying to follow his older brother, who scampers ahead of the trailing toddler. Both the devotee-poet and the mother are overwhelmed with unconditional love for the divine baby, asking nothing in return and simply delighting in his charm.

I.7.1

Like the slow plodding of an elephant, its three ichors flowing,
As gold bells hanging from chains 'cross its back toll, "clang, clang,"
The Śārnga bow bearer toddles, jingling ankle chains
and drum shaped hip jewels,
Carefully placing his two chubby feet;
won't he walk, tripping and tottering?

I.7.2

With a new cool white tooth rising
from the gums of his coral red mouth
Shining like the new crescent moon rising
from the red horizon, he laughs,
He who sleeps on Ananta toddles,
wearing a turtle charm on a string of bone beads,
Vāsudeva, the hue of a perfect jewel;
won't he walk, tripping and tottering?

I.7.3

Like the white moon and its shimmering rays
glowing through the encircling aura,
A pīpal-leaf pendant of gold hangs from a gold braid ‘round his hips
Wrapped in a saffron-dyed raiment. Hṛṣīkeśa toddles
with a gold torque at his neck
And shines like a lightning-laden dark cloud;
won’t he walk, tripping and tottering?

I.7.4

Laughing with saliva oozing like syrup from a hole in a pot,
He toddles forward to give me a kiss,
the cloud-colored One with Tiru at his chest.
He is mine; when he gives me nectar
from his sweet mouth, it thrills me.
He, who tramples on the heads of his defiant foes,
won’t he walk, tripping and tottering?

I.7.5

As a big white mountain runs scampering ahead
A little black mountain comes behind, carefully placing each step.
So runs Baladeva, his endless fame praised the world around,
With his brother toddling behind;
won’t he walk, tripping and tottering?

I.7.6

With the sign of the conch imprinted on one foot
and the sign of the disc on the other,
He makes these marks here and there with his feet,
as if he is drawing as he steps.
Kāma’s grandsire rains down delight
over and over in a flood which keeps rising.
He whose hue is of a dark storming sea,
won’t he walk, tripping and tottering?

I.7.7

Like little dew drops rolling off a full blooming lotus blossom,
From his red mouth, saliva oozes, beads, drips and falls.
The Śārnga bow bearer toddles,
    jingling waist jewels like a bell on a bull's neck,
Carefully placing his two chubby feet;
    won't he walk, tripping and tottering?

I.7.8

As if describing a mountain stream on the slopes of a small dark hill,
A string of shells hangs on his hips, moving up, then down.
Vāsudeva whose hue is of a perfect jewel,
    took the form of a jewel-like infant
Unknown in the human world before;
    won't he walk, tripping and tottering?

I.7.9

Like a black elephant calf tossing white dust on itself
Trīvikrama plays in the fine dust sweating 'til it sticks in spots.
So his little feet, like bright lotus buds, won't hurt when he steps,
He toddles on a quilt cooled with petals;
    won't he walk, tripping and tottering?

I.7.10

Like the orb of the moon over rolling sea waves,
    red-eyed Māl, Keśava wears
A jewel on his sweat-washed brow which glitters as it sways to and fro.
With more sacred force than the Ganges itself,
    where flooding waters swell in waves,
Water trickles from his small penis as he toddles;
    won't he walk, tripping and tottering?

I.7.11

Those who can recite this fine verse
of Viṭṭucittaṉ, praised by the Vēyars,
These songs of the collyrium-colored Lord
who appeared in the cowherd clan
As he toddled, tripping and tottering,
for his mother's joy and his rival's fall,
They will have children who will worship
the jewel-hued feet of Māyaṉ.

First Ten, 8th tirumoḻi – A mother's delight

The Āḻvār uses the common Tamil interjection of wonder, amazement and delight, '*accō*,' four times in each of the double-length last lines of each verse in this song. The sense imparted is that Yaśodā is amazed at having Kṛṣṇa for her son and cannot believe her good fortune, just as the devotee-poet is enchanted by the image of the divine baby in his mind. In this *tirumoḻi*, Yaśodā calls out descriptive exclamations or utters incomplete sentences, leading the commentator to say[140] that she is so overwhelmed, she is at a loss for words and spontaneously exclaims *accō* without being able to finish her thoughts. In keeping with this expressive tone, "Oh, my! Oh, my!" is probably the best translation of the exclamation following her incomplete thought. Much of the episodal content in the verse is from outside the baby Kṛṣṇa cycle, including references from the *Mahābhārata* and the dwarf incarnation myth. The story of Kṛṣṇa curing the hunch-backed girl is found in I.8.4. Verse 8 mentions a son of Māvali named Namuci who objected to his father giving land to the dwarf; no other Āḻvār mentions this episode. The story of Śiva's curse, as discussed in the section on mythology, is referenced in verse 9. The swan incarnation, which is of minor importance in Sanskrit texts, is mentioned twice in the *Tirumoḻi*, I.5.11 and below in I.8.10, as well as in earlier Tamil literature.

I.8.1

Decked with golden bells and jewels on his head,
He fills the air with a soft jingling sound
As he rushes toward me like a cloud filled with lightning.
When he runs to my hip … Oh, my! Oh, my!
    When our Lord comes to me … Oh, my! Oh, my!

I.8.2

Black curls swarm 'round his coral-lipped face
Like bees sucking nectar from a red lotus blossom.
He bears the bow and club, the conch, sword and disc.
With those beautiful hands … Oh, my! Oh, my!
When he comes to hold me tight ... Oh, my! Oh, my!

I.8.3

As a messenger for the Five, he had a hand in the Bhārata War.
And he entered the pond where lay the poison-spitting serpent;
He leapt on his horrible head to grant his gracious mercy.
That collyrium-colored One … Oh, my! Oh, my!
Lord of the cattle fold … Oh, my! Oh, my!

I.8.4

He said, "Give us some fragrant sandal paste."
Shrewdly, she anointed his blessed body,
And her swollen hump then shrank inside.
Her shape was straight that day… Oh, my! Oh, my!
That our Lord may come to me … Oh, my! Oh, my!

I.8.5

Deceitful Duryodhana surrounded by warriors wearing war anklets
Saw you shining like the sun, and unconsciously
He began to rise but quickly sat himself down again.
His glare that was like fire … Oh, my! Oh, my!
His lovely hand with the disc … Oh, my! Oh, my!

I.8.6

To level the field in the Great War
and to remove the burdens on the earth,
He drove the chariot for Vijaya, with verdant victory garlands,
He with wide black eyes and black body like a cloud.
When he comes to hold me tight … Oh, my! Oh, my!
Battle bull of the cowherds … Oh, my! Oh, my!

I.8.7

At the sacrifice of Māvali, who was praised as great by many,
Warning, "This is not to your advantage," Śukra forbade the boon.
The Lord poked out his eye with a piece of straw.
His hand that bears the disc … Oh, my! Oh, my!
And the left with the conch … Oh, my! Oh, my!

I.8.8

"What is this trickery? My father didn't know!
Take your former form to measure the land."
So said stubborn Namuci whom he sent spinning into the sky.
He of the glittering crown … Oh, my! Oh, my!
Liberal Lord of Vēnkaṭa … Oh, my! Oh, my!

I.8.9

"All the known seas and mountains, as well as the seven worlds,
Will not suffice to fill this skull, Cloud-colored One. Oh, no!"
So entreated Īśa with the tightly tangled locks.
The Lord filled up that skull … Oh, my! Oh, my!
He with the mark on his chest … Oh, my! Oh, my!

I.8.10

When the world was wrapped up in a great thick darkness
Completely concealing the four eternal Mysteries,
He removed that darkness which enveloped the world.
When he was a swan … Oh, my! Oh, my!
He returned the rare Mysteries … Oh, my! Oh, my!

I.8.11

Those who incessantly sing these songs of the Bhaṭṭa king,
Who dwells in Putuvai, adorned with multi-storied mansions,
The words of the herdess, "That he
may come to me … Oh, my! Oh, my!"
Singing to Nārāyaṇa who stands before his adorers,
they will rule the vast heavens.

First Ten, 9th tirumoḻi – Hugging mother's back

Periyāḻvār's representation of god as a child makes the deity accessible without penance or renunciation, scholarship or yogic meditation. God is directly available to mothers and children, and as shown by the final signature verse in this *tirumoḻi*, devotional contemplation of Kṛṣṇa in his child form is perceived as a means of bringing to a mother children of her own. In this song, Yaśodā is understood to be, like many village women in India, going about her daily chores sitting or squatting on the ground, while her youngster scampers about. And as toddlers exploring the greater world are want to do, Kṛṣṇa periodically returns to his mother, grabbing her from behind as she leans over her work, illustrating Yaśodā's close relationship with the imminent god. Verse I.9.1 presents what must be a realistic scene in which the toddler pees down his mother's back; the verse incorporates the Sanskrit word for 'ruby' *māṇika* to suggest the Tamil word for 'penis' *māṇi*, to complete the meaning of the verse. In verse I.9.4, which refers to the *Mahābhārata* war, Dhananjaya and Vijaya are both names for Arjuna, one of the Pāṇḍava brothers. Verse I.9.9 tells the story of Satyabhāma, one of Kṛṣṇa's wives.

I.9.1

Like pearls sprouting from the tip
Of a ruby bud rising from a round orb,
Little drops trickle like drizzling rain
As my baby comes and hugs my back; Govinda hugs my back.

I.9.2

Anklebells tied at his feet, coral beads tied at his wrists,
A bracelet adorning his arm, and a chain hanging 'round his neck –
With all of his golden trinkets, he comes dancing and prancing.
My Kaṇṇaṉ hugs my back; our Lord hugs my back.

I.9.3

He appeared there to ruin the clan of the army commander
Who, teeming with evil, ruled the land
Refusing to yield wealth he hoarded.
The Lord comes and hugs my back;
the Bull of the herders hugs my back.

I.9.4

For Dhananjaya who humbly begged refuge
And to terrify the kings of that land
The Prince with the Nandaka sword drove Vijaya's chariot.
The charioteer hugs my back; the King of heaven hugs my back.

I.9.5

Beneath a parasol of peacock feathers, dark and many eyed,
He came in clever play, tied with a bronze leaf pendant,
As were sung many melodies and "Many Years" was chanted.
He who took the worlds hugs my back; Vāmana hugs my back.

I.9.6

As a lone brahmācarya bearing an umbrella,
From him who stood at the sacred northern altar,
While the warriors watched, he took all the land.
That embodiment of blessings hugs my back;
He who measured the earth hugs my back.

I.9.7

He turned the bowl of the mortar face down, then he climbed on top
And gulped down all the sweet milk and the butter from that pot
Until his blessed belly was completely full.
The Lord comes and hugs my back; the Discus bearer hugs my back.

I.9.8

He climbed upon a sandy hill so all the elders could see
And performed a delightful dance, while playing a song on his flute.
While worshipped by those to whom the Mysteries have been revealed,
And as immortals praise him, he hugs my back;
          our blessed Lord hugs my back.

I.9.9

When his beloved longed for the *kaṟpaka* tree
          growing in Indra's grove,
He said, "I'll give it to you right now,"
And firmly fixed it in her own moonlit courtyard.
He who planted it hugs my back;
          the King of celestials hugs my back.

I.9.10

Those who can recite these twice-five Tamil verses
          joyfully given by Viṭṭucittaṉ,
These words of the herdess whose bamboo-like shoulders
Were hugged from behind by the Lord with the disc,
They will rejoice in begetting good children.

Second Ten, 1st tirumoḻi – Making scary faces

While the First Ten concerns Kṛṣṇa's infant-toddler stage, the Second Ten portrays him as a little older child, one who is prone to mischief and willfulness. The verses shift focus to the concept of god's *līlā*, 'divine play,' the view of the universe as god's playground where events are a result of divine whimsy. In the verses of *Tirumoḻi* II.1, the poet writes in the voice of a girl being tormented by Kṛṣṇa who, as an obnoxious little boy, is jumping out and startling the speaker while making a bug-eyed scary face. The identity of the speaker is revealed in the phrase, he "took our flowery silk saris" (verse 4). This *tirumoḻi* provides a good example of Periyāḻvār's innovative use of doubled fourth lines as a refrain to focus the song on Kṛṣṇa's childhood antics and personality. Each fourth line twice contains the phrase, *pūcci kāṭṭukiṉṟāṉ*, literally, 'he's showing bugs.' A related phrase suggests the true action in the verse. *Pūcciyāṇṭi* and its shorter form *pūccāṇṭi* refer to a bogeyman or ghost, literally a 'buggy-beggar,' and *pūcciyāṇṭi kāṭṭu*, refers to scaring a child by making frightening faces.[141] The response, *ammaṉē*, literally 'Oh, Mother' or 'Oh, Goddess,' is simply an exclamation of surprise, translated here as 'Eeek!' Several of these verses refer to episodes from the *Mahābhārata* epic, while II.1.8 presents the touching story of Rāma giving up his kingdom to his brother, Bharata, and being exiled into the forest. The words *Bhārata* and *Bharata*, varying in vowel length, have quite different meanings and are not to be confused.

II.1.1

With the well-blown conch at his left, he who blows a bamboo flute
Had a hand in the Bhārata War long ago,
        when not even ten cities could be had
For the patient king who had lost all in the devious gambling match.
That messenger is making scary faces.
        Eeek! He's making scary faces.

II.1.2

To destroy the One Hundred who made others tremble –
Kings with stone-hard shoulders, great charioteers and more –
He stood at the fore of the great chariot as Pārtha bent his bow.
That red-eyed chatterbox is making scary faces.
Eeek! He's making scary faces.

II.1.3

He went into the churning waters and climbed a *kadamba* tree,
Then jumped on Kāliya's fiery hoods. With his anklebells jingling,
He blew his bamboo flute and danced there – what a wonder!
That cowherd boy is making scary faces.
Eeek! He's making scary faces.

II.1.4

He was born at midnight to end the fears of the simple cowherd folk
And to overthrow and kill the cruel demon, Kaṃsa.
But one day he came and took our flowery silk saris.
That rascal is making scary faces.
Eeek! He's making scary faces.

II.1.5

He who shattered the oxcart stole the ghee collected
By Nanda's wife who then beat him with the churning rod.
Then he tried to leap free, and wriggled and writhed in pain.
The boy who was tied is making scary faces.
Eeek! He's making scary faces.

II.1.6

He who was born without blemish to Lady Devakī,
Whose soft young breasts are like copper pots,
Was brought to the herder village where he ate ghee, milk and curds.
That darling is making scary faces.
Eeek! He's making scary faces.

II.1.7

She adopted him, didn't she? Or did she bear him herself?
All of Yaśodā's thoughts are of her young lion –
The fierce lion of the cowherders, his black mane full of flowers.
The Lord is making scary faces.
Eeek! He's making scary faces.

II.1.8

At a word from her with a breast-like hump,
His elephants of worldwide praise, his horses and kingdom,
Everything, he gave to Bharata, then went into the harsh forest.
He of lovely eyes is making scary faces.
Eeek! He's making scary faces.

II.1.9

That bull elephant, when caught in the fierce crocodile's mouth,
Raised its trunk in prayer, crying, "Kaṇṇaṉ, my Kaṇṇaṉ,"
Who came riding a bird and there ended its pain.
That Mighty One is making scary faces.
Eeek! He's making scary faces.

II.1.10

Those who sing these ten "scary face" songs,
Words of eloquent diction written by Viṭṭucittaṉ
Spreading the fame of the archer
who sent arrows to trouble guarded Lanka,
They will reach Vaikuṇṭha and there be forgiven.

Second Ten, 2nd tirumoḻi – Calling Kaṇṇaṉ to suckle

Modern Westerners might feel that a boy who is old enough to tease others by making scary faces (as in the previous song) but who still nurses from his mother's breast would get teased himself. But in predominantly agricultural, traditional cultures, breastfeeding until the age of 3 or 4 would be common. With episodal content at a minimum, this song focuses on Yaśodā's darling and her overwhelming affection for him. The Aḻvār writes in her voice in direct speech to the deity, as she calls him to her. Her pressing need to nurse him due to the swelling of her breasts with milk is a powerful metaphor for the urgent longing and overflowing love of the devotee-poet for his god. Both the Āḻvār's and mother's desires are thwarted by god's playful capriciousness.

II.2.1

Bull of the cowherds who sleeps on a serpent,
 wake up now to suck my breast.
You went to sleep without eating last night
 and now it's nearly noon, is it not?
I don't see you coming; your tummy must be grumbling.
 Drops of milk trickle from my breast.
Come cling close to me, kicking up your feet
 and drink, sucking with your blessed lips.

II.2.2

Since the day you were born, my Lord,
 I've known nothing of getting a drop
Of stored ghee or heated milk or thick curds or fragrant butter.
You get to do whatever you want; I do nothing. Just don't fuss.
Show me a smile with your pearl-like teeth,
 and sighing through your nose, drink from my breast.

II.2.3

If you make the children cry, their mothers cannot stand it.
When they come with complaints about you,
    you thrive on it, Vāsudeva.
Your father won't punish you properly, and I can't scold you at all.
Little Beauty of Nanda Gopāla, drink from my swollen breasts.

II.2.4

When you kicked the treacherous cart which was contrived by Kaṃsa,
I feared for your fine soft feet, King of the immortals.
The cowherd clan's fear knew no limit when,
    through your own deceitful means,
You captured Kaṃsa that day. Come and drink from my breast.

II.2.5

Evil-minded Kaṃsa is full of rage against you;
If he sees you weak and captures you through deceit,
    I can't live, Vāsudeva.
It's your duty to heed your mother's words,
    and I said, "Don't go!" emphatically.
Jeweled Lamp of the herder village, stay and drink from my breast.

II.2.6

Villiputtūr is made sweet by the humming of bees
    creeping on the loosened locks
Of ladies with lightning-thin waists; but the sweetest thing is you.
When people see you, they say,
    "What penance did she do who bore him in her womb?"
So such words may be said, Hṛṣīkeśa, come drink from my breast.

II.2.7

The women who live just to watch you with longing,
say, “Let me bear one just like you.”
They can’t part from you, but stand staring with eyes opened wide.
Those ladies with bee-laden buds in their hair,
long to sip nectar from your lips
And stand waiting for a chance to take you.
Govinda, drink from my breast.

II.2.8

When the mountain-like wrestlers opposed you,
you made their bodies burn.
To fill yourself up to your shining broad chest, come climb onto my hip
And nursing first from one breast while softly caressing the other,
By turn and turn again with a snuffle and sigh,
drink from both my breasts.

II.2.9

Beads of sweat on your pink lotus face are like scattered pearl drops
Inside the bud of a lotus flower. Don’t make mischief in the courtyard,
Wallowing in the dust ‘til your whole body is covered.
King of immortals who pleased immortals with nectar,
come drink from my breast.

II.2.10

You hum and sing with jingling ankle bells tinkling
As you come running, and I think, “This is Padmanābha!”
But don’t run off again, Lord Supreme, doing your little dance
With your shaking and swaying. Come drink from my breast.

II.2.11

Those who know the song whose ancient praise adorns the world,
The song of the Bhaṭṭa Lord of Villiputtūr,
        fragrant with blue lilies in the pools,
These words of the herdess with beautiful bound breasts,
        calling, “Mādhava, come and eat,”
Their thoughts will ever cling to bright red-eyed Māl.

Second Ten, 3rd tirumoḻi – Piercing Kaṇṇaṉ's ears

Tirumoḻi II.3 is interesting on several levels. For one, it refers to a practice, common until recent times, of piercing the ears at an early age, then inserting heavier and heavier earrings so that the lobes will gradually lengthen. Kṛṣṇa will have no part of it, even though his mother coaxes, threatens and pleads. Also, here is the first time in the text that the poet writes in the voice of Kṛṣṇa, himself. While the first verses in this *tirumoḻi* are in the voice of his mother, as in previous songs, by II.3.7 the listener hears Kṛṣṇa's taunting response to her. In verses 7 through 12, Kṛṣṇa's retort is in the first part of each verse, and his mother's further response is in the latter part, creating a conversation between them. In order to highlight the argumentative "give-and-take" between them, Periyāḻvār used a poetic structure, *antāti* meaning 'end-beginning,' in which the first word or words in a verse are a repetition of the last words of the previous verse, as Kṛṣṇa throws his mother's own words back at her in sarcastic comebacks. The poet further enriched the song and lengthens the *tirumoḻi* by using one of the twelve names of the deity in each of twelve verses, occurring in the traditional order as follows: Keśava, Nārāyaṇa, Mādhava, Govinda, Viṣṇu, Madhusūdana, Trīvikrama, Vāmana, Śrīdara, Hṛṣīkeśa, Padmanābha, and Dāmodara.[142] Verse II.3.5 contains the only reference in the *Tirumoḻi* to the name Viṣṇu (Tamil *viṭṭu*) for the Vaiṣṇava deity celebrated in the text, except as it occurs in the poet's name, Viṭṭucittaṉ (Sanskrit *Viṣṇucitta*).

II.3.1

Your hard-working father stays out late; there's no one to protect you
From Kaṃsa, cruel and courageous in battle, but you wander out alone.
Crazy boy who ate the demon's breast milk,
Prince Keśava, I've prepared betel nut.
All the ladies of the cowherd, Sea-hued One,
have come to pierce your ears.

II.3.2

Nārāyaṇa who's never far from the minds
of those who worship your flower-like feet
Where anklebells ring sweetly along with
the coral jewels tied 'round your waist.
Come, Lord so hard to comprehend;
I'll put the thread through your ear without pain.
These ear studs are auspicious to the eye and made of beautiful gold.

II.3.3

I've brought ear jewels in the shape of the *makara*
which dwells in the ocean covering the whole earth.
If your ears burn when I put in the thread,
I'll give you anything you want.
Bright Light who appeared to protect the cowherd clan,
My little cowherd sprout,
You who madden the young milkmaids' hearts,
Mādhava, please come here.

II.3.4

The well-behaved children of the herders
have put on fine diamond ear studs
So their ear lobes enlarge and lengthen.
But, Govinda, you don't heed my pleas.
If you put on this pair of fine ear studs,
I'll give you sweet-tasting jack fruit.
Come here, Praiseworthy Prince, and I'll give you
my fine saffron-smeared breast to nurse.

II.3.5

Even if I plead and call you "Praiseworthy Prince,"
you don't listen; shall I praise you, young man,
When you go off with those curly-haired girls
to clasp hands in the *kuravai* dance?
If you allow me to put in this thread, Lord,
I'll give you these huge rice cakes.
Your black locks are longed for by bamboo-limbed ladies;
Viṣṇu, please come here.

II.3.6

When you wailed so all the heavens heard,
I stared intently into your mouth.
I saw the whole world, and my heart trembled;
I knew then this is Madhusūdhana.
My Prince, there'll be no scar; your ear will just pinch a bit.
Be good for just a split second!
Kaṇṇaṉ, Protector, my sea-hued One,
my dark cloud, come nurse from my breast.

II.3.7

"I don't want your breast or anything," you said
and ran, plucking out and tossing the studs.
But you grazed the cattle and protected them from hail stones
by easily lifting a mountain.
You're the one who broke the bow, Trīvikrama;
You're the Lord of the whole herder village.
When you couldn't lift your tiny head, I left your ears alone.
It's really my fault, isn't it?

II.3.8

"Stop saying, 'My fault.' When I ate dirt one day,
what a loving look you had
When you caught me and beat me for everyone to see."
Vāmana whose flag bears the foe of the serpent,
you're the one who allays all pain.
Put this thread in your ears or the holes will close up.
My Lord, I'm telling the truth.

II.3.9

"The truth? You believe every word they say.
'You snatched and ate butter,' you said
And catching my hand, tied me to a mortar for all to see, didn't you?"
If you stand their smirking, reciting all I've done,
the holes in your ears, Śrīdara, will close.
Take this thread from my hand and put it in yourself
so these ladies here won't laugh.

II.3.10

"You and these ladies, what's it to you
if my ears burn and swell up?"
It's unbearable, his head will hurt, so I didn't do it before.
It's all my fault, isn't it?
Kaṇṇaṉ, Hṛṣīkeśa who destroyed the bull and threw the calf,
See all the kids in the village with their lovely ear lobes lengthened.

II.3.11

To soothe their eyes, ladies with hair scented with blooms,
seek you everywhere,
Great Lord, our sweet Ambrosia who remains always in our thoughts.
I'll give you ripe fruit to eat and painlessly put the thread in your ears.
You kicked and splintered the demon cart.
Padmanābha, please come here.

II.3.12

"'Come here,' you say and grab my hand,
then force the studs in my ears.
What's it to you if it hurts? I can't stand the pain."
But I've brought you some nice jambo fruit;
My Prince, just look at these.
You kicked the cart; sucked the demon's breast and killed her,
Dāmodara, please come here.

II.3.13

These words of Yasódā to Tirumāl -
her wish to put in *makara* ear jewels
To make his ear lobes hang long –
words composed by the king of Putuvai
Of ancient fame which fills the earth and even shines in the mind,
Those who say these twelve names in twelve *antāti* verses
are servants of Acyuta.

Second Ten, 4th tirumoḻi - Kaṇṇaṉ's bath

In a fairly conversational tone, the Āḻvār presents in this song a weary-worn Yaśodā coaxing Kṛṣṇa away from his mischievous pastimes to come take a bath. The reader gets a fairly detailed picture of the oil bath: the child is rubbed with oil to clean and soften the skin, then tamarind juice is used to remove the dirty oil. After this, the child is rinsed in warm water with gooseberries used as an astringent. Fragrant sandal paste cools the skin after the bath and collyrium is reapplied to the eyes to cut glare and counteract any "evil eye" directed toward the child. Yaśodā bribes Kṛṣṇa with treats to get him to come, but also uses other strategies. In II.4.7, she points out that if she has to scold him in front of others, it will reflect badly on his birth mother, Devakī. The Tamil word *naṟṟāy* is derived from *nal* – 'good' and *tāy* 'mother,' but means specifically 'one's own mother.'[143] I believe the modifier *ciṟanta* 'superior, noble' suggests that Yaśodā is not speaking of herself, a dairy woman, but about Kṛṣṇa's birth mother from the warrior class. Verse II.4.9 references Nappiṉṉai, 'our little girl'; as Yaśodā's brother's daughter, she is Kṛṣṇa's "cross cousin" and destined by Tamil kinship practices to be Kṛṣṇa's bride. Yaśodā threatens her son that his future wife might laugh at him if he doesn't take his bath. This song is one of many in the text in which the Great Āḻvār presents the mother's efforts to catch her son as a metaphor for the devotee's endeavors to grasp and understand the unconditioned behavior of the deity.

II.4.1

Since you've played in the dust, and you reek of churned butter,
I can't let you go to sleep tonight until I've scrubbed you hard.
I've gotten the oil and the tamarind all ready;
how long must I wait here?
Lord , so hard to reach, Nāraṇa, come take your bath.

II.4.2

If you catch black ants to put in the ears of the calves to make them run,
They'll scatter and go astray; let's see if you gulp butter then!
Ōṇam, the star of your birth is today, so you should come and bathe.
You who fell the fig tree, Our Lord, please don't run away.

II.4.3

Though I saw you suck the harpy's breast, my heart did not falter;
And though the milkmaids cried out, I still gave you my breast.
I've filled up the copper boiler with warm water and gooseberries.
You the hue of a well-praised jewel, come here to take your bath.

II.4.4

You kicked over the cruel cart which was contrived by Kaṃsa;
You put your mouth to her breast, Lord, so the deceitful demoness died.
I've brought you turmeric powder, collyrium and sandal paste,
And a garland of red lilies. My beauty, come and bathe.

II.4.5

I've made little rice cake snacks and mixed sugar into the milk.
I've kept them good and hot! So if you'd like to eat, my Prince,
Come here, Praiseworthy Lord. You should have a good bath,
Or the girls with copper-pot breasts will laugh and gossip about you.

II.4.6

You tip over the pots of oil, you pinch and wake the babies,
Then you roll your eyes back into your head, Lord of mischief.
Beautiful Prince, whose hue is of the flooding waters in the roaring sea,
I will give you ripe fruit to eat. Come here and take your bath.

II.4.7

Since your birth, my Lord, I know nothing of fresh milk and curds
Or of having newly churned butter hanging high in the nets.
Since others would slander your noble birth mother,
　　　　I won't forget myself
And speak about this in front of them. Just come and take your bath.

II.4.8

It seems you tied palm leaves to a calf's tail
and threw it to knock down ripe fruit.
Then you went after a huge snake, caught it and danced on its head.
My Prince, I don't have your strength. Please don't run away.
It's the blessed day on which you were born.
Come here, Nārāyaṇa! You should bathe well today.

II.4.9

Your body turns gold with dust after you've been in the cowshed;
I'm happy to see you like that, but others who see you will scold.
You don't have one bit of shame! If Nappiṉṉai sees you, she'll laugh.
My beautiful Ruby, my Jewel, come here to take your bath.

II.4.10

Those who are able to master these fine Tamil verses,
Songs of the Bhaṭṭa lord, King of Putuvai,
its ancient fame filling the earth,
Telling how Yaśodā with full girdled breasts
rejoiced when calling Lord Kaṇṇaṉ for a bath,
His body dark like a monsoon cloud, they will have no evil fate.

Second Ten, 5th tirumoḻi – Combing Kaṇṇaṉ's hair

Tirumoḻi II.5 seems to reflect a practice of directing a small child's attention to the antics of a crow in order to get the child to sit still long enough to have his hair combed. Kṛṣṇa's tangled curls are wet and loose after his bath of the previous song and, in traditional South Indian culture, it is considered unlucky to see someone with their hair down, as if they are in mourning or possessed by spirits. The final signature verse makes it clear that Yaśodā is worried about the neighbors seeing Kṛṣṇa with his hair undone and wants the crow to help her fix it quickly. It is much like *Tirumoḻi* I.4 in which Yaśodā calls the moon to catch Kṛṣṇa's attention long enough for him to fall asleep. II.5.4 contains a subtle threat to the crow as Yaśodā refers to two incidents in which Kṛṣṇa destroyed bird demons: Bakāsura, a demon heron whose beak he split, and Pūtanā, a harpy (demon bird woman), who disguised herself as a wet nurse who came to poison Kṛṣṇa. The Tamil text uses the term *pēy*, meaning 'demon'; however, I have translated this here with the English *harpy* to transmit the bird imagery indicated by the original. The suggestion here is that the crow's life will be in danger if it does not entertain Kṛṣṇa.

II.5.1

He lies in Tirupēr, the husband of Piṉṉai;
He, alone, is the Primal Seed even for the celestials.
This king has taken in service our whole clan, including me.
Crow! Come help me comb his hair.
Crow! Come comb the hair of Mādhava.

II.5.2

This child, who first drank from the demon's breast
Then broke a cart and a laurel tree,
Is black-haired Kaṇṇaṉ, the color of the *kāyā* flower.
Crow! Come comb his hair neatly.
Crow! Come comb the hair of this Pure Jewel.

II.5.3

The butter stored in the pots swaying high in the nets,
Our Lord gulped down and then scurried off to sleep,
That great King of the celestials, Kaṇṇaṉ of the cowherd.
Crow! Come help me comb his hair.
Crow! Come comb the hair of this Black Cloud.

II.5.4

When he saw a cunning demon disguised
As a bird fishing in a waterhole, he thought,
"It's only a bird," and quickly split its mouth.
Crow! Come comb the hair of that child.
Crow! Comb the hair of him who sucked the harpy's breast.

II.5.5

The Supreme Lord, while grazing the calf herd,
Grabbed a calf and threw it for fruit.
Don't hop up and run off cackling.
Crow! Comb his hair everyday.
Crow! Comb the hair of the Discus bearer.

II.5.6

When he decided to destroy with his disc
The indestructible kings of the East,
He cut them down in the wink of an eye.
Crow! Comb his hair neatly.
Crow! Comb the hair of Govinda.

II.5.7

Don't wander off wishing to eat
The *piṇṭa* balls or boiled rice to give to the goblins.
The Great Lord of the heavenly immortal -
Crow! Comb his black bee-like hair.
Crow! Comb Māyavaṉ's hair.

II.5.8

It is he who created fair four-faced Brahma
In a shapely blossom rising from his navel.
I've smeared on tamarind juice to straighten his knotted locks.
Crow! Comb his hair with an ivory comb.
    Crow! Comb the hair of Dāmodara.

II.5.9

He measured the whole world long ago
Thrilling even the king's wives.
I've laid his precious head on the flowery bed.
Crow! Comb his hair at the back.
    Crow! Comb the hair of him of one-thousand names.

II.5.10

These words of the herdess so those who see him won't chide,
"Crow, come comb his hair, this swarm of dark locks,"
The words of the Bhaṭṭa king of high-walled Villiputtūr,
Those who celebrate them in song will never near misfortune.

Second Ten, 6th tirumoḻi – A staff for Kaṇṇaṉ

Yasódā continues to get Kṛṣṇa ready to go out with the other kids in the herder village and calls for a herding staff to be brought to him. But to whom is she talking? In previous songs, the poet has directed her voice to Kṛṣṇa himself, to her village neighbors, to the moon and to a crow. The reader initially may assume that she is addressing another person, but might question that when reading verse 7 with its reference to a *Rāmāyaṇa* episode. In that verse, Yaśodā threatens that Kṛṣṇa may put out the person's eye if the staff isn't brought quickly! Periyāḻvār clarifies the scene in the final signature verse; he says that this is a song of the herdess calling for the crow of the previous *tirumoḻi* to bring a staff for her son. What kind of staff can a crow bring? Readers familiar with the large crows of India will attest to their cleverness and abilities. The staff is similar to the little boy's bow mentioned in II.6.1 - a toy one "from the hedge." The picture is complete with the understanding that Yaśodā continues to direct Kṛṣṇa's attention to the crow pecking at sticks while she gets her son dressed. He will be ready then to go out to play, carrying a twig as his little toy herding staff.

II.6.1

He takes his toy bow – a twig from the hedge row –
He, with the leaf pendant 'round his broad neck
And a tuft of peacock feathers tied at the back.
Bring a staff for the boy going out with the herd;
  bring a staff for the Sea-hued One.

II.6.2

Fragrant Kuṭantai, Kōṭṭiyūr and Tirupēr,
My son wanders everywhere at play.
For his broad hand, which bears the conch,
Bring a staff, finely made and well-shaped;
  bring a staff rubbed with red lac.

II.6.3

He killed Kaṃsa who angrily stood against him; losing patience,
He split the mouth of the bird which fought against him.
For him who runs ahead, his curly locks flying,
Bring a staff for this little calf herder;
bring a staff for the Lord of the gods.

II.6.4

To Duryodhana, his crown thick with jewels,
Who kept saying only one thing and in a single word,
He pledged his hand to join in the Bhārata War.
Bring a staff for this little calf herder;
bring a staff for the Sea-hued One.

II.6.5

As a unique messenger to Duryodhana,
Angered by the denial of a single city,
He, incarnate on earth, pledged his hand in the Bhārata War.
Bring a staff for Pārtha's charioteer;
bring a staff for the Lord of the gods.

II.6.6

He who lies on the banyan leaf, who lies on a serpent bed,
Has slept for many eons upon the blue sea.
When he was a young man, he granted grace to Pārtha.
Bring a staff for the beautiful Lord;
bring a staff for the Sleeper in Kuṭantai.

II.6.7

On Citrakūṭa mountain, which glitters like gold,
The furious Lord with a curly hair knot
Took one eye from that disguised demon.
Bring a staff quickly so your eye isn't next;
bring a staff for the jewel-hued Prince.

II.6.8

For the sake of Sītā with a lightning-thin waist,
He bent with his foot and strung the bow without equal,
Then fell the ten jeweled heads of the King of Lanka.
Bring a staff for the lightning-crown bearer;
bring a staff for the One who dammed the sea.

II.6.9

He cut the head and arms of the King of Lanka,
Then to Prince Vibhīṣaṇa, whose jewels shine like lightning,
He said, "Rule so that my shining name reaches afar."
Bring a staff for the Lord with a lightning-like chain;
Bring a staff for the Nobleman of Vēnkaṭa.

II.6.10

Those who can master this Tamil Ten
Recited by the Bhaṭṭa of Villiputtūr,
The lady's words, "Crow, bring a staff for our Prince,"
They'll beget good children and live happily in this world.

Second Ten, 7th tirumoḻi – Adorning Kaṇṇaṉ with flowers

A central focus of Hindu worship in a temple or household shrine is the offering of flowers by placing them before the deity or on the image in a garland. In fact, traditional histories indicate that Periyāḻvār was himself the gardener in the temple in Śrīvilliputtūr whose duty it was to provide fresh flowers daily and to weave garlands for the deity. In this *tirumoḻi,* he transforms his devotional routine by taking the voice of Yaśodā speaking directly to the living god, Kṛṣṇa, to come and be adorned with flowers. In translating this song, I have attempted to find common English names for most of the flowers based on the scientific name from the Fabricius *Tamil and English Dictionary* and with the help of Professor Emeritus Almut Jones, Department of Plant Biology at the University of Illinois-Urbana. In cases where there is no common English term, a descriptive phrase is used to enhance the meaning of the verse. Verse II.7.8 requires a special note: regarding the reference to Kṛṣṇa's slaying of Śrī Mālikaṉ, the commentator Aṇṇankarācāriyar explains that he has researched numerous texts and has not been able to identify the source or more details of this episode.[144]

II.7.1

When you go out to graze the cowherd,
your dark body tires from wandering the groves,
Then you'll gulp raw milk straight from the pots,
making all the hecklers laugh at you.
Sweetness of honey, you don't know
that you're a rare remedy for our sorrows.
Come let me crown you, Lord, with fragrant magnolia blossoms.

II.7.2

If eyes see a dark cloud, it's as if they see you
Who was born incarnate to devour the seven worlds.
Bridegroom of Sītā who sleeps in Śrīrangam,
Come let me crown you with a string of fragrant jasmine.

II.7.3

You climbed to the upper story and entered the ladies' apartment,
Then tugged on their bordered bodices
    and tore the edges of their dresses.
You continually create mischief, Father of holy Vēnkaṭa.
Come let me crown you with trumpet flowers and sage.

II.7.4

Don't stand in the middle of the street
    making mischief for the young milkmaids.
You, like a cloud-colored calf, your browed forehead full of black curls
Will be fragrant with a fine garland of marjoram and sage.
Beautiful Prince, come here and let me crown you with these.

II.7.5

You split the bird's mouth and broke the tusk of the battle elephant;
You cut off the nose of the ogress and the head of her protector.
Yet I, your servant, beat you without fear
    when you grabbed and gulped down the butter.
Come let me crown you with red lilies which rose in the clear pool.

II.7.6

Since you fought the oxen, my Prince, you want for nothing, it seems.
You did the mischief you had in mind
    when you leapt and grabbed Kaṃsa by the leg.
After you made mischief in the streets,
    you charged off to fight with the wrestlers.
Come let me crown you, Golden One, with these laurel flowers.

II.7.7

Our King who can dance with pots raised high,
My son who can charm the sweet moon-face maids,
You gouged open Hiraṇya's chest and cleaved it in two.
My King who lies in Kuṭantai, let me crown you with creeper buds.

II.7.8

Even though you had befriended Śrī Mālikaṉ,
You decided that he must die, and took his head with your disc.
Lord who knows the future, you put an end to my confusion.
Let me crown you who lies in jeweled Śrīrangam
with dark jasmine flowers.

II.7.9

You sit in a heavenly palace surrounded by the celestials;
You abide in your servants' hearts, Bridegroom of the pure Lotus Lady;
And you sleep on a banyan leaf, with the seven worlds consumed.
So I may delight in seeing you, let me crown you with dark buds.

II.7.10

This ten of the lord of the Bhaṭṭas, king of melodious Villiputtūr,
Is a garland of words of the glad herdess to him who seized the earth:
"I've brought you dark and white jasmine,
magnolia and red water lilies.
Now come and let me crown you with all the flowers I've mentioned."

Second Ten, 8th tirumoḻi – An amulet for Kaṇṇaṉ

As dusk falls in the herder village, fear of lurking danger rises; wary Yaśodā's maternal instincts tell her to put an amulet on her child to ward off evil. She reflects on the strange demonic attacks that have already beset her child, like the demon cart and harpy; an amulet is certainly in order! She also cautions her son to avoid known dangers, like the open crossroad (II.8.2) and the wandering Śaivite begger (II.8.8) portrayed as a bogeyman. Her understanding of Kṛṣṇa as the all-powerful deity is clouded by her overwhelming human love for him as her little son. Here the Āḻvār voices the same sentiments found in his *Tiruppallāṇṭu*, literally 'many years,' the benediction sung to protect the deity. In the first verse of that short song, Periyāḻvār offers the deity *kāppu* 'protection,' making it clear that the poet is actually blessing the god with prosperity and long life. In Yaśodā's song, the verses end with the repeated line, *kāpp(u)iṭu* 'to give protection' with an amulet. Another phrase is also repeated in each verse addressing the image established in a standing posture in Veḷḷaṟai, one of the 108 Vaiśṇava pilgrimage sites in Tamil Nadu.

II.8.1

Indra, Brahma and Īśa and all the celestials have come
Offering auspicious flowers and are standing invisibly nearby.
You who stands in Veḷḷaṟai with wise men in moonlit mansions,
My Beauty, dusk is falling; let me put this amulet on you.

II.8.2

I neglected all the cows which were bellowing to enter the calf shed
And came out here to call you, but you have no care for me.
Don't stand in the crossroad at nightfall,
you who stands in walled Veḷḷaṟai.
You know what I say is right. Come let me put this amulet on you.

II.8.3

You would eat no rice after I scolded you for ruining
The play dishes and houses of the girls with smooth copper-pot breasts,
You who stands in Veḷḷaṟai
where wise men worship the gods thrice daily.
This time I won't do anything, Lord.
Come let me put this amulet on you.

II.8.4

"He jumped on us and kicked sand in our eyes."
Countless children come complaining again and again.
Kaṇṇaṉ who stands in Veḷḷaṟai, you tease anyone who sees you.
It's indeed the stormy sea you resemble, Liberal Lord.
Come let me put this amulet on you.

II.8.5

The mischievous children in this city number in the thousands,
But there's nothing that won't be blamed on you,
so come here, my Lord.
You who stands in Veḷḷaṟai of the Good, Brilliant light of Knowledge,
Come let me praise and bless your body
while I properly put this amulet on you.

II.8.6

Angry Kaṃsa commanded a dark harpy with red hair
To come here and deceive you; this has caused some talk!
You who stands in walled Veḷḷaṟai,
its jeweled mansions in creeping mist,
My Beauty, I'm scared for you stay there;
come let me put this amulet on you.

II.8.7

You gave a vicious kick to splinter the laurel trees and demon cart.
After that, King of children, you caught
the harpy and sucked her breast.
You who stands in radiant Veḷḷaṟai, I don't know what's going on!
It's getting to be bedtime, Supreme Lord.
Come let me put this amulet on you.

II.8.8

To the celestials, you are precious and make their happiness soar,
King who killed the rutting elephant,
Death in the depths of cruel Kaṃsa's heart,
You of Veḷḷaṟai with walls of perfect gold, Child raised with riches.
Beware the mad monk with the skull bone bowl!
Run fast to get this amulet on you.

II.8.9

Bearing holy water in a conch, the sages of the Ṛg Veda await you.
Don't be brash, my Prince, standing out in the street;
listen to your mom a little longer.
You who stands in radiant Veḷḷaṟai,
let me adorn you with an auspicious amulet.
Come; I'll light the fire in the evening lamp so then we can see.

II.8.10

These words of Yaśodā, eminent among women,
as she puts an amulet on her son,
The One of Veḷḷaṟai who is joined by the tender Treasure of the lotus,
This garland of song of Viṭṭucittaṉ
who's reaped the fruits of the Vedas,
Those who reap the fruits of these lines
are *bhaktas* whose sins will vanish.

Second Ten, 9th tirumoḻi – The neighbors' complaints

In this *tirumoḻi,* Periyāḻvār presents a charming scene of village women bringing complaints to Yaśodā about the mischief of her son. The verses are chatty and informal, making the religious message of the verse accessible to all levels of society. The neighborhood ladies feel Yasódā is shirking her responsibility to control Kṛṣṇa, but she cannot restrain god and loves him unconditionally regardless of his behavior. The listener hears in one verse the neighbor's complaint and then, in the next verse, Yaśodā's response. In verse 4 after Yaśodā's comments, the poet also interjects his own observations as a narrator in the second half of the verse. Verse 6 presents the phrase, *kōtukalam uṭai kūṭṭaṉēyō: kōtukalam* is from Sanskrit *kautūhala,* meaning 'curiosity or a curiosity, something of interest';[145] in Tamil, however, the word in various spellings (*kautukam, kōtukam, kōtukalam, kutukulam)* comes to mean 'delight,' but also 'jugglery, legerdemain, or magic tricks.'[146] The epithets Yaśodā uses describe her son lifting Mount Govardana and dancing with pots on his head, both clever tricks of balance, which I have chosen to reflect in the translation, "You're just a kid full of tricks, aren't you?" as she excuses his bad behavior yet again. Throughout this *tirumoḻi,* the devotee-poet describes god at play, his actions explained in II.9.11 as 'fun' (Tamil *kirīṭai,* Sanskrit *krīḍā*), a spontaneous expression of divine joy, which is incomprehensible to mortals. The Āḻvār presents Yaśodā as the model devotee whose unconditional love is not affected by the deity's capriciousness.

II.9.1

He gulped down the butter, then smashed
the empty pot on the floor to hear it crash.
We can't stop Lord Kaṇṇaṉ's bad habits.
You should control your son.
Like squirting tamarind juice in a wound,
he does mischief in house after house.
You've got a son with a keen eye, Yaśodā.
My lady, please call your son.

II.9.2

Come here! Come on! You should come.
Prince Vāmaṇa, you should come here.
Come here, Prince Kākutstha, your red-lipped face
encircled by black curls.
Even now, Ladies, he is dear to me. Kohl-colored child, come here.
I can't bear the insolence of the neighbors.
Ah, Poor me! Please come here.

II.9.3

There's no way to stop the mischief
of this blessed child, this beautiful boy.
He gulped down the butter and shattered the pot,
and now stands there looking innocent.
Such injustice to neighbors – is it just, Yaśodā?
Please call your son to come. Madhusūdana won't let us live.

II.9.4

"Cloud-colored One, come here; Child of the temple, come here.
Come here, Nārāyaṇa who lies in Tirupēr
encircled by crashing white waves"
He dashed into the house of the herdess, lisping, "I already ate!"
And she ran forward to lift him to her.
Such are the lessons Kaṇṇaṉ's learned.

II.9.5

As my daughter, wrists laden with bangles,
put the fresh milk on the stove,
I went next door to borrow a hot coal
and stood talking for, I swear, just a second.
The Prince with the Śālagrāma tipped and drank the pot,
and now stands there looking innocent.
Yaśodā, with pressed sugarcane speech, my lady, please call your son.

II.9.6

You know you should come. You know you should come.
Don't say, "I won't!" You know you should come!
I won't listen to anything said by these neighbors who'll say anything.
You're just a kid full of tricks, aren't you? You lifted the mountain;
you danced with the pots.
Come here, My Lord of Vēnkaṭa, Sage who's the essence of the Vedas.

II.9.7

I made sweets of red paddy and green pulse, fragrant ghee and milk
For the twelve day Ōṇam festival. But I have long known this child!
"I want more," he said as he devoured it all,
and stood there looking innocent.
Please call your son, my lady. Yaśodā, this is only a part of it!

II.9.8

Keśava, come here. Don't say, "I won't!" Just come!
Don't play in the houses of these unfriendly people.
Come away from where women and servants say insults.
Doing what Mom says is your duty. Dāmodara, you come here!

II.9.9

I had sugar candy and treats in a bowl
with snacks and sesame seed balls.
I thought they'd be safe in my own house,
but he sneaked in, took them, and slipped away.
He came back later and, spying my pots,
found and ate my shining white butter.
Please call your son, my lady. Yaśodā, this is only a part of it!

II.9.10

You're as haughty as a queen when we complain, my lady,
  but that trickster is *your* son!
He came in my house and called to my daughter,
  then snatched her bangle off her arm.
He gave the bangle to a girl who was bringing
  black plums from the grove to sell.
He took a fine fruit from her and now laughs and says, "It wasn't me!

II.9.11

Those who can sweetly sing these songs
  about the fun had by him of Śrīrangam
In the south where the Kaverī flows through groves buzzing with bees,
Singing the verses of Viṭṭucittaṉ, the Bhaṭṭa Lord,
  those servants of Govinda
Stand like beacons for the eight directions
  with their feet on my humble head.

Second Ten, 10th tirumoḻi – The maids' complaints

In *Tirumoḻi* II.10, the poet presents a series of Kṛṣṇa episodes as sung by village girls complaining to Yaśodā. The song begins with the story of Kṛṣṇa taking the girls' clothes and refusing to return them, an episode later repeated and made popular throughout northern India by the Sanskrit *Bhāgavata Purāṇa.* In the refrain, the girls protest that they are "at their end" because he is teasing them. Periyāḻvār continues using this setting to describe several other favorite episodes from Vaiṣṇava mythology: slaying the demons Kāliya, Dhenuka and Pūtanā, stealing butter, lifting Govardhana Mountain, descending as the dwarf and boar incarnations, and rescuing the elephant caught by the crocodile. The phrase repeated twice in the fourth line, "Now we are at our end," is ambiguous, but in the final verse, the poet clarifies that the girls are making complaints (Tamil *muṟaippaṭu*), and are not pining maidens lamenting. Therefore, I feel they are at their wit's end with him, rather than dying from lovesickness.

II.10.1

When we were playing on the river bank
He threw mud at us and took our bangles and clothes,
Then ran like the wind into his house.
Because he won't reply to us, now we're at our end;
    because he won't tell us of our bangles, now we're at our end.

II.10.2

With earrings dangling near his hair locks
    which hang over a dangling chain,
He is praised and adored by bowing lords of the eight directions.
He snatched the clothes of those whose flowered locks hum with bees.
Because of the one in the sky high tree, now we're at our end;
    because he won't give what we need, now we're at our end.

II.10.3

He stirred up the pond filled wide with lotuses
And caught and pulled the tail of the venomous snake,
Then he jumped up onto its soft hooded head.
Because of him whose body swayed in dance, now we're at our end;
    because of him who stood on its head, now we're at our end.

II.10.4

With his thick broad arms – which had once tossed Dhenuka
Up onto the palm fruit so his breathing ceased –
He checked the rains which fell by command of the celestials' king.
Because of him who protected the cows, now we're at our end;
    because of him who saved the cows, now we're at our end.

II.10.5

He ate a mix of curds and milk from the house of the herdess.
That bamboo-armed lady, in return, searched and caught him,
So he was unable to have the pure white butter.
Because of him who stayed stuck there, now we're at our end;
    because of him who was beaten and cried,
    now we're at our end.

II.10.6

When he was a tiny boy, tottering as he walked,
He saw and understood what was in the heart of hearts
Of the lying harpy, and so he took her life.
Because of him who sucked the demon's breast,
    our now we're at our end.
    because of him who felt no affect, now we're at our end.

II.10.7

He came to Māvali's sacrifice in the form of a dwarf.
"Give me three feet," he said, as he begged a boon,
And with his first step, he took the whole earth.
Because of him who stretched out his second foot,
now we're at our end;
because of him who measured the world,
now we're at our end.

II.10.8

The Great Lord of the celestials ended the suffering of the elephant
Which was troubled and entrapped by a cruel crocodile
In a broad pool full of fresh water lilies and aloe.
Because of him who discharged his disc, now we're at our end;
because of him who blessed the elephant,
now we're at our end.

II.10.9

Like a rain cloud which moves through the heavens,
He roamed the forests here and there frolicking in play
In the form of a boar which rooted up the earth.
Because of him who put it in its place, now we're at our end;
because of him who dug up the earth, now we're at our end.

II.10.10

All of these complaints of the worthy girls
Reported to Yaśodā about her lotus-eyed child
Are the words of the Bhaṭṭa king of Putuvai;
For those who can say them, there will be no suffering.

Third Ten, 1st tirumoḻi - Yaśodā's doubts

As with the beginning of the Second Ten, the Third Ten begins a new chapter in Kṛṣṇa's life. His mother realizes that he is no longer a child, as she sees that his mischief more and more involves the neighbors' virgin daughters (Tamil *kaṉṉiyar*, Sanskrit *kanyā*). She repeats, "Now that I know you," I can no longer consider you a baby. Periyāḻvār introduces to the *Tirumoḻi* a theme which became popular in later Vaisnava poetry, Kṛṣṇa's sport with the milkmaids – sneaking behind their parents' backs, creeping into their houses and whisking them away into the forest – all causing gossip in the village. Verse III.1.10 provides a glimpse of timekeeping from this era. The poet describes Kṛṣna spending "three times seven night *nāḻikai*" embracing a maiden. Each *nāḻikai* (Sanskrit *nāḍikā*) is about 24 minutes;[147] multiplied times 21 is over 8 hours of the night! Clearly Kṛṣṇa's activities have undergone a shift as the Third Ten begins.

III.1.1

With a thousand playmates following,
you come staggering with each step
After gulping the milk and golden ghee - a creeping thief full of lies.
You set your mouth to the breast, Lord,
to kill that cunning maid, her waist like lightning.
Now that I know you, my dear, I'm afraid to give you my breast.

III.1.2

I bathed you in golden turmeric, then I fed you and went out.
Before I got back, you'd kicked and broken this huge, heavy cart.
After you went in the house next door,
their fine-waisted virgin was never the same.
Now that I know you, my love, I'm afraid to give you my breast.

III.1.3

You gulped down the butter and well-boiled pulse,
then tipped the curd pot and drank it.
Now you have killed the demons disguised as magic laurel trees.
Princely child well practiced in magic, they say that you are my son.
Now that I know you, my darling, I'm afraid to give you my breast.

III.1.4

You aroused those modest milkmaids, with lovely collyriumed eyes,
And crept behind to snatch their floral designed saris;
you play pranks again and again.
I've heard enough talk behind your back, you liar, it would fill a book!
Now that I know you, my Lord, I'm afraid to give you my breast.

III.1.5

You gulped down the butter and curds I'd collected
from all three churnings of the day.
Then you toppled and drank the pots which were carried
on poles 'cross the herders' shoulders.
Like a baby wailing for breast milk, now you weep with sob after sob.
Now that I know you, my boy, I'm afraid to give you my breast.

III.1.6

When a herd of cows and calves pillaged the fields
of tall sugarcane and ripe red paddy,
You threw one unwelcomed calf, Lord, to fell a woodapple fruit.
You trapped and transformed one virgin,
her soft hair humming with bees.
Now that I know you, you rascal, I'm afraid to give you my breast.

III.1.7

In the groves of the herder hamlet, you put
to your lips your alluring sweet flute,
While maidens with curly soft hair
encircle and adore you, my Radiance.
I have no fortune, my Lord, but the misfortune of getting you.
Now that I know you, you scoundrel, I'm afraid to give you my breast.

III.1.8

Even when you do nothing, the neighbors won't look at you
after you've aroused their daughters,
Embracing their shoulders and sporting with them;
you've done unspeakable things!
The cowherd clansmen won't stand for this conduct;
I'm ruined! I have no life.
Now that I know you, Nanda's son, I'm afraid to give you my breast.

III.1.9

Their mothers go out to sell buttermilk;
their fathers go out behind the herd.
The young virgins of the herder hamlet, you carry off at your leisure.
Giving the grumblers satisfaction,
you wander where they'll see and gossip.
Now that I know you, herder boy, I'm afraid to give you my breast.

III.1.10

Taking one maiden, her hair bunched in blossoms,
you entered the dense forest grove.
Her pearl-laden breasts, you embraced all the night,
and emerged only after eight hours.
People will say what they will, but I can do nothing to scold you.
Now that I know you, my Lord, I'm afraid to give you my breast.

III.1.11

To our Lord with the black-hued body
said the herdess, her hair fragrant with flowers,
"I'll give you unending ambrosia, but I won't give you my breast."
These verses of the Bhaṭṭa king of Putuvai,
its ancient fame filling the world,
Those who sing this garland of sweet music
are servants of Lord Hṛṣīkeśa.

Third Ten, 2nd tirumoḻi – Yasódā's regrets

Throughout this *tirumoḻi,* Yaśodā misses the closeness of Kṛṣṇa in his baby days. As she is forced to recognize that his mischief is upsetting the village, she sends him to work herding the calves, but regrets having to be away from him and sighs as she berates herself, "What a shame!" in each final line. While Periyāḻvār predominantly expressed devotion as delight in nearness to god, in this song he presents the devotee's sadness in remaining separated from god and the devotee's sense of unworthiness to be united with him.

III.2.1

To keep him from wandering at will in every one of the houses,
That collyrium-colored One, tender sprout of the cowherd,
I gave my little boy his bath and sent him out behind the calves,
Which made sore his ankleted feet that kicked Kaṃsa. What a shame!

III.2.2

To keep him from wandering everywhere, playing tricks in the village,
Smashing the sand houses of the girls,
their skin glowing with saffron paste,
Why did I send my child out behind the calf herd
To the midst of the forest full of hunters and dust from the calves?
What a shame!

III.2.3

To keep him from wandering everyday with the girls
of goodly jeweled girdles
And playing out in the dust 'til it's covered his gold-adorned body,
I sent out behind the calf herd my child with a jeweled hue
To the midst of the howling forest on the jeweled mountain.
What a shame!

III.2.4

To keep him from wandering everywhere in the village
doing all the things
That provoke the black-haired women to come casting dispersions,
I sent out behind the calf herd into the midst of the forest
Him who is sweet to the eye, but hard to comprehend. What a shame!

III.2.5

To keep him from entering each and every house
as an intimate of the herders' wives
Giving them his sweet *kovvai* fruit lips
and making them each suspicious,
I sent out behind the calf herd the celestials' great Leader
To the midst of the forest full of hunters with cruel bows.
What a shame!

III.2.6

To keep him from wandering the village everywhere
committing many crimes,
Gulping down fresh butter, dripping it down his chin,
I sent my child out stumbling, following the herd of calves
Into the midst of the forest where wander bull elephants.
What a shame!

III.2.7

To keep him from wandering, playing and frolicking with his friends,
Making so many women with creeper-fine waists spread slander,
I sent the Lord who rides the bird out behind the calves
To the midst of the hot forest full of dried milkweed. What a shame!

III.2.8

In the same way that he was kept twelve months in the womb
I've cared for him and fed him the nectar of my breasts.
But I sent my young lion behind the calves into the forest
In the early morning heat so his golden feet got sore. What a shame!

III.2.9

Without giving to Dāmodara an umbrella or his sandals,
This cruel women sent her child out behind the calves
To the midst of the harsh hot forest where upon the ground
Were jagged burning rocks which hurt his feet. What a shame!

III.2.10

These words of Yaśodā, "I sent out behind the calves
My Jewel who is always so sweet to me,"
By the Bhaṭṭa king of Putuvai of brilliant golden houses,
There's no suffering for those who master this sweet Tamil garland.

Third Ten, 3rd tirumoḻi – Yaśodā's relief

Periyāḻvār's expressions of longing and lament are far fewer than his verses of joyful intimacy with god. Shifting from the previous song in which Yaśodā spent the day in regret, the poet describes her delight in her son when he returns with the herd. But the Āḻvār seems to suggest that her mind wavers back and forth regarding her fitness to be Kṛṣṇa's mother. At one moment she rejoices in having "the best son" (III.3.1) and begs a kiss (III.3.2), yet she calls herself a sinner (III.3.3), feels dazed by his divine feats (III.3.6), and at times even fears him (III.3.8). And the amount of food he consumed at the Indra festival (III.3.8) makes her panic about her own larder! After going through a range of emotions felt by an ardent devotee (joy, love, wonder, apprehension, and unworthiness), she ultimately loses herself in Kṛṣṇa's *māyā*, his illusion, of being a herder boy, and she remains simply a loving mother, asking her son to stay home - out of trouble – and to just keep clean.

III.3.1

A rag ring stretches one ear lobe and a red lily is on the other,
With a bordered waist band on his clothes
        and a string of cooling pearls.
See the bearing of that sea-hued boy coming behind the herd.
The one who got the best son in the world is I, Ladies, no other.

III.3.2

In southern Śrīrangam on the Kaverī River
        encircled by walled flower gardens
Are you eternal, Madhusūdhana, my Keśava.
        I, a sinner with an easy life,
Fed you early this morning and sent you out to graze the calves.
No woman's heart hurts like mine; little boy, come give me a kiss.

III.3.3

You went to the grove to watch the calves graze,
        Dāmodara, adorned with dark lilies.
Just look at you - covered with calf dust, Groom of peahen-like Piṉṉai.
I got your bath all ready; wash yourself up and come eat.
Your father has not eaten yet; he will eat now with you.

III.3.4

Lord of lovely Vēnkaṭa full of fragrant groves, Black battle bull, Māl,
You went out forgetting your favorite umbrella,
        your sandals and your flute
Into the harsh, hot forest behind the calves,
        burning your little lotus-bud feet.
My Lord, your eyes are all red now, and you're completely exhausted!

III.3.5

Battle bull who blew the conch, Pāncanjanya,
        which struck fear in your foes,
Little lion of the herders, Bridegroom of Sītā,
        my tiny little red-eyed Māl,
You went off with the other calf herders to graze the calves, it seems,
Leaving your little shawl and toy dagger up on the top of your cot.

III.3.6

Beauty who bears in hand the beautiful fiery disc,
I survived your entering that pond to fight the serpent, spitting poison.
What can I do? You make my stomach whirl!
        You have no fear of anything.
What you did delighted Kaṃsa's mind, You of the blue *kāyā* bud's hue.

III.3.7

You became a boar, a tortoise and a fish,
You whose hue is of the Milky Sea.
You caught with your hands a demon disguised
as a calf grazing in the field,
And then, it seems, you threw it to fell fruit from a woodapple tree.
Those who make trouble for my boy always end up like that!

III.3.8

Keśava, I heard something unheard of –
that you took the rice, curry and curds
It seems that the herders had offered to Indra,
then ate them up all at once.
I don't have that much to feed you!
Maybe raising you is too hard for me.
Vāsudeva of unfading fame, from today I've started to fear you.

III.3.9

Bearer of the roaring white conch,
your birth star, Ōṇam. is seven days hence.
I've called ladies of melodious speech
and had the "Many years" proclaimed.
To prepare for the festival, I sprouted auspicious seeds,
and I cooked curry and rice.
Starting from tomorrow, don't go out behind the calves;
stay here and, please, keep clean.

III.3.10

The good herdess, Yaśodā, of serpent-thin waist,
rejoiced on seeing her son,
Govinda, as he came from grazing the calf herd.
All the words of her bidding
Are the verses of Viṭṭucittaṉ of southern Putuvai
where prosper those without hate.
Those who can sing these "calf" songs
will gaze on the feet of the sea-hued Lord.

Third Ten, 4th tirumoḻi - The maids see Kaṇṇaṉ

Here the poet depicts both a village girl gawking at the handsome young god, captivated by his charisma, as well as her mother, irritated at this shameful behavior. But her mother is not impassive to physical attraction to him either. Isn't she the one commenting on his tight clothes and his bulging "dagger" (III.4.2)? Through this device, Periyāḻvār creates a significant shift in the devotional approach of the poem. As discussed in the introduction, his contribution to the Vaiṣṇava religion is his innovative expression of devotion to god as a mother unconditionally loves a child, even a capricious child. That type of devotion, later known as *vātsalya bhakti*, is distinguished from the mood presented here, and in later *tirumoḻis* of this poet and in other Āḻvār texts, in which god takes on the *personae* of a romantic lover, the devotee assuming the mental role of a young girl passionately in love and out of control.

III.4.1

Govinda comes with a gang of boys,
spreading music all around
On a flute with hanging peacock feathers,
on hand drums and huge drums with peacock fans.
The maids lean on their windows as they wonder,
"Is that a dark thundercloud coming?"
They push through the crowd; they stand like statues.
They fast; they faint; they've fallen in love.

III.4.2

His hair is festooned with peacock feathers
midst sweet jasmine and kino tree flowers;
His clothes as fine as a creeper's new leaf fold on his flawless hips
Where a dagger bulges in a wide waistband,
clinging as tightly as a lizard on a wall,
As he comes home at sunset midst a crowd of cowherds.
Don't stand there gawking at that boy
with all your bangles falling off!

III.4.3

He blows his conch to call the cows,
his arm draped over his friend's shoulder
While the others bring his shawl, club and dagger,
his taut bow and rounded mace.
She looked at his saffron-clad waist and shapeliness;
my girl stood right next to him and simply stared.
Now that the city has seen this,
they will surely insinuate something!

III.4.4

Come see the Lord who, born as a herder boy,
protected the cattle by lifting a mountain,
As he comes down the path with his comrades,
grazing the calves and playing a flute.
Ladies, I've never seen anyone like him.
Girls, come see for yourselves!
My bangles slip off; not one will stay put!
I can't stop my young breasts from rising under my dress.

III.4.5

I saw him singing and dancing at the head of the herder boys,
With the eye of a feather adorning a curl,
as the herders 'round him held leaf shades.
Since that day, I can't tolerate marriage talks
for anyone, but Māyan̲ of Māliruncōlai.
"She's for the victorious Lord," they say.
"Give her to him! If you don't, there'll be trouble."

III.4.6

The forehead of that herder boy glitters
with vermilion, a *tilaka* and curls.
From the leafy green, cool fields he descends
with the herders, swinging a staff.
If he decides to come down our street, we'll yell,
"He stole our ball," and surround him.
Then we'll surely get a glimpse, my friend,
of the smile on his coral lips.

III.4.7

Behind the cattle herd, below the forest canopy,
his blessed body glows;
His hair-tuft smells of blue lilies and is decked with a peacock feather.
He sings and dances with the herders
and blows his flute, his lotus eyes wide.
When my daughter got a glimpse of this noisy boy,
his beauty simply left her faint.

III.4.8

This cow herder comes with a peacock plume
adorning his curls clinging tightly to his brow,
Where a sacred mark has been made with vermilion
using the tip of a leaf.
When she stands right in front of that Indra-like boy,
I say, "Don't let your bangles slip off."
Just look at her, ladies – out in the open road;
both her bangles and clothes have come loose!

III.4.9

That herder boy comes with garlands
    of forest and wild jasmine in his hair;
With a red lily tucked on his right ear,
    he puts a flute to his lips and blows sweetly.
Just look at my girl standing right in front of him;
    she can't keep a proper distance.
Seeing his grace, she's filled with desire;
    her white bangles slip as her limbs become thin.

III.4.10

Those *bhaktas* who sing in happy melodies this garland of ten verses,
Written by Viṭṭucittaṉ, king of Putuvai, its groves humming with bees,
Of the love felt by the young herder girls
    who saw Kaṇṇaṉ coming behind the cowherd,
Worshipped intently by heavenly immortals,
    they will dwell in highest Vaikuṇṭha.

Third Ten, 5th tirumoḻi – Govardhana, a victory umbrella

The focus of this song is the story of Kṛṣṇa lifting Govardhana Mountain as an umbrella to shield the cowherd village from the torrent of the angry rain god, Indra. The episode, which appears in early Sanskrit literature, the *Viṣṇu Purāṇa* and *Harivamśa* from the 3rd to 5th c. CE,[148] suggests a shift from an agricultural religion which worshipped the rain god, Indra, to a pastoral religion devoted to nature, cattle and Kṛṣṇa. A full retelling of the episode which provides the context of the verses in this song is in the introductory material to this book. The latter half of each verse provides praises of the mountain in charming descriptive scenes. Verse III.4.9 states that the mountain bears the same name as Kṛṣṇa, *Govardhana,* meaning 'bounty of the cowherd' which describes both the mountain and Kṛṣṇa.

III.5.1

A heaping mountain of rice, a pool of curds
    and a lake of ghee, he ate to the last drop;
He, the hue of the raging sea, defied the army of rain clouds.
The mountain, where young hill girls
    catch simple fawns with wide, round eyes
And give them milk with a twist of cotton,
    Govardhana he bore as a victory umbrella.

III.5.2

Madhusūdana checked the rains which poured for seven days
As ordered in anger as a show of strength
    by the king of the faultless celestials.
That mountain, where the anxious elephant
    placed her calf between her legs
And faced a lion hastening to attack,
    Govardhana he lifted upside down as a victory umbrella.

III.5.3

Our Father with the shining disc in his hand
was entreated with, "Give us refuge,"
By the weeping cattle, herders and milkmaids,
their wide eyes lined with kohl.
The mountain, where stout shouldered hunters bend their bows,
teasing, "Look, deer in the meadows,"
Seeing deer-eyed ladies who beg refuge,
Govardhana, he bore as a victory umbrella.

III.5.4

The great Lord of the celestials put his hand
at the base of the hill and plucked it up
Like someone tossing a ball of rice
to a cruel-mouthed, angry-eyed elephant.
The mountain, where rain flowed from clouds
which had tumbled to the sea to draw water
And risen to pour it down like from a pitcher,
Govardhana, he raised as a victory umbrella.

III.5.5

Īśa, our Father, took up that clod of dirt as he did in the form of a boar,
As if challenging the heavenly celestials,
"Come take it if you're strong enough."
The mountain, where a maddened forest elephant which lost its tusk
raised its ichor-smeared trunk
And look with longing at the curved crescent moon,
Govardhana, he bore as a victory umbrella.

III.5.6

Tirumāl, possessed of perfection,
with the five fingers of his hand as the ribs
And his long jeweled arm as the handle
made an umbrella for the cowherd.
The mountain, where clear streaming cascades form a glittering robe
Hung with strings of shining pearls,
Govardhana, he bore as a victory umbrella.

III.5.7

Dāmodara bore the vast mountain
spreading the five fingers of his broad hand,
Like the King of serpents, his many hoods spread,
calmly bearing up the vast earth.
The mountain, where monkey mothers cradle their young,
lulling them with songs of Hanumaṉ
Who subdued Lanka and destroyed its glory,
Govardhana, he bore as a victory umbrella.

III.5.8

Clenching that unyielding shield, Nārāyaṇa faced in open battle
A multitude of massive clouds roaring,
pouring rain arrows from all sides.
The mountain, where in thatched bamboo huts
sit powerful sages, scratching the necks
Of murderous-mouthed tigers 'til they sleep,
Govardhana, he bore as a victory umbrella.

III.5.9

Dāmodara, whose lips sucked the harpy's breast,
bore like a pillar bracing a weight
That mountain which was known throughout the world
by his own name, 'Bounty of the cows.'
The mountain, where troops of male monkeys
lead the way with their young on their backs
And teach them to reach for branches, then leap,
Govardhana, he bore as a victory umbrella.

III.5.10

The beauty of his fingers on his well-marked lotus hand
neither failed, nor faltered;
Nor did the nails of the jewel-hued One feel pain;
it must have been magic!
The mountain, where rain poured in profusion and settled,
its peak covered in a cluster of clouds
Like sacred ash on its brow,
Govardhana, he bore as a victory umbrella.

III.5.11

This garland of Ten was written by the Bhaṭṭa lord of Puttūr,
where prosper nobles learned in the Mysteries,
About the victory umbrella, Govardhana,
where jasmine creepers cling to spiny shrubs,
The mountain of him who rides the serpent's foe,
has a serpent bed and dispelled the serpent;
Those devotees who fill their minds with its praise,
will abide in supreme Vaikuṇṭha.

Third Ten, 6th tirumoḻi – Kaṇṇaṉ's flute

The *Tirumoḻi* of Periyāḻvār, in keeping with its classical roots as discussed in the introduction, at times engages in wonderfully descriptive natural images. Seemingly placed in the voice of a herdess, this verse describes the magic of the music from Kṛṣṇa's flute and its captivating effect on not just the milkmaids, but also on heavenly celestials, forest creatures and the forest itself. Several celestial performers are mentioned by name, each feeling unworthy to continue after hearing Kṛṣṇa's flute. Nārada, Tumburu and the Kinnaras play stringed instruments, while the Gandharvas are celestial singers. Menakā, Tilottamā, Rambhā and Urvaśī are heavenly dancing girls. Also mentioned by name in III.6.4 are the demons Dhenuka, the ass demon, Pralamba, a demon disguised as a cowherd boy, and Kāliya, the black serpent. It is this *tirumoḻi*, and specifically verse III.6.9 imitated in *Bhāgavata Purāṇa*, which most closely demonstrates Periyāḻvār's direct influence on that later Sanskrit text.[149] Compare *Tirumoḻi* III.6.9 to the following from the *Bhāgavata Purāṇa:*

Ladies, listen to this wonder!
He of winning smile and glittering chest,
Nanda's son who brings gaiety to troubled people,
when he blew his flute,
Pastured bulls, cows and deer, grouped afar,
their minds bereft by the flute playing,
With ears cocked and just-bitten mouthfuls,
were as if asleep or drawn in a picture.
(Bhāgavata Purāṇa 10.35.4-5)

Not only is the content of *Bhāgavata Purāṇa* 10.35 very similar to *Tirumoḻi* III.6, but it also is structured as twelve four-line verses, somewhat uncommon for that text. It is completely unique in its use of Tamil-derived second syllable rhyme to unite each four-line verse, giving it the look of a Tamil *tirumoḻi*.

III.6.1

Ladies living in the land of the roseapple, listen to this marvel!
At the sound of the flute at the pure lips of Tirumāl,
        he who bears the pure right-whorled conch,
The limbs of the Gopāla girls grew limp
        and their soft, young breasts thrilled.
Breaking free from their guardians,
        they rushed out like a string of blossoms
        and stood shyly tilting their heads.

III.6.2

As Govinda blew the flute at the corners of his mouth,
        left cheek leaning on left shoulder,
Both hands busy, eyebrows dancing and his belly puffed out like a pot,
The maidens, like does 'round a dancing peacock,
        stood quivering, their bright eyes fixed
As their flower-laden hair fell loose
        and their fingers clutched their slipping saris.

III.6.3

When the king of heaven, Vāsudeva,
        king of Mathurā, darling of Vaikuṇṭha,
Young prince of king Nanda, darling of the herders,
        Govinda played his flute,
Heavenly maidens came quickly in crowds
        with melting hearts, their bud eyes bedewed;
With fragrant hair falling loose, they stood
        with glistening temples, straining their ears.

III.6.4

He crushed and trampled those poisonous weeds
named Dhenuka, Pralamba and Kāliya.
As he roamed and strolled through the grove,
that little dark boy blew his flute.
In the Celestial City, Menakā, Tilottamā, and Rambhā
and Urvaśī were reserved and confused.
They were simply unable to open their mouths
and renounced song and dance completely.

III.6.5

Their ears were caught in the music of flute
at the mouth of Madhusūdana,
Who as a Man-lion awed the kings of the three worlds
when he destroyed the demon's strength long ago.
Thus did Nārada and Tumburu each forget their well-strung *vīṇās*;
The Kinnara couples declared, "We will not touch our lyres!"

III.6.6

Listen to the longing of those who heard the tune of the flute he blew,
Our Supreme with red eyes and stout shoulders,
the celestials' lion, Devakī's little one.
All the Gandharvas who wander in the heavens
were caught in the net of that nectar of song.
Confused, they gasped, "We have nothing to do,"
and pitifully turned up their palms.

III.6.7

Listen to the wonder I saw in this world!
As the group of Gopālas grazed the herd,
When the Sleeper on the serpent blew his flute,
the music rose up to the heavens,
Making the immortals forget their food offerings
and come hastening to crowd in the cowherd village.
With their ear-tongues enjoying the taste of the tunes,
they grew fixed on Govinda and were powerless to move.

III.6.8

When Govinda blew his flute, he caressed it,
with fingers skipping up and down,
Glancing from the corners of his bright eyes,
glistening brows arched and red lips puckered.
Flocks of birds left their nests
and came circling to perch in the grove,
While herds of milk cows laid with legs stretched,
heads lowered, not twitching an ear.

III.6.9

He, the hue of low hanging thick clouds, blew a tune on his flute,
His face, where hangs dark curly hair,
like a red lotus encircled by bees.
A herd of dazed deer forgot to graze,
the just-nipped grass slipping from their lips;
Listening, they stood transfixed, immobile, a scene from a painting.

III.6.10

This herder, like a rare jewel, decked with a dark-eyed peacock plume,
A fine golden garment tied 'round him, the Great Lord blew his flute.
The trees showered down star-shaped flowers;
their limbs grew limp and let fall blossoms;
And turning their gaze toward Tirumāl,
they closed their weeping bud-eyes.

III.6.11

Those who master these Tamil verses
composed by Viṭṭucittaṉ, king of Putuvai,
On the music of the flute – a river of nectar swelling,
bubbling and bursting from the holes –
The flute placed at the soft lips of Govinda,
his black hair curling thickly at his hairknot,
They will be admitted to the assembly of sages;
their speech will be sweeter than the tune of the flute.

Third Ten, 7th tirumoḻi – Her mother's worries

In this song, the Āḻvār takes the reader through a range of deliberations considered by a village mother chatting with her neighbors, as she comments on her daughter falling in love with Kṛṣṇa. She first can't believe that her little girl has really grown up, then she blames her daughter's openly infatuated behavior on her shameless girlfriends. She worries about what the neighbors will say, and finally realizes that there is nothing she can do. She decides that it is best to let her daughter go with Kṛṣṇa before there is a bigger scandal. The conversational tone of the verse is enhanced by an engaging series of pithy proverbs and idioms. She refers to her daughter as a ladle flung loose from the handle, which in English might be rendered 'a loose cannon,' i.e. uncontrolled. She also suggests that her daughter is becoming immersed in an infatuation from which she cannot gain anything, because "the ladle cannot taste the salt." She compares her daughter to a plant which has unexpectedly come up from the previous year's seed that an English-speaking gardener would call a 'volunteer.' She suggests that Kṛṣṇa, as the farmer, can take advantage of whatever benefit he might like to gain from her. And finally the realistic mother decides that she had better concede to her daughter's desires before the girl is "past a cure," i.e. pregnant anyway. In keeping with the casual nature of the verse, I have translated *kaittalattuḷḷa māṭaḻiya* 'wasting wealth in the palm of the hand' with the modern English idiom 'consuming all our cash on hand' to maintain the conversational tone. Several verses explain what the daughter is feeling for Kṛṣṇa in a phrase literally translated as 'she is feeling *māl*,' a play on words with *māl* being not only a Tamil name of Nārāyaṇa, but also meaning 'bewilderment, mental aberration, love or lust.'[150] To convey both love and confusion, I have translated this phrase using the colloquial English, 'she's gone mad for him.' The poet clarifies the meaning a little in the final signature verse when he states that the girl rejoices in her feelings (Tamil *makiḻntaṉaḷ*), so the listener understands she relishes her infatuation for Kṛṣṇa and is not suffering in longing for him. One more note of interest: Verse 4 provides one of the few examples within the *Four Thousand Divine Works* in which ardent devotion is referred to as being immersed. The maid is described as having been pushed into the 'depths' (Tamil *āḻam*) of a river, which suggests the later use of the term *āḻvār* 'those who are deeply immersed' to refer to the devotional Vaiṣṇava poets.

III.7.1

She plays in the dust 'til her body's covered; her speech is all a-jumble.
She's not ready yet to cover her chest with a red-threaded half sari;
She can't live without her toy winnowing fan
    or a little toy pot in her hand.
Yet now she comes hand-in-hand with him
    whose bed is the hooded serpent.

III.7.2

Her lips show gaps in her teeth; her head doesn't have much hair.
She's been drawn to a few other girls
    whose little heads never bend modestly.
She returns from a forbidden liaison, but speaks as honorably as usual.
She's gone mad for Māyaṉ, the hue of a beautiful dark jewel.

III.7.3

With a pile of fine white sand, she would build
    a toy hut in the courtyard;
Now she makes nothing but the bow, staff, sword, conch and disc.
Thinking of her with Govinda – her breasts still not yet rounded –
How my fearful heart falters, daily more riddled with doubt.

III.7.4

Deceiving my little daughter, a simple innocent child,
Her many girlfriends have done such mischief!
    But to whom can I complain?
They have pushed her into the deep stream, "Discus bearer"
    where she remains immersed.
And she does not know the old saying,
    "The soup ladle cannot taste the salt."

III.7.5

Adorned in garlands of *tulasī* she roams,
            recognized by city and countryside.
She searches each and every spot where Nārāyaṇa has gone.
There are those who would ruin us, so people are concerned.
Again and again, they worry, "Watch her when she's with Keśava."

III.7.6

A pendant for her forehead, golden ear studs,
            and both anklets and bells for her feet;
I raised her with everything she wanted, but now she doesn't want me.
She dashes outside in public, saying,
            "My dark *pūvai* flower–hued Lord!"
Ladies with long curly locks, she's gone mad for him.

III.7.7

She's the innocent girl of this innocent woman,
            whose modesty even keeps me from speaking.
Yet like a ladle that's flown loose from the handle,
            she stands at the head of those shameless maids.
She sounds like a parrot, repeating, "Keśava, Imperishable Lord."
Ladies of long fragrant locks, she's gone mad for him.

III.7.8

Adorning herself with a golden neckband, she looks in the mirror,
            jingling the bangles on her hand.
Arranging her raiment, she's weak with excitement
            and reddens her *kovvai* fruit lips.
She calms herself with thoughts of his godliness
            and babbles his one-thousand names.
She's gone mad for him whose hue is of an immutable dark jewel.

III.7.9

What's to be gained by holding her back
to conduct a marriage ceremony
And consume all our cash on hand? We will be disgraced!
Like a farmer with a "volunteer" sprout in the field,
he can do whatever he wants with her.
Let her go grow up with him the hue of a thick dark cloud.

III.7.10

While we were busy planning to keep her in our home,
Intending to conduct a huge wedding, she had ideas of her own.
So before we hear the old saying, "She's past the time for a cure,"
Place her at the side of him who once measured the earth.

III.7.11

"She's gone mad for Nārāyaṇa who sleeps on a banyan leaf,
After devouring the entire earth;" this speech made by the mother
Was composed by Viṭṭucittaṉ, king of Putuvai
encircled by beautiful groves.
To those who can master all ten, never will there be suffering.

Third Ten, 8th tirumoḻi – Her mother's questions.

The subject of this *tirumoḻi* is a direct reflex of the classical theme of a mother's lament on the elopement of her daughter. The 5th c. CE Tamil text on poetics,[151] *Tolkāppiyam*, Book III, identifies one literary theme as "the mother expressing her concern and love about the lover and her daughter," also clarifying that "there are mothers who go themselves in search of their daughters along the streets of …the cities."[152] Periyāḻvār modeled this 9th century devotional song on classical love poetry of that theme by presenting the speech of the anxious mother who, according to the signature verse, is questioning neighbor ladies along the road as she follows the lovers, Kṛṣṇa and her daughter, on their way to Mathurā. She wonders if her daughter will be officially married by circling a branch of the sacred fig tree, if she will just end up doing tedious work in the household, if her mother-in-law will treat her well, and if she will have status in the clan even though she is a junior wife among several spouses. As the mother follows along their path, she makes disparaging comments about the way Kṛṣṇa has behaved with regard to her daughter and her family. She says he has not been respectful and has caused a scandal. However, the final verse brings the realization that even though she has doubts about god, she is still following along the "path to Māyavaṉ." Kṛṣṇa's move to Mathurā along with his new bride brings an end to Periyāḻvār's recounting of Kṛṣṇa's life in the cowherd village; further verses in his *Tirumoḻi* focus on other Vaiṣṇava devotional themes. The subject of this *tirumoḻi* is particularly poignant in Periyāḻvār's song as listeners remember the story of the poet's own adopted daughter, Āṇṭāḷ, who left her father to become a bride of god in the Śrīrangam temple. The Āḻvār writes in verse III.8.4, "I have only one daughter and I raised her like the goddess; … it was red-eyed Māl who took her!" Another point of interest is verse III.8.5 because it identifies Nanda, Kṛṣṇa's foster father, as the bride's maternal uncle (Tamil *māmaṉ*), i.e. the mother speaking in the poem then is Nanda's sister and Kṛṣṇa's aunt. This type of "cross cousin" marriage is still a favorable match in South India today. If the girl of this verse is taken to be the Nappiṉṉai figure of earlier verses of the Periyāḻvār *Tirumoḻi*, other Āḻvār verses and even earlier Tamil texts, then verse III.8.5 can provide significant information about the sometimes contentious study of Piṉṉai, her kinship and her role.

III.8.1

As the dew drops on that day's flower
blossoming in the lovely lotus pond,
The pollen and petals fall away: its beauty fades, does it not?
Just so, hasn't this house become ghostly?
I can't find my daughter anywhere?
Has she gone with him who destroyed the wrestlers
to enter the city of Mathurā?

III.8.2

Like a totally ignorant, completely homely herder
Stealing away a calf, he took our virgin girl
Using clever trickery; hasn't Nārāyaṇa's mischief
Become a constant curse to our kin and clan?

III.8.3

Will they conduct a marriage proper for a virgin?
adorn her? seat her on the dais?
Will they announce that she's for Dāmodara
so kin and neighbors will know?
And make this goddess of the immortals' Lord
circle a fig tree branch?
Will the drums be beaten to an uproar?
Will there be festooned archways, I wonder?

III.8.4

I have only one daughter and I raised her like the goddess
Who is praised by all the world; it was red-eyed Māl who took her!
Will Yaśodā, noble lady of her clan, the one who got that boy,
Be pleased when she sees the bride and do her post-wedding duties?

III.8.5

Will Nanda Gopāla, her uncle, greet my daughter with kindness
And tell her to stand up proudly. When he sees her *kayal* fish eyes,
Red lips, rounded breasts and waist, and her soft bamboo-like arms
Will he know that the mother who bore this girl
will no longer be able to survive?

III.8.6

Will our Lord simply set up house with her
with just a union of mutual consent
And do whatever he wants with her, like those lowly hunter folk?
Or will he who struck dead the wheel demon properly attain her hand
By conducting a formal marriage,
acknowledged by city and countryside.

III.8.7

Will the great Lord of the heavenly immortals, the Bearer of the discus,
Belittle my daughter's belongings and treat her with disrespect?
Or will he give her a prosperous family life,
proclaiming her queen of the cowherds
And will he defend my daughter in front of his previous wives?

III.8.8

He has not done things respectfully, Ladies,
as expected by one born of his clan.
Nor has Nanda Gopa's son, Kaṇṇaṉ,
done anything according to custom!
Will my daughter grow weaker and weaker
with both sides of her waist giving in,
Weeping as she tugs on a churning rope
which raises welts on her hands?

III.8.9

Can she rise up early before dawn, without her eyelids drooping,
To go to work at churning the curds, foaming thick and white?
Will he who once measured the earth,
his red eyes like bright lotus buds,
Make her do work below her and treat her with disrespect?

III.8.10

Those who can say this pure Tamil ten
composed by the Bhaṭṭa of cool Putuvai,
These words spoken by the mother and the questions that she asked
Along the way in the cowherd village, following the path of Māyavaṉ,
They will become devotees of the pure jewel-hued Lord.

Third Ten, 9th tirumoḻi – The Untipaṟa game

In 1900, G. U. Pope published a translation of Māṇikkavācakar's *Tiruvācakam*, a 9th century CE text devoted to Śiva,[153] which included a series of three-line verses with a repeated line, *untīpaṟa*. Pope translated this phrase as 'fly aloft, Unthi' providing his opinion that *unti*, subject of the verb, referred to a ball or something like a badminton birdie.[154] At approximately the same time as Māṇikkavācakar, Periyāḻvār wrote *tirumoḻi* III.9 with the final signature verse describing this song as the words of ladies who *untipaṟa*, the girls being the subject noun. Clearly Pope's translation does not work here. The phrase is a combination of two verbs, two actions occurring simultaneously: *unti* 'jumping or leaping up' and *paṟa* 'fly, move swiftly or run nimbly.' Periyāḻvār's verse, then, is the song of ladies who are playing a game involving jumping up quickly and running. In the body of the verse, the repeated phrase is *pāṭi-p-paṟa*, literally 'singing run;' therefore, one can assume that the game involves singing as well. Prof. G. Vijayavenugopalan, currently a Senior Research Fellow with the École Française d'Extrême-Orient-Pondicherry, provided an interesting insight on this text. He described a modern game popular among girls in which a team sits on the ground in a row with enough space between the players for a person to run. One other girl from another team is chased and one girl from the seated team does the chasing, or in English terms is "it." The person being chased can run between the seated girls, but "it" can only run around them and cannot cross over the line they create. However, the girl who is "it" can push a seated teammate out of her position and take her place on the ground. The previously seated girl is now "it" and continues the chase from her position of advantage. One can easily envision that in this situation, "it" might yell, "*Untipaṟa*" - 'leap up and run' – as she pushes her teammate out and takes her place with the line of girls singing. Based on this understanding, I have translated the *tirumoḻi* as a song sung while playing this type of tag, the repeated phrase, *pāṭi-p-paṟa* meaning 'run and sing.' The verses themselves alternate between descriptions of episodes in the Kṛṣṇa and Rāma incarnations of Nārāyaṇa: Kṛṣṇa stealing Indra's tree, kidnapping Rukmiṇī, participating in the Bhārata War, killing the serpent Kāliya, and living as a herder; and Rāma defeating Paraśurāma, slaying Tāḍakā, being exiled by Kaikeyī, making his younger brother, Bharata, regent, attacking Śūrpaṇakhā, defeating Rāvaṇa and crowning Vibhīṣaṇa king.

III.9.1

With the help of that strong lordly bird,
    he plucked up the tree with fresh flowers
Under the gaze of its lord with his lady who had refused
To give its flowers of love to the goddess of our Lord.
Run and sing of the strength of my Lord;
    run and sing of the strength of our sovereign.

III.9.2

"Come see the strength of my bow," said his rival,
And he seized both his power and his bow.
Before when he bent a bow, he took the demoness' life.
Run and sing of the strength of his bow;
    run and sing of Dāśarathi's stature.

III.9.3

With feelings of passion rising for the lady, Rukmiṇī,
He swept her up into his chariot and carried her away.
He crushed the pride of his enemy who then opposed him.
Run and sing of him who shaved his enemy's head;
    run and sing of Devakī's lion.

III.9.4

His step-mother approached him and said, "Be gone into the forest!"
His own mother followed behind, crying "Oh, our Lord,"
As he departed into the fearful forest
    as his cruel mother had commanded.
Run and sing of the wrathless Lord;
    run and sing of Sītā's groom.

III.9.5

He assisted in the Bhārata War as a messenger for the Five.
He entered into the pond with the poisonous snake
And blessed him by leaping up on his fearful serpent hoods.
Run and sing of the kohl-colored One;
run and sing of Yaśodā's lion.

III.9.6

"You bear the crown that rules the three worlds;
Have mercy on me, your servant,"
Said the incomparable Bharata as he followed.
Run and sing of him who left his sandals;
run and sing of the Ruler of Ayodhya.

III.9.7

He jumped in and churned up Kāliya's pond
And danced on his five hooded, high heads
To mete out his grace and redeem that snake.
Run and sing of the Sage's strong arms and bravery;
run and sing of the pure jewel-hued Lord.

III.9.8

He gave his kingdom to a brother too young for the royal wreath,
Then went to the Daṇḍaka forest on the word of that hurtful woman.
Śūrpaṇakhā, of curved waist, he made roar.
Run and sing that he cut her nose and ears off;
run and sing of the King of Ayodhya.

III.9.9

He kicked the demon wheel and broke the laurel tree.
He went out with the herders to protect the cattle herd,
That Sage who blew on a jeweled bamboo flute.
Run and sing of him praised by the herders;
run and sing of him grazing the cow herd.

III.9.10

He blocked off the black sea and entered into Lanka;
The disrespectful one's nine and one golden crowns
And the kingdom he gave to the brother not in the battle.
Run and sing of the never-satiating Nectar;
run and sing of the Monarch of Ayodhya.

III.9.11

These words of the brightly adorned ladies who jumped up and ran,
Telling of Nanda's son and Kakutstha's descendent,
Are the pure Tamil words of Viṭṭucittaṉ of southern Putuvai.
For those who master the five plus five, there will never be any sorrow.

Third Ten, 10th tirumoḻi – Hanumaṉ's proof

The Great Āḻvār presents this verse in the voice of the monkey Hanumaṉ, Rāma's devoted and loyal servant. In this scene, Hanumaṉ has found Rāma's wife, Sītā, captive in Lanka and tries to persuade her that he is a friend and that she will be rescued. But she does not know ally from enemy and wants proof that he is from Rāma's camp. The poet uses this situation as a device for retelling the wonders of the Rāma incarnation of Nārāyaṇa, and in the process creates dramatic tension as Hanumaṉ tries over and over to convince Sītā to trust him. The final resolution occurs in an emotionally charged stanza expressing Sītā's elation. While Periyāḻvār certainly included references from the Rāmāyaṇa in his works, this *tirumoḻi* provides the poet's only fully developed episode from that myth. Why this one? Perhaps Periyāḻvār's message here is that god presents, in numerous ways in everyday life, proofs of his love. Sītā's happiness was the same joy the poet feels when seeing any and every small sign that god is near. A summary of *Rāmāyaṇa* episodes referenced in the *Tirumoḻi* can be found in the introduction and may help the reader follow the stories mentioned.

III.10.1

Sweet lady with dark curly hair, I am your servant. Salutations!
I know he attained you when he broke the bow
        of Janaka whose crown abounds with jewels,
That he blocked the way of one of rare powers
        who slew the race of kings
And destroyed both his powers and thick bow: this is one proof.

III.10.2

Lady in whose hair lie lovely waterlilies,
        I bow at your feet. Salutations!
Give me leave to speak; please graciously listen,
        sweet deer with wide blossom eyes.
It was evening at that special place, a time for sweet pleasures,
When you laced for him a jasmine wreath: this is one proof.

III.10.3

With an agitated mind, Kaikeyī asked a boon
Of the king, his mind distraught that he could not deny her,
And so he ordered, "Royal Prince, to the forest go and dwell."
So with Lakṣmaṇa he went: this is one proof.

III.10.4

Sweet lady with beautifully bound breasts,
    Lady of Videha! Salutations!
Graciously listen, great goddess of the Lord,
    King of Ayodhya encircled by chariots.
On the Ganges was Guha, well-skilled with a sharp-tipped spear,
Who gave his gracious friendship: this is one proof.

III.10.5

Lady of soft deer-like gaze, Lady of Videha! Salutations!
When you dwelled in the woods, its forest paths full of stones,
On Citrakūṭa slopes with honey groves,
    came Bharata with milk-sweet words
Who bowed there in reverence: this is one proof.

III.10.6

While on Citrakūṭa Mountain, a little crow touched your chest,
So he sent forth an arrow which chased it 'round the world
'Til it cried out, "Wise Lord Rāma, you are my only refuge."
That arrow pierced its eye: this is one proof.

III.10.7

Lady with lightning-thin waist, I'm your true servant. Salutations!
A golden-hued deer entered the forest and there it sweetly played;
In keeping with your wishes, our Lord followed with his bow;
Later Lakṣmaṇa left: this is one proof.

III.10.8

Lady with dark hair full of blossoms, Lady of Videha! Salutations!
When the King of Ayodhya came seeking you,
he met the king of monkeys of equal praise,
To whom he told these incidents which are the proof.
But the most fitting token I bring is this – his ring!

III.10.9

He came to the fire ritual held by the ruler of the four directions,
That day he broke the strong bow in the presence of the huge assembly.
When Sītā saw that ring, she raised it high, rejoicing.
She of flower-laden locks cried, "Oh, Hanumaṉ, it's the perfect proof!"

III.10.10

Those who sing the songs of the Bhaṭṭa lord of Putuvai,
praised throughout the world,
The proof of what was known and told by brave and noble Hanumaṉ
When he saw the Lady of Videha with beautifully bound breasts,
They will dwell with the celestials in beautiful Vaikuṇṭha.

Fourth Ten, 1st tirumoḻi – Some hints

While earlier verses in the *Tirumoḻi* have predominantly been presented in the voice of a character from within Vaiṣṇava mythology, with the Fourth Ten, the poet shifts to directly address the reader in his own right. In IV.1, he examines the Vaiṣṇava concept of divine descent of the Supreme Deity through earthly incarnations, explaining in simple terms that Kṛṣṇa, Rāma, Narasimha the Man-lion, Varāha the Boar, and Tirumāl are the same deity, incarnate in various forms. Devotees, *bhaktas*, are urged to seek their Lord in every form in order to comprehend the Supreme Deity. What is most important, however, is his imminence on earth where 'there are those who saw him."

IV.1.1

If you seek the place of Rāma, whose greatness none can oppose,
Whose high crown burns as brightly as the rays of a thousand suns,
There are those who saw him as a lion, his hands covered with blood,
Tearing at the chest of Hiraṇya
with battle shoulders and anklets shaking.

IV.1.2

If you seek the place of great Rāma,
who bears the Śārnga bow with a thundering string,
The club, the conch, the divine disc, and the Nandaka sword,
There are those who saw him break the bow
at the sacrifice of Janaka, Rāja of kings,
For the sake of Sītā, whose fingers were folded
like the five-petalled glory lily.

IV.1.3

If you steadily seek the deity who shot the fig trees with his bow,
Who destroyed in battle the army of his enemy
and plucked the tusk from the ferocious elephant,
There are those who saw him seated majestically
on the shore washed by waves,
Where a clan of monkeys carried on their heads
stones to dam up the sea.

IV.1.4

If you seek the mystic babe who yet has an ancient form
And is surrounded by the vast waters, come; I'll give you a hint.
There are those who really saw him angrily in battle
Destroy seven strong bulls for Piṉṉai, the sweet milkmaid.

IV.1.5

If you seek Lord Tirumāl whose fame is praised in turns
By four-face Brahma and blue-necked Śiva,
from whose red locks the waters rise,
There are those who fixed their gaze on him
doing battle midst the enemy army
When he carried off in his chariot Rukmiṇī, her girdled breasts heaving.

IV.1.6

If you seek the place where dwells the beautiful jewel-hued One
Who deftly killed the evil demoness by putting his lips to her breast,
There are those who saw him seated on his lion throne surrounded
By thousands of goddesses and all of Dvāraka, dashed by the salty sea.

IV.1.7

If you ask for the place of him in whose hands are found
The white conch trumpet and the bright fiery disc,
    come; I'll give you a hint.
Some saw him lend a hand in the Bhārata War
    as a shrewd ally to the army,
Standing at the head of the chariot
    with white horses and a monkey banner.

IV.1.8

Devakī's child, he with war weapons, compelled time to elapse,
Standing in front of the kings who were waiting, counting the minutes.
There are those who saw him next to the well-armed warrior
Who made Jayadratha's head roll on the field
    when the Lord hid the sun with his disc.

IV.1.9

If you steadily seek the god who consumed the world completely-
The earth, mountains and rolling seas - then spit it out again,
There are those who saw him as an inconceivably rare boar
Who dug out the spacious Earth and married that dark-haired goddess.

IV.1.10

This garland of ten was composed by the lord of the Bhaṭṭas
    learned in the Mysteries which celebrate Tiru,
Who dwells in Putuvai, where fertile fields
    yield red paddy, drooping like horse heads,
Giving some hints to see Māyaṉ whose body is like a black rain cloud;
Those *bhaktas* with worshipful hearts will reach
    the feet of our Supreme Lord.

Fourth Ten, 2nd tirumoḻi – Tirumāliruncōlai Mountain I

Periyāḻvār, like many Vaiṣṇava and Śaiva poets, devoted some of his songs to specific shrines and sacred cities. Tirumāliruncōlai is a mountain pilgrimage site near Madurai, known in modern Tamil Nadu as Aḻakar Koyil. Each verse contains not only references to episodes from the Vaiṣṇava myth, but also detailed descriptions of the mountain. In verse IV.2.1, the Āḻvār gives the reason the river there is named Cilampu, 'ankle bracelet.' Periyāḻvār, a gardener who wove garlands for the image in the Śrīvilliputtūr temple, generally only mentions flower offerings. Verse IV.2.9, however, references spirits making blood offerings at Tirumāliruncōlai, which might suggest that animal sacrifices were being made at some Vaiṣṇava temples at that time, as in the later verse IV.7.6 which also describes the northern temple at Kaṇṭam being filled with smoke from sacrificial fires burning near rows of posts where sacrificial animals were tied. As discussed in more detail in the introductory material, verse IV.2.7 is central to the study of Periyāḻvār, as it is the most significant tool available for dating his life and works. Here is mentioned King Neṭumāṟaṉ of Kūṭal (an earlier name for Madurai), assumed to be a contemporary of the poet; however, there is speculation as to which Pāṇṭiyaṉ king this refers. The two possible rulers lived from the late 8th to the early 9th c. CE. The Fourth Ten, with its shift in voice and subject matter, might be a late composition in Periyāḻvār's life, and the reference to King Neṭumāṟaṉ generally places the poet near the early 9th c. CE.

IV.2.1

The mountain of the King who stands as the lamp of his clan,
Who destroyed the roving ogre clan
which raided, terrorized and murdered,
Is Tirumāliruncōlai of the South where the Cilampu River flows
With the sound of ankle bracelets of celestial maidens dancing.

IV.2.2

The mountain abode of him who sliced off the strong one's arms,
The heads of the sword-bearing demon
and the nose of his wicked sister
Is the famous southern mountain named Tirumāliruncōlai
Where is heard the blessing "Many Years" spreading in all directions.

IV.2.3

The golden mountain of the Noble who sent on the path to Hell
Those furious fiends which afflicted men of excellence and of honor
Is cool Māliruncōlai where dark forest paths are transformed
For devotees constantly coming to give service there.

IV.2.4

The mountain of him who lifted the Govardhana mountain
To end the festival of the celestial king
which was celebrated by the herder clan,
Is southern Tirumāliruncōlai where a river of fragrance flows
As if from the blossoms of the *kaṟpaka* tree
which grows in the land of heaven.

IV.2.5

The mountain where dwells the One
who took the life of Kaṃsa's elephant,
He who also had mercy on the elephant in the pond,
Is cool Tirumāliruncōlai where the dark elephant renounced his mate
To wander repeating his vows to the dark sea-colored One.

IV.2.6

The mountain of him who destroyed with four sandal-scented arms
The wrestlers who boldly opposed him, according to their orders,
Is Tirumāliruncōlai of the South where celestials and good sages
Say, "He has appeared" and do service in worship.

IV.2.7

The mountain of him who drew water from a subterranean stream
When he stood on the chariot for his cousins
to confound the enemy kings,
Is southern Tirumāliruncōlai praised by him of the South,
King of southern Kūṭal, Neṭumāraṉ, his sharp spear skilled in killing.

IV.2.8

The gold mountain of the Noble who destroyed
the homes of the enemy kings
And drove them by narrow footpaths into the dark harsh forest
Is Tirumāliruncōlai of the South where sing in the early dawn
The striped six-legged beetles, reciting his one-thousand names.

IV.2.9

The mountain of our Father where spirits appear at dusk
To give sacrificial offerings, spilling red blood in swells,
Is Tirumāliruncōlai of the South where on jungle slopes
Creep *indragopa* beetles, red as the Lord's fruit lips.

IV.2.10

The mountain where the Immaculate Lord is majestically enthroned,
Encircled by countless goddesses, lighting the eight directions,
Is Tirumāliruncōlai of the South where as evening falls
Young she-elephants nudge and jostle to couple with the bull.

IV.2.11

Those who resolutely recite these words of Viṭṭucittaṉ
Who dwells in Villiputtūr where he took a vow of worship,
They will gaze at both feet of Kaṇṇaṉ, the dark sea-colored Lord,
Who resembles the mountain whereon he dwells,
Māliruncōlai, decked with laurel groves.

Fourth Ten, 3rd tirumoḻi - Tirumāliruncōlai Mountain II

The third *tirumoḻi* continues with a celebration of the pilgrimage site, Tirumāliruncōlai. Episodes are generally from the later part of Kṛṣṇa's life and include specific mention by name of several enemies: Rukmin, Bāṇa, Naraka, and Śiśupāla, whose stories are retold in the introductory material. Verse 4 includes a reference to hill women of the Kurava tribe singing *kuṟinci* songs about Kṛṣṇa. *Kuṟinci* is the name of one of the five classical themes of early Tamil love poetry, which are classified according to the five geographic divisions of Tamil Nadu. The *kuṟinci* theme is associated with the mountainous region and with love in union, suggesting that the hill women are in love with Kṛṣṇa. The final verse, IV.3.11, includes a reference to the deity's "four famous divine forms" which the commentator Aṇṇankarācāriyar suggests refers to Vāsudeva (i.e. Kṛṣṇa), Sankarṣaṇa (an epithet of Kṛṣṇa's brother, Balarāma), Pradyumna (Kṛṣṇa's son) and Aniruddha (Kṛṣṇa's grandson), the last three perceived to be emanations, or *vyūhas*, of the first in his Supreme form.[155] Vasudha Narayanan in her study of Āḻvār religion, *The Way and The Goal*, refers to Periyāḻvār's *Tirumoḻi* IV.3.11 in support of her theory that the Āḻvārs had "considerable knowledge"[156] of the practices of the Pāncarātra tradition which focused on worship of divine images in temples, as opposed to rituals and sacrifices, and produced a large body of literature including philosophical discourse on the *vyūha* concept.

IV.3.1

The mountain of him who chased and chastised Rukmin
Who had pursued him, intent on returning Rukmiṇī,
Is vast Māliruncōlai where the golden rain tree on its top
Gladly gives out gold as leaf rings and petal coins.

IV.3.2

The mountain of the jewel-hued One
who grew to destroy his deceivers,
Kaṃsa and Kāliya, the elephant, the bull and the laurel trees,
Is Tirumāliruncōlai where the venom-spitting serpent rises
To strike at the cool moon and lick it with a fiery red tongue

IV.3.3

The mountain of the sea-hued Lord who first surrounded Naraka,
Then seized and split him, and carried off all the maids,
Is Māliruncōlai, girded in gold – a garland of flowery groves
Of laurel trees and magnolia, woody kino and silk-cotton trees.

IV.3.4

The mountain which resembles the warrior who attacked all alone
And released from captivity the daughter of Bāṇa, Māvali's son,
Is Māliruncōlai where gather crowds of Kurava girls
Dancing and singing *kuṟinci* songs of our Gopāla Govinda.

IV.3.5

The mountain of the beautifully-jeweled Lord
who put an end to the insolence
Of Śiśupāla who had denounced him, uttering many insults,
Is Tirumāliruncōlai, a royal mountain, an elegant peak,
A huge cool mountain, a victor, a fertile and towering height.

IV.3.6

The mountain of our Father who placed
upon the wives of the One Hundred
All the pains of Pāncālī, the wife of the Pāṇḍavas,
Is ancient Māliruncōlai, the mountain with deep spring wells
Where swarm the bees to drink nectar and sing fine melodies.

IV.3.7

The mountain of our strong-armed Rāma
who for the sake of Sītā, with gold earrings,
Impaled on stakes the race of ogres
and showered down arrows in battle,
Is lofty Mount Māliruncōlai, where circle
multitudes from the broad earth
Who come to bathe in the clear cascades
which cast up gold on the shores.

IV.3.8

The mountain of the King who ended the blustering of Lanka's leader
By showering from his well-bound bow arrows scattering fire,
Is the mountain Tirumāliruncōlai where Indra and all the celestials,
As well as the wheeling orbs, come to circle in adoration.

IV.3.9

The mountain of the Pure One who played at
digging and taking the earth on his tusk,
Measuring and taking the earth in his hands,
eating and expelling it again,
Is Māliruncōlai where ripples the cool Cilampu River,
Carrying a store of offerings to lay at the feet of our Lord.

IV.3.10

The mountain where reigns the sleeper on Ananta,
with one thousand hooded heads,
His one thousand arms extending,
his one thousand crowns like lightning,
Is the mountain Māliruncōlai with one thousand flowering gardens,
Where flow one thousand streams,
and many thousands of pools run deep.

IV.3.11

The mountain-like Lord of the mountain which is named Māliruncōlai,
His four famous divine forms, this Sea of nectar of the four Vedas,
This heavenly Lamp which shines on the great meaning of Vedanta,
This heavenly *kaṟpaka* tree, him has Viṭṭucittaṉ exalted.

Fourth Ten, 4th tirumoḻi – The people of Tirukōṭṭiyūr

In IV.4, which celebrates the pilgrimage site Tirukōṭṭiyūr, Periyāḻvār ponders the question of why god created nonbelievers. He sees them as burdens to their parents, their community, and the earth itself, a waste of good food and water. But devoted believers, *bhaktas*, bring joy and blessings to themselves and their neighbors. Verse 1 depicts the deity as the Primal Lord who perfects or guides the deeds of the other three gods, Indra, Brahma and Śiva. In verse IV.4.6, the poet describes the perfection of devotees in their five senses (touch, taste, smell, vision and hearing) and five sense organs (skin, mouth, nose, eyes and ears) through which they perceive the five elements (earth, water, fire, wind and the atmosphere) in the performance of the "five sacrifices." Narayanan discusses the occurrence of this phrase in other Āḻvār texts as a reference to five rituals performed in the Pāncarātra tradition.[157]

IV.4.1

In Tirukōṭṭiyūr dwell those who daily offer feasts,
those whose tongues never speak of petty deeds,
Those who repeat the Vedas, and those who perform pious deeds.
And there are those of sinful deeds who never think of the Primal Lord
Who perfects the deeds of the other Three.
Why did the Creator create them?

IV.4.2

In Tirukōṭṭiyūr dwell those of generous palms
who are ever devoid of hatred,
Who as patrons of the sages increase their fame and destroy their faults.
There are also those who do not praise
the pure jewel-hued One who ate the seven worlds.
They were born only to cause great pain
to the bellies of their mothers who bore them.

IV.4.3

In Tirukōṭṭiyūr, where are erected many shaded rest pavilions,
Inlaid with precious emeralds and other fine jewels of rare hue,
Are those who never think of Tirumāl,
counting his names on their fingers,
Which they only use to push rice wads into their filthy mouths.

IV.4.4

In Tirukōṭṭiyūr, full of red lotus fields
where fly flocks of young swans to nestle,
Each like the white conch fixed in the hand
of him whose soft bed is the serpent,
There is a kind of human whose tongue
never calls his name, "Hell Destroyer";
The clothes they wear and the water they drink
are committing sins, aren't they?

IV.4.5

In Tirukōṭṭiyūr where frolic the young *vāḷai* fish in the ponds
Making mischief, leaping over the turtles' backs
and shaking the white lily blossoms,
From those burdens of the earth whose hard hearts
never think of the disc-handed One
Remove the food from their mouths as they eat
and simply shove in grass!

IV.4.6

In Tirukōṭṭiyūr dwell those of generous palms
who are without any faults
In their five senses and five sense organs,
which know the five elements and five sacrifices.
They wander repeating and praising his names,
saying, "Nātha," and "Narasimha."
The earth itself feels fortunate to bear the dust from their feet.

IV.4.7

In Tirukōṭṭiyūr live those who know well
the four Mysteries, singing praises night and day,
Who celebrate the festivals by joining in dance
with him who broke the wild lime tree.
In that city do loving *bhaktas* stand humbly,
their hands joined in prayer
To him whose hue is of a dark rain cloud.
What penance could those dwelling there have done?

IV.4.8

In Tirukōṭṭiyūr does red-eyed Māl incessantly receive service
From those of sweet temper, of unwavering love,
of dignity and wisdom.
In this land where dwell in harmony
those who sing the praises of Govinda,
Demons would not dare to steal even the smallest grain as it grows.

IV.4.9

In Tirukōṭṭiyūr, full of fertile paddy fields
and surrounded by walls of rose gold
Where flocks of cuckoos fill the branches in the groves
with songs of the goodness of Govinda,
When I see those who praise him, repeating his names,
"Our God who became the man lion,"
I think, "Each one is the sign of the Lord,"
and all of my longing is ended.

IV.4.10

In Tirukōṭṭiyūr prosper those of bounteous palms
who earn the praises of the earth
By giving rice without expecting a return
when a handful could be sold for good money.
Those who say, "Keśava" and "Puruṣottama,"
"Oh Shining Light, Oh Dwarf"
Are servants of our Lord and gain the right to sell me.

IV.4.11

Those who flawlessly say these verses
on Tirukōṭṭiyūr with fertile fields and fresh ponds,
About those who are devoted to the Primal Lord
and those who stray from devotion
Songs by Viṭṭucittaṉ, king of cool Putuvai,
the Bhaṭṭa lord who is without fault,
They will become devoted servants of our Lord Hṛṣīkeśa.

Fourth Ten, 5th tirumoḻi – On the edge of death

Periyāḻvār wrote the First and Second Tens with such palpability that the readers might feel like they are actually watching Kṛṣṇa as an adorable child, listening to his patient and loving mother, or chatting with the neighbor ladies. That sense of life-like realism returns with IV.5 in the poet's description of dying from which he leaves out nothing: itchy lesions, flies, drool, incontinence, spasms, and greedy relatives. Was Periyāḻvār influenced by early Buddhist canon which exhorted monks to attentive mindfulness of the impermanence and repulsiveness of the body, to meditate on their physical beings as a collection of disgusting body parts?[158] Periyāḻvār himself suggests influence from such a text, the *Satipatthāna Sutta,* the title of which in Sanskrit means 'approaching mindfulness,' when he states in the signature verse that his song about the odiousness of death was written with 'strong singleness of mind' (Tamil *cittam naṉkorunki*) and should also be sung by devotees with 'strong singleness of mind.' The poet juxtaposes this type of "corpse meditation" with the joy of devoted thoughts of Nārāyaṇa, which he says will result in dwelling in heaven after death. Such devotion, says the Āḻvār, will keep the dying person from suffering tortures by snakes, snapping dogs and tridents. Is the poet referring to Hell? While that exact term does not occur in this song, the Sanskrit word *naraka* 'hell' does occur elsewhere in the *Tirumoḻi,* as in the subsequent verse IV.6.

IV.5.1

Those who are on the edge of death
        with minds confused and hung on hopes,
Yet calling not, "Mother! Father! my son!
        my lands! Lady of fragrant locks!"
But who say, "Keśava, Puruṣottama,
        Faultless Lord who became a boar,"
The greatness that they reach is not within our power of speech.

IV.5.2

Before you reach the edge of death, maddened by lesions that itch
Which are thick with pus and swarming with flies
that mix in the growing mire,
Join your hands above your head and call aloud, “Namo Nāraṇa!”
Even if given a guarantee of this earth after you go,
it won’t be allowed.

IV.5.3

Before your time arrives when you can’t even open your mouth,
When questioned all around you with, “Tell us!
Is there stuff you’ve stashed away and forgotten?”
Fix the god, Mādhava, in the temple that you build of your heart.
Those who offer flowers of love will be spared torture by snakes.

IV.5.4

Before your rising breath rushes out and your windpipe collapses,
Before spasms seize your arms and legs
and your eyes close on their final sleep,
Let rise in your heart the three measures
of the one sound – AUM - the Cause,
And if you long for the sea-hued Lord, your dwelling will be in heaven.

IV.5.5

Your throat will close; porridge poured at your lips
will drip out again down the sides of your chin;
Before piss passes unchecked through your clothes
and your eyes close on their final sleep,
Be firm in prayer to Hṛṣīkeśa
so dogs won’t snap at your thighs,
So tridents won’t leap out at you,
and you won’t lose the clothes on the way.

IV.5.6

Before the five senses abandon the body
and those crowded around depart
Having tested for breath, but turned up their palms,
and slowly lowered their heads,
May those who persist in one act –
placing in their hearts Madhusūdana,
Māyan̲ who sleeps in the ship-filled sea – may they persist evermore.

IV.5.7

Before the underlord's heartless lackeys come to drive them like oxen,
Catch and tie them with a stout rope, and drag them away backwards,
Those intent on ending darkness in their hearts
who say, "My king, Madhusūdana,"
And count his qualities with "Such a one is he,"
they will be his servants in heaven.

IV.5.8

Before your family clusters in bunches,
lauding your feats, leaving out your faults,
Before they cover you in a shroud and lament
while they put you on a bier
Like a pot of honey for a pack of jackals,
let your heart rejoice and join him,
Govinda, the *kaustubha*-jewelled,
then escape passed that notorious place.

IV.5.9

As pain swells at the sides of their mouths
and their eyes flutter, sunken and rheumy,
As on one side is Mother, one side is Father,
and on one side weeps the wife,
Before the fires catch at their sides, those who keep red-eyed Māl
At their side as their closest relation will escape the torture of snakes.

IV.5.10

Those who master this garland of Ten
sung with singleness of mind on Tirumāl
By strong-armed Viṭṭucittaṉ, king of Śrīvilliputtūr,
On the rewards of the *bhaktas* who at death
think of the divine Lord and their deeds
With singleness of mind, the thoughts of them
will ever dwell on Tirumāl.

Fourth Ten, 6th tirumoḻi – The mother of a "Nāraṇa"

Namāvali is the practice of repeating god's names as an expression of devotion and as a means of gaining karmic merit. The most blessed chant for Periyāḻvār is "*Namo Nārāyaṇa*" which in the *Tirumoḻi* is often shortened to "Namo Nāraṇa." In *tirumoḻi* IV.6, Periyāḻvār makes the simple point that by giving children the names of god, such as "Nāraṇa," considering the number of times mothers in every century and culture call to, yell at and nag their children every day, those mothers will be performing *namāvali* on a continual basis. He can't understand why someone would do otherwise. When the goal of life is to be born in heavenly Vaikuṇṭha, why would people name their children after a human who failed in that goal and was reborn on earth? The solution seems obvious to the Āḻvār – name your children after Nārāyaṇa. In the refrain, "The mother of a 'Nāraṇa' will never go to hell," the Sanskrit word for 'hell' *naraka* (Tamil *narakam*) has been used. Regarding his counsel to pregnant women in Verse 3, the two elements of the phrase *eccam polintīṟkāḷ* can be combined in various ways. *Eccam* means 'remainder, refuse, dung, and spit' but euphemistically also means 'child;' the verb *poli* means 'to increase, prosper, or enlarge.'[159] While the phrase could be translated, 'prosper with children,' or 'enlarge with child,' I have chosen 'swell up with filth' to convey the original negative meaning of *eccam* and to maintain the overall tone of rebuke.

IV.6.1

You fools who give your children useless names full of false hope
For a few coins, a bunch of grain and clothes full of filth,
Give the name "Keśava" or "Nāyaka" and you will be blessed!
The mother of a "Nāraṇa" will never go to hell.

IV.6.2

You fools who give your children names of decaying human kind
With greed for a rag to wrap around your loins,
If she calls, "Hey, Śrīdara" or "Tall red-eye Māl,"
The mother of a "Nāraṇa" will never go to hell.

IV.6.3

You who like oil baths and wear bangles and jewels,
But swell up with filth, why do you give strange names?
Even if you're a beggar, you can mutter the names of our Lord.
The mother of a "Nāraṇa" will never go to hell.

IV.6.4

If you who are born as humans give to your human babes
The names of other humans, there's no chance for your salvation.
If she calls her child, "Govinda, my Mādhava, Ruler of heaven,"
The mother of a "Nāraṇa" will never go to hell.

IV.6.5

If you who are born of filth give to your filthy spawn
The names of other filth, there's no chance for your salvation.
If she calls her child, "Good Govinda, Govinda of noble birth,"
The mother of a "Nāraṇa" will never go to hell.

IV.6.6

Don't give the name of some man famous
throughout city and countryside,
Then slip in the grave-pit to suffer, falling in along with him.
Direct your desires toward Dāmodara,
our Leader who kicked the wheel demon.
The mother of a "Nāraṇa" will never go to hell.

IV.6.7

You weak-minded men without any purpose,
You give names of men born of earth who become earth again.
Consider the names of the cloud-colored One who is so sweet to see.
The mother of a "Nāraṇa" will never go to hell.

IV.6.8

You might give a country folks' name,
like "Nambi" or "Bimbi" or something,
But the Nambis and Bimbis will vanish
as simply as one-two-three-four!
If she calls the name, "Hey, Kaṇṇaṉ! You of large lotus eyes!"
The mother of Nambi's "Nāraṇa" will never go to hell.

IV.6.9

As if you are pouring ambrosia into a pit full of filth,
Give the tongue-pleasing name "Dark Cloud" to your piss-soaked baby,
Then all clasp hands together and whirl around in a riot, dancing.
The mother of nice-sounding "Nāraṇa" will never go to hell.

IV.6.10

Whoever is able to say these ten perfect Tamil verses
Composed by Viṭṭucittaṉ, whose skill is glorified of old,
This advice: "Give to your children the names of effulgent Māl,"
They will ever be cherished in the vast heavens of Vaikuṇṭha.

Fourth Ten – 7th tirumoḻi – The protected city of Kaṇṭam

Periyāḻvār was the only poet in the *Divine Works* to celebrate the pilgrimage site of Kaṇṭam-kaṭi-nakar 'garrison protected city.' The poet seems to have chosen fairly militaristic episodes and imagery to use in these verses in keeping with the name of the site. Battles, weapons, and destruction of demons prevail here. Nārāyaṇa's Nandaka sword is mentioned by name in IV.7.4. Verse 5 also includes the pestle and the plough with Nārāyaṇa's standard arsenal, weapons ascribed to Kṛṣṇa's brother, Baladeva, who is also considered an emanation of Nārāyaṇa Vāsudeva. The pilgrimage site is presumed to be modern Devaprayag, a village in the Himalayan Mountains on the confluence of the Alaknanda and Bhagirathi Rivers which unite there to flow into the great Ganges. The verses of this *tirumoḻi* are full of dynamic and picturesque images of the sacred waters and the religious activities of pilgrims. Verse 10 is unclear in its description of devotees who understand "The three letters, what is made of three letters and the making of it with three letters." Perhaps this describes the esoteric knowledge of the mantra AUM, made with the three sounds, A-U-M, with the three letters signifying those three sounds. The same verse further plays with the number three by referring to Nārāyaṇa in his dwarf incarnation in which he rescued the universe in three steps – on earth, in heaven and beyond – and that he appears in three forms. One suggestion might be that he appeared on three levels: on earth in multiple incarnations, in heaven as Nārāyaṇa-Viṣṇu, and "beyond" as the formless Supreme.[160] Verses 2 and 3 refer to a shrine to Śiva also located nearby in Kaṇṭam.

IV.7.1

The place of our Puruṣottama who rules as far as his fame,
Who, as Dāśarathi, severed the king's head
    and the nose of the king's sister,
Is the protected city called Kaṇṭam
    revered on the banks of the Ganges
Which removes cruel fate with the words, "Ganga, oh, Ganga."

IV.7.2

The dwelling of Māl Puruṣottama
whose jewel-hued form rose, expanding,
Frightening the sun, its maw spitting fire,
and the moon, a ball of cool dew,
Is the protected city called Kaṇṭam where mix in the Ganges flood
The *tulasī* leaves from Nārāyaṇa's feet
with golden rain buds from Śiva's fiery locks.

IV.7.3

The place of our Puruṣottama who made roar the right-whorled conch
And threw his fire-spitting discus to fell that demon's head
Is the protected city called Kaṇṭam
where the Ganges flows full of jewels
From the hands of the four-faced god, to the feet
of our four-armed Lord, and through Śankara's locks.

IV.7.4

The city of our Puruṣottama who bore
Nandaka to send to Death's dwelling
The enemy army that boldly opposed the celestial's majestic rule
Is the protected city called Kaṇṭam
on the banks of the great river, Ganges,
Both banks, from the Himalayas to the ocean,
resounding with bathers, cleansed of sin.

IV.7.5

The dwelling of Māl Puruṣottama,
armed with the plough and the pestle,
The flaming discus and conch, the bow, the axe and the sword,
Is the protected city called Kaṇṭam
on the banks of the great river, Ganges,
Which removes within an instant all the sins of seven births.

IV.7.6

The dwelling of Māl Puruṣottama,
who in Mathurā with a mountain umbrella
Averted pounding torrents which poured
from water-laden clouds above, roaring,
Is the protected city called Kaṇṭam
where the Ganges casts ploughs on the shore,
And where pious sages perform their ablutions,
plunging in the roaring waves.

IV.7.7

The dwelling of Māl Puruṣottama
who broke the bow and beat the elephant,
Crushed the head of the elephant driver,
fought the wrestlers and kicked the king,
Is the protected city called Kaṇṭam
where the Ganges mixes *kaṟpaka* buds
With the ichor of fabulous Airāvata
and sandal paste of celestial maidens.

IV.7.8

The place of Hari Puruṣottama,
King of walled Dvāraka on the crashing sea
Who blessed his brother-in-law
with the kingdom of the conquered kings
Is the protected city called Kaṇṭam
where both banks of the Ganges are scented
By smoke from incessant holy fires rising
from rows of tall sacrificial posts.

IV.7.9

The place of our Puruṣottama,
who is in Sālagrāma and northern Mathurā,
In Vaikuṇṭha, Dvāraka and Ayodhya, and in unbounded Badarī,
Is the protected city called Kaṇṭam
where the crashing Ganges churns the waters
With waves that dash down tree tops,
shatter the earth and shake huge mountains

IV.7.10

The place of our kind Puruṣottama
with compassion for those who embrace
The three letters, what is made of three letters,
and the making of it with three letters,
Is the protected city called Kaṇṭam
with wooded groves on the Ganges' shore
Where he took three steps, appeared in the three
and, in those three, took three forms.

IV.7.11

For those who retain on their tongues
these Tamil verses composed with love
By fervent Viṭṭucittaṉ, the king of Villiputtūr, devoid of sorrows,
About the feet of Puruṣottama who dwells
in Kaṇṭam on the banks of the rolling Ganges,
Their rewards will be equal to bathing
in the Ganges at the feet of Tirumāl.

Fourth Ten, 8th tirumoḻi – His city of Śrīrangam

One of the largest shrines in India today is the Śrīrangam temple, located on an island formed by the Kaverī River and one of its tributaries near the modern city of Tirucchirāppalli. It was a major pilgrimage site during the Tamil devotional period and was celebrated by eleven of the twelve Āḻvārs. The second half of each of the following verses is dedicated to the natural description of the city, its surroundings and the river, maintaining continuity with classical Tamil landscape poetry. Some typical episodal content is found in the first lines of some of the verses, but in others, the stories are less familiar to the Āḻvār texts. Focusing on the deity's compassion, the first three verses relate stories of Nārāyaṇa returning children to life: the stories of Sāndīpani (IV.8.1), of returning the Brahmin's children (IV.8.2), and of Parikṣit (IV.8.3) as retold in the introductory material on Vaiṣṇava mythology. The commentator Aṇṇankarācāriyar suggests that the reference in verse 10 to Viṣṇu burning two bodies is an allusion to him slaying the demons, Madhu and Kaiṭabha.[161]

IV.8.1

The city of him who gave as a teacher's fee
    to that guru of great austerities
The revived form of his dear son, who had died in the swelling seas
Is called Śrīrangam where the waters,
    flowing with honey and laden with pollen,
Dash against the bathing steps to cleanse the clothes
    of those learned in the pure Mysteries.

IV.8.2

The city where dwells he who retrieved and in a split second reunited
All the four children who had died right in the birthing room
Is called blessed Śrīrangam where dwell eminent sages,
Those who kindle Vedic altar fires,
    and those who are gracious to guests.

IV.8.3

The city of him who restored to life the offspring of his nephew,
Who, with a sage's visage, kept his cousins
from being thrown on the sacrificial fire,
Is called Śrīrangam where in the waters face in battle
Blue lilies like his body and pink lotuses like his face.

IV.8.4

The city of him who heard the harsh words
of the wicked woman and her hunch-backed slave
Who then left his kingdom and the kind mother who bore him
To follow the path to the forest and destroy the Kaṇṭaka demons
Is called blessed Śrīrangam, its groves full of honey-laden blossoms.

IV.8.5

The city of the protector of this world
who fought and destroyed in battle
Rāvaṇa, full of evil who had gained great powers,
Is called blessed Śrīrangam, the place where my Tirumāl stays,
Where coocoos call in cool groves
with bottlebrush blossoms and silk-cotton buds.

IV.8.6

The city of the destroyer of underworld demons
who blocked their rise from below
By discharging his discus to destroy even their unborn in the womb
Is Śrīrangam where ever hum with a sweet sound like the stringed lute
Swarms of bees adorned with white pollen
from the petals of the screwpine buds.

IV.8.7

The city of Perumāṉ who reduced to corpses the evil demon horde
So that their thickly flowing blood swelled, foaming in floods,
Is lovely Śrīrangam at whose feet the roaring Kaverī worships,
Offering from the vast mountains sandal trees too huge to embrace.

IV.8.8

The city of him who split the limitless world
        and split the demon's chest
As a strong-tusked boar and as a sharp-toothed lion
Is well-walled Śrīrangam where at evening the large winged beetles
Sing praises of our Lord and sip the white conch-like jasmine.

IV.8.9

The city of tall Māl whose hue is of dancing peacocks,
Of the blue lily buds and of roaring waves,
        of the clouds that cluster 'round the hilltops,
Is well-walled Śrīrangam where ever creep
        the southern breezes through the courtyards,
Wandering through hill groves, caressing
        the breasts of creeper-waisted ladies.

IV.8.10

We are devoted to those who praise the One
        who burned the two bodies,
Those who sing this Tamil Śrīrangam verse composed by Viṭṭucittaṉ
On the blessed Lord who rules Tirupati
        and who fought and destroyed in battle
Him who gained great powers and raised a battle roar.

Fourth Ten, 9th tirumoḻi – The temple in Śrīrangam

Tirumoḻi IV.9 continues Periyāḻvār's celebration of the famous temple at Śrīrangam begun in the previous *tirumoḻi*. The episodal content presents several points of interest and is more difficult to interpret than elsewhere. Verse 2 seems to suggest that Tiru, Śrī Lakṣmi, might be jealous of the devotees, making accusations against them, but that Nārāyaṇa stands up for his own people. That same verse references the traditional reason given for the image in the Śrīrangam temple facing south, rather than east, as is more common. Temple mythology states that Rāvaṇa's brother, Vibhīṣaṇa (Tamil *vipīṭaṇaṉ*), was taking an image of Rāma to Śrī Lanka for worship there. Since Rāma did not want his image installed in Śrī Lanka, the image became stuck in Śrīrangam on the way and faces Śrī Lanka to the south in recognition of Vibhīṣaṇa's devotion.[162] Verse IV.9.3 presents a description of what occurs at salvation: the poet envisions Nārāyaṇa's grace drawing him up into the blinding light of heavenly Vaikuṇṭha and then removing any means – here, a ladder (Tamil *ēṇi*) - for him to go back down, i.e. be reborn on earth. Verse IV.9.5 refers to the *Harivamśa* episode of the sage Nārada praising a turtle who seemed to be meditating on a log. The turtle humbly says the River Ganga is more worthy of praise; Ganga says the ocean is more worthy; and so on. Thus Nārada praises by turn, the earth, mountains, Brahma, the Vedas, the sacrifice, the offering and finally Nārāyaṇa.[163] The story of Parikṣit is referenced in verse 6, with his mother, Uttarā, mentioned by name. A complete list of Nārāyaṇa's ten incarnations is provided in verse IV.9.9: the fish, turtle, boar, man-lion, Vāmana, Paraśurāma, Dāśarathi Rāma, Kṛṣṇa, Balarāma, and Kalki. While lists of incarnations vary by Āḻvār and date, Periyāḻvār's list constitutes what has become generally accepted.[164]

IV.9.1

The temple of Tirumāl, earth's ruler, who placed
his sandals as a pledge to his brother
Then, to save the celestials, performed his duty in the place of battle
Is radiant Śrīrangam where in the wind
wave and sway graceful dark lilies,
Like the flower eyes of Lady Tiru,
like the Lord's body and his blessed feet.

IV.9.2

Even if the Lady of the lotus tells falsehoods against his devotees,
He'll say, "My servants wouldn't do that;
if they did, they did it for good."
They serve no other but him of Śrīrangam where his bud-like eyes
Strain toward well-walled Lanka for sake of steadfast Vibhīṣaṇa.

IV.9.3

He heard cheers when he smashed the angry elephant and the wrestlers,
The wheeled wagon, Pralamba, the evil horse
and the laurel trees in the dark grove.
Through the realm of fiery rays dispelling darkness,
he raises his devotees in grace,
Then removes the ladder to accept them as servants;
the city where he dwells is jeweled Śrīrangam.

IV.9.4

The temple where he sits majestically as the master of Dvāraka,
Where he is served as the groom of sixteen thousand queens,
Is Śrīrangam of the river where fresh lotus flowers,
to imitate the blossom in the great Lord's navel,
Suppose themselves its equal and stand proud,
then bow to give their pollen-gold.

IV.9.5

The temple where he sleeps, praised in song by cheerful Nārada,
Who first praised by turns the turtle, the Ganges and the deep sea,
the earth and the huge mountains,
Four-face Brahma and the four Mysteries, the sacrifice and its offering,
Is Śrīrangam of the river where flocks of birds perch
in the flowers to sing the glories of the bird-king.

IV.9.6

The temple where dwells Life's ruler,
who restored to life the son of Uttarā,
Who made crowned as kings his cousins,
so their wife could tie up her hair,
Is blessed Śrīrangam which stands as a beacon
to all directions throughout the vast lands,
Where bow and pray both *bhaktas* and *bhagavas*,
siddhas and sages, learned in the ancient Word.

IV.9.7

The temple of our Lord who as a brahmācharya dwarf
Crush Māvali's pride and took his kingdom,
then in a second, gave him Hell for a home,
Is Śrīrangam illumined by jewels
on the couched serpent's splendid hoods
That rise like the morning sun over a radiant jeweled mountain.

IV.9.8

The temple of him who roared, mouth wide,
when he seized proud Hiraṇya's chest
And pierced it with pointed claws,
crushing his crown 'til his eyes bulged
Is cool Śrīrangam where rise fertile lotus flowers,
like the reddened feet which measured the earth,
To which rows of red paddy growing in the paths
bend their stalks to bow their heads in prayer.

IV.9.9

The temple of him who was a divine fish and turtle,
a boar, a lion and a dwarf
Who became three Rāmas and Kaṇṇaṉ,
and who will conclude with Kalki,
Is Śrīrangam of the river where a swan plays
swinging on the red lotus blossoms,
Embracing her mate on a flower bed,
besmearing their bodies with red pollen.

IV.9.10

Master of the battle-bird, Master of the earth,
Bearer into battle of the sword named Nandaka,
Master of the Mysteries, the strong-armed Master,
Master of the undefeated armies,
Master of the darkness, Master of the day,
Master of the sacred places of the seven worlds,
Master of Śrī, Master over me –
it is he who sleeps sweetly in Śrīrangam.

IV.9.11

Those who master these Tamil verses of Viṭṭucittaṉ,
a true servant with a truthful tongue,
On the feet of him of Śrīrangam,
ever praised by the North and the South,
The temple favored by him with the fiery disc
who stopped the suffering of the elephant,
They, ever united with his blessed feet,
will never be estranged from our Lord.

Fourth Ten, 10th tirumoḻi – Sleeper in Śrīrangam

The Āḻvār thinks ahead to his own death in *Tirumoḻi* IV.10 and worries that he will not have the presence of mind at that time to call on his Lord. He presents this song to put Nārāyaṇa on advanced notice that it will be Nārāyaṇa's responsibility through his grace to protect Periyāḻvār from Yama, Death, taking him to the underworld. This surrender to god of the burden of responsibility for salvation is an expression of the Śrī Vaiṣṇava concept of *prapatti*, "surrender to God and reliance on God's unmerited grace."[165] As discussed in more detail in the introductory material, the conflicted poet describes himself as undeserving in verse 1, while in verses 3 and 6, he points out that he deserves at least a little karmic credit for his own efforts in chanting and meditating on Nārāyaṇa's divine names. Throughout these verses, the caricatures of Yama's assistants are vivid and unmistakable to all audiences.

IV.10.1

When one becomes weakened, the strong whom he entreats
        will surely be his saviors.
So even though I'm undeserving, I reach out to you
        who once saved the elephant.
When I'm suffering from fatigue, I won't remember you at all,
So I'm speaking up right now in advance,
        Sleeper on the serpent in Śrīrangam.

IV.10.2

Bearer of the conch and disc, look out for me at the time of death;
Yama's attendants, their tongues curled with rage,
        intend to inflict endless tortures.
As I go, not one thought of you will enter my mind!
        What's left is the misery of *māyā*.
So while I'm still able, I'll speak up in advance,
        Sleeper on the serpent in Śrīrangam.

IV.10.3

When I reach the gates of Yama's borders,
  if his forces grip and kick me,
Bearer of the conch and disc, there'll be no way to say, "Stop!"
Whenever I could speak, I said all of your names;
  take note of me for that.
Don't let me suffer. You must protect me,
  Sleeper on the serpent in Śrīrangam

IV.10.4

To him of the bull and him of four heads, your glories are unknown;
Primal Lord, only you became the whole world and the three letters.
When Yama's horrid henchmen come to take me,
  thinking, "The days of this one are done,"
That's the day you must protect me,
  Sleeper on the serpent in Śrīrangam.

IV.10.5

Manifest Supreme asleep on the Milky Sea
  with the hooded serpent for a couch,
Wanting to create and sustain the world,
  you produced from your navel four-faced Brahma,
And knowing that worldly men are imperfect, you also created Time.
My Father, you must protect me, Sleeper on the serpent in Śrīrangam.

IV.10.6

The mercenaries of merciless Yama
  will inflict continuous cruel tortures.
You who became the earth, water, fire, wind and ether,
When I could think, I thought all your names; take note of me for that.
My Lord, you must protect me, Sleeper on the serpent in Śrīrangam.

IV.10.7

Master of the gods who is also the meaning
        of the perfect Word-Mysteries, Our Lord,
My Father, my never decreasing sweet Nectar,
        you who rules the seven worlds,
When Yama's deceitful servants grab me, prick and prod me,
Say, "Don't fear!" You must protect me,
        Sleeper on the serpent in Śrīrangam.

IV.10.8

When Yama's lackeys snatch and push me,
        send me crashing with, "Move on, Flesh''
I won't be able to think of you, I, who know nothing of your mystery.
Lord of the heavenly celestials, great Māyaṉ born in Mathurā,
Whatever happens, you must protect me,
        Sleeper on the serpent in Śrīrangam.

IV.10.9

You protected the herd by lifting a hill, Grazer of the cattle, Our Lord.
From the beginning to the end, I've not forgotten you,
        rare and primeval Radiance.
When Yama's cruelest comrades grab me, prick and prod me,
Then and there, you must protect me,
        Sleeper on the serpent in Śrīrangam.

IV.10.10

Those of pure heart who are able to say
        this garland of ten verses by Viṭṭucittaṉ,
King of Villiputtūr, praised by the Vēyars,
        about the Sleeper on the serpent in Śrīrangam,
About Māyavaṉ, Madhusūdhana, Mādhava, Acyuta, Bull of the herders
Worshipped by those learned in the Mysteries,
        they are servants of the jewel-hued Lord.

Fifth Ten, 1st tirumoḻi – The Āḻvār's entreaty

Periyāḻvār tries to explain in this *tirumoḻi* his uncontrollable and unconditional love of god and beseeches his Lord for divine blessing. In several verses, he says that being a religious servant is simply in his nature, like "a spot on a deer," and he has no choice but to write devotional verses to Nārāyaṇa, no matter what god may think of him. He apologizes for any faults in his poetry and asks god to be patient with him. In verses 5 and 6, he says he has given up the world for a life of devotion, which at that point is the only way he knows to live. In the final verses of this *tirumoḻi*, Periyāḻvār entreats god to bless him with experience of divine love.

V.1.1

Since my words are so impure, Mādhava, I can't place you on my lips,
But my tongue knows nothing but you. I fear I can't control it!
Even if you're angry and think I'm an idiot, I still can't stop my tongue.
Primal Cause with the Garuḍa banner,
even the croaking of a crow is auspicious.

V.1.2

With a foolish tongue I've sung these poor poems,
you whose hands bear the conch and the disc.
But isn't it the duty of the Great to be patient
with their servants' words, even if wrong?
I have no eyes but that see you; my mind will grasp no other.
You who ate and expelled the seven worlds,
a spot on a deer isn't a flaw, you know.

V.1.3

Of goodness and evil, I know nothing –
nothing but to ever say, "Nāraṇa."
This is not just scheming flattery, you know, spoken emptily to you.
Tirumāl, I know no way to perceive you,
I who incessantly say, "Namo Nāraṇa."
Real strength is the strength of a Vaiṣṇava
living in your temple, you know.

V.1.4

You who measured seven worlds with your height,
Tall One, Faultless Lord.
Don't hesitate to accept this servant;
I've no need for food or clothing, you know.
Due to my standing in your service, these will appear then and there,
You who killed cruel Kaṃsa and freed your father from his fetters.

V.1.5

My house, garden, shed, the compound,
the pond and the well, the field lands,
All of these, leaving none, I have gathered and given up at your feet.
It's hard for me to associate with worldly men of many desires.
To fell the elephant, you broke its tusk,
Boar who took the earth on your tusks.

V.1.6

Kaṇṇan, Primal Cause, Dark One,
You who created the four-faced Lord,
On a day that I do not eat at all, I, your servant, feel no hunger.
But a day that I do not revere the Ṛg, Yajur or Sāma Veda,
Or a day that I fail to approach your feet with flowers,
that day is a fasting day for me.

V.1.7

With longing, my heart does languish
to see the means of your feigned sleep
Upon the vast serpent couch in the midst of the milk-white sea.
Rejoicing meets with weeping; I cannot go to sleep.
My hair is on end; tears flow from my eyes.
Tell me the way to reach you.

V.1.8

Madhusūdana who checked the rain with a dark mountain umbrella,
Kaṇṇaṉ who released an elephant from torment,
Primal Lord who killed an elephant,
You remove the pain of those who revere you;
your great fame is hard to praise.
My Lord, bless me daily with the fortune to exalt and be near you.

V.1.9

Trusted friend, Man-lion, Lord of those who've mastered your praise,
King of heaven who measured seven worlds,
you're the eons, the Cause, the Sea-churner.
With the discus long ago, you released
the trembling elephant from torment.
My Lord, Sweet Nectar who is master over me,
end the pain of this poor fool.

V.1.10

Those who repeatedly say his names –
Madhusūdana, Mādhava, Vāmana, My Emerald,
Black-haired boy so sweet to see, Lion to his foes, Father of Kāma –
As written in these ten songs in perfect Tamil
by Viṭṭucittaṉ, king of prosperous Putuvai,
They will promptly enter the heavenly world of Nārāyaṇa.

Fifth Ten, 2nd Tirumoli – The guarded harbor

Periyāḻvār wrote in many voices in the *Tirumoḻi* and spoke in his own right, as well, addressing other devotees and God. In this *tirumoḻi*, however, the poet speaks directly to "Disease," warning that his body is protected by Nārāyaṇa dwelling in his heart and that it cannot be breeched. The poet seems to have particularly chosen the word *paṭṭiṉam*, 'shore village, harbor' as a metaphor for his body, as it lends to the sense that his body is now a safe haven. Sickness and old age are encouraged to flee and give up their fruitless attacks. Specifically mentioned in verse 2 are Death's messengers; knowing that the Āḻvār is protected, they altered the tally of his sins kept by the underworld accountant, Citragupta, countermanding Death's orders to seize the Āḻvār.[166] The image of creating a temple of the heart is common in poetry of several Āḻvārs,[167] but Periyāḻvār depicts a bedchamber with Nārāyaṇa in mystic repose in his heart, with all of god's attendants and weapons keeping a watchful vigil over the Āḻvār (V.2.9).

V.2.1

Disease which takes hold and spreads all around
Like ants on a butter pot, go! Escape while you can.
The Lord of the Vedas, who lies on a hooded serpent couch,
Has possessed me and entered my heart;
    unlike before, this harbor is guarded.

V.2.2

The messengers of the Underworld king
    changed the orders fixed with his seal
On the ledger of the accountant, Citragupta, then took flight to hide.
I am a servant of the Nectar of devotees,
    Primal Ruler of the ancient wisdom,
Lord of the pearl-filled seas; unlike before, this harbor is guarded.

V.2.3

He smashed the cattle pen of the womb
and conquered the strong bulls of my senses,
Then freed me from lust for these sinews and bones,
and untied the noose from my feet.
My Father, who took the earth between his tusks,
teaches me night and day.
He trained me in his service; unlike before, this harbor is guarded.

V.2.4.

Disease of corroding harsh fate, there's a harsh fate for you, you know!
Don't come in here! Don't come in! It's not easy now. Don't come in!
My body is a holy temple where lies my own Lion Lord.
Escape without disgrace; unlike before, this harbor is guarded.

V.2.5.

I cherished Māyaṉ as a Brahmin dwarf, and brought him
Into my heart, where I've kept him – but no other.
See my Ruby Treasure, you of evil, pain and power.
Don't stop to think; just walk away!
unlike before, this harbor is guarded.

V.2.6

Disease which brings affliction, I'll tell you something, so listen.
My body is a temple honoring the Lord who grazed the cows.
I'm saying this once more, Profound fate, but for the last time.
There is nothing for you here; just go!
unlike before, this harbor is guarded.

V.2.7

Wandering low-hill breasts, I slipped and into a hole, I fell.
I entered a cave and got stuck, and lay there weak and bewildered.
The Lord, the hue of the ship-laden sea, reversed my hardened fate
And made me without shame; unlike before, this harbor is guarded.

V.2.8

He who dwells in my heart as my brahma guru,
The Lord of yellow raiments fully removed all my faults.
He entered into my purified heart, leaving the emblems of his feet
On the top of my head; unlike before, this harbor is guarded.

V.2.9

Don't sleep, don't sleep, bright shining disc!
        Don't fall asleep, Oh, conch!
Sharp well-wielded Nandaka sword, lovely Śārnga bow, Oh, mace!
Protectors of the eight directions who never know destruction,
Don't fall asleep, Oh, King of birds; watch over this bedchamber.

V.2.10

Viṭṭucittaṉ praises the Lord who sleeps in the crashing sea,
Who came into his heart along with the Lotus Lady,
With the vast ocean of milk and with his serpent couch,
Because he has become the guardian of the harbor.

Fifth Ten, 3rd tirumoḻi – Father of Tirumāliruncōlai

In *Tirumoḻi* V.3, Periyāḻvār suggests that salvation is a result of both god's grace and the devotee's efforts. While in verse 7, he openly states that his salvation is by the grace of god's name, he also gives numerous examples of the his own actions which have brought him close to god: he has freed himself from his bodily meshwork of bones and sinew (V.3.1), he has grasped god (mentally and emotionally) and won't let him go (V.3.2), and he gains personal power (Tamil *tavam*, Sanakrit *tapas*) performing service in the temple (V.3.3). However, once the Āḻvār is established in his relationship with god, he says he can only survive near Nārāyaṇa. Again and again, he affirms that he won't allow god to leave him, clearly suggesting that it is within the devotee's power to hold the deity near.

V.3.1

I cut asunder this meshwork which lay
caught in a whirlpool of suffering,
And entering where you had entered, I saw you. Now can I let you go?
To her who had lost six children, dashed down onto a stone,
You came with resolve and were born of her womb,
My Father of Tirumāliruncōlai.

V.3.2

I've caught you now and won't let you go.
If you hide using your trickery –
But for your vow to Tiru – you are faithful to no one,
My Father of Tirumāliruncōlai where circle in prayer sacred streams
Which bless and wash away sins of city and country folk alike.

V.3.3

I have gained power through service to you.
If I now go to someone else
And serve him at his front gate, it will damage your reputation,
My Father of Tirumāliruncōlai where hill folk
pluck millet fresh from the fields
To eat and give as an offering, saying, "Hail to your golden feet."

V.3.4

For me, who has wandered many miles, bewildered,
nowhere is there shade, nor is there water.
I see no other place to survive, but in the shadows of your feet.
As a messenger for the Pāṇḍavas, you spoke of insincere kinships;
Creating a quarrel, you made corpses abound,
My Father of Tirumāliruncōlai.

V.3.5

I can't lift my legs; tears never stop. My languishing limbs tremble.
I can't lift my voice; hair thrills never cease. My shoulders ever droop.
My mind races in bewilderment. To survive, I've united with you,
My Father of Tirumāliruncōlai where fish race in deep clear springs.

V.3.6

The Bearer of the bull banner and Brahma, Indra and all the others
Do not know the remedy for this disease called, "birth."
You're the doctor, jewel-hued Lord, to remove all future births.
Let me enter your temple gate, My Father of Tirumāliruncōlai.

V.3.7

I was growing weary and sinking on the far side
of the Sea of Pointlessness.
By the grace of your name, I climbed out on this side.
With, "Don't fear!" you stretched out your hand,
You with the disc, wide hands and wide eyes,
with a golden-colored raiment,
You whose hue is of the red evening sky,
My Father of Tirumāliruncōlai.

V.3.8

"These many ages! These many eons!
Today and tomorrow," I counted.
All this time, I had been ensnared! Now I won't let you go!
You who made your cousins prosper ruining their one-hundred foes,
My Father of Tirumāliruncōlai, don't you know my mind is on you?

V.3.9

I, who have always adored you from the days I lay in the womb,
I came here today and saw you. Now can I let you go?
With your blessed disc, you killed Bāṇa,
cleaving his one-thousand arms
Which fell in every direction, My Father of Tirumāliruncōlai.

V.3.10

Those who master these nine-and-one verses,
this petition for service at the feet of the Lord
Of Tirumāliruncōlai where all the world comes
to bathe deep in mountain springs,
By Viṭṭucittaṉ, king of Putuvai, shining with radiant gold mansions,
They will belong to the One who measured the vast world.

Fifth Ten, 4th tirumoḻi – The Lord's home

According to later philosophers, besides his ten earthly incarnations and his descent into the sacred images, Nārāyana also descends into the heart of the devotee as the *antaryāmin* 'the inner ruler,' a concept clearly depicted in this final tirumoḻi.[168] The Great Āḻvār says in verse 4 that he opened his mouth and drank himself full of god, and again in verse 5, that they are now in each other. His heart is not only a shrine, but Nārāyaṇa's home, his permanent dwelling. While some Āḻvārs gave passionate expression of the pain of separation from the deity and the heartrending longing to be with god, Periyāḻvār predominantly sang of his joy in devotion; this final song is a serene and fulfilled expression of his contentment with being near god and god being in him.

V.4.1

You of the cool peaks of high Vēnkaṭa Mountain,
Lord who enlivens the world, Dāmodara, our Fortune,
I fixed the sign of the disc on myself and all that is mine.
I have been blessed by your grace. What is your holy plan now?

V.4.2

Supreme Lord who rides the bird, after you took me in hand
Great bliss has made empty the ocean named Birth;
The forest of deadly sins has been set afire and burned.
This river of nectar named Knowledge
    rises over my head and flows through my lips.

V.4.3

My king, my leader, Lord of my clan, who in this world can gain
Such goodness as gained by me, me who is one with you?
All the sins of the world were like ghosts,
    falling and pressing upon me,
Which couldn't breathe and so abandon me
    to run and jump in the thickets.

V.4.4

As if filling a pot of with nectar churned from the Milky Sea,
I molded my body and opened my mouth and drank myself full of you.
Now ruthless Death won't be able to come close to my domain,
Disc-bearer with mountain shoulders, Warrior with the Śārnga bow.

V.4.5

Like rubbing gold on a touchstone so its color will appear,
I placed you on my poor tongue and rubbed, but with no change.
I have kept you in my heart and even placed myself in you,
My Father, my Hṛṣīkeśa, Guardian of my life.

V.4.6

All of your heroic deeds without omitting one,
I have inscribed on the sides of the walls of my heart.
Prince Rāma who on his right bears the king-conquering axe,
Now that you've come to me, Lord, where else is there to go?

V.4.7

As the king of the Pāṇṭiyas carved his *kayal*-fish mark on the mountain,
You have put upon my head the mark of your blessed feet.
"You broke the tusk; you killed the wrestlers,"
again and again these praises
With practice have polished my tongue. You have made me your own.

V.4.8

Slighting your serpent Ananta, as well as Garuḍa, the bird,
You came to stay in my mind; you gave me life, my Lord.
Just contemplating this melts my heart; my eyes stream with tears.
And by contemplation, Tall Lord with the disc, all my efforts are over.

V.4.9

You quit your habit of sleeping on a couch in the cool sea
To come running to me, my Prince, to live in the sea of my mind.
As the matchless sea, matchless orb, and matchless earth
Are your homes, Lord of illusion, you've have made me your own.

V.4.10

Like a bright white banner shining high on a mountain,
My Lord of light, you are the lamp of my heart.
Scorning the hill in the North, Vaikuṇṭha, and walled Dvāraka,
Leaving all of these, you took me for your home.

V.4.11

Those who can sing of the celestials' King,
Ambrosia of the Antaṇar priests,
The One whose hue is of thick cool clouds, the Bull among the herders,
Gopāla who has made a temple in the heart of Viṭṭucittaṉ
Who was born in the clan of Vēyars,
they'll be as near to the Lord as his shadow.

பெரியாழ்வார் திருவடிகளே சரணம்

Periyāḻvār Tiruvaṭikaḷē Caraṇam

In the shelter of Periyāḻvār's blessed feet.

Notes to Introduction

[1] Ramanujan, A.K., *Hymns for the Drowning* (Princeton: Princeton University, 1981) ix.

[2] Zvelebil, Kamil, *Smile of Murugan on Tamil Literature of South India* (Leiden: E.J. Brill, 1973) 199.

[3] John Carmen and Vasudha Narayana, *Tamil Veda: Piḷḷān's Interpretation of the Tiruvāymoḻi* (Chicago: University of Chicago) 3-7.

[4] Farquhar, J. N., *An Outline of the Religious Literature of India* (Delhi: Motilal Benarsidass, 1967) 241.

[5] Zvelebil, Kamil, *Tamil Literature.* Handbuch der Orientalistick 2.1 (Leiden: E.J. Brill, 1975) 154.

[6] Cīṉivācaṉ, Ma. Pe., *Periyāḻvār* (New Delhi: Sahitya Akademi, 1999) 12.

[7] Monier-Williams, Monier, *Sanskrit-English Dictionary* (Oxford: Clarendon, 1970) s.v. "bhakti."

[8] Richman, Paula, *Extraordinary Child* (Honolulu: University of Hawai'i, 1997) 4.

[9] "University of Madras Tamil Lexicon," Digital Dictionaries of South Asia. <http://dsal.uchicago.edu/dictionaries/tamil-lex> s.v. "vēyar."

[10] See Raghava Iyengar's "Date of Periyāḻvār" and "Date of Śrī Āṇṭāḷ," Sankar's "Contemporaries of Periyāḻvār," and Ramanujam's *History of Vaiṣhṇavism,* 207-11. Ramanujam (206) has also briefly discussed the reference to 'Celvaṉ' in *Tiruppallāṇṭu* #11; however, he does not find sufficient evidence on this reference to draw any definitive conclusions regarding a specific historical person to whom it refers.

[11] Nilakanta Sastri, K. A., *History of South India*, 3rd ed. (Madras: Oxford University, 1966) 172.

[12] Hardy, Friedhelm, *Viraha-bhakti: The early history of Kṛṣṇa devotion in South India* (New Delhi: Oxford University, 1983) 208.

[13] Aṇṇankarācāriyar, P.B., *Tivyaprapanta Pakavat Katāmrutam* (Kanci: V.N. Tēvanātan̲, 1971) 116-20.

[14] Narayanan, Vasudha, *The Vernacular Veda* (Columbia: University of South Carolina, 1994) 9.

[15] Hardy, *Viraha-bhakti* 407.

[16] *villiputtūr man̲ viṭṭucittan̲ tan̲ kōtai (Nācciyār Tirumoḻi* 2.10*); putuvai man̲n̲an̲ paṭṭarpirān̲ kōtai (Nācciyār Tirumoḻi* 5.11*)*. Aṇṇankarācāriyar, P.B., *Nālāyira Tivviyap Pirapantam* (Kanci: V.N. Tēvanātan̲, 1971) 91 & 95.

[17] Aṇṇankarācāriyar, *Katāmrutam* 116-20.

[18] Aṇṇankarācāriyar, *Katāmrutam* 121.

[19] Cīn̲ivācan̲ 17.

[20] Narayanan, *Vernacular Veda* 11.

[21] Hardy, *Viraha-bhakti* 412.

[22] Hardy, *Viraha-bhakti* 248.

[23] Unless otherwise noted, all translations are my own.

[24] Kaliyanam, G., *Guide and History of Sri Andal Temple* (Srivilliputtur: Sri Nachiar Devastanam, 1971) 18.

[25] Narayanan, *Vernacular Veda* 63.

[26] Ramanujam, B.V., *History of Vaishnavism in South India upto Ramanuja* (Annamalai Nagar: Annamalai University, 1973) 10.

[27] Cīn̲ivācan̲ 25.

[28] Nilakanta Sastri 423.

[29] Nilakanta Sastri 423.

[30] Aṇṇankarācāriyar, *Nālāyira* 380.

[31] Narayanan, Vasudha, *The Way and the Goal: Expressions of Devotion in the Early Sri Vaiṣṇava Tradition* (Washington, D.C.: Institute for Vaishnava Studies, 1987) 165.

[32] Farquhar 188.

[33] Narayanan, *Way* 197, n. 25.

[34] Dehejia, Vidya, *Slaves of the Lord: the Path of the Tamil Saints* (New Delhi: Munshiram Manoharlal, 1988) 99.

[35] Fabricius, J.P., *Tamil and English Dictionary,* 4th ed. (Tranquebar: Evangelical Lutheran Mission, 1972) s.v. "kā."

[36] Vēnkaṭakiruṣṇaṉ, Ma. A., *Periyavāccāṉ Piḷḷai aruḷiceyta Tiruppallāṇṭu Viyākkiyāṉam* (Cennai: Cennaip Palkalaik Kaḻakam, 2006) 34.

[37] Vēnkaṭakiruṣṇaṉ 53.

[38] Aṇṇankarācāriyar, P.B., *Tiruppallāṇṭum Periyāḻvār Tirumoḻiyum* (Kancheepuram: Granthamala Office, 1962) 10.

[39] Zvelebil, *Tamil Literature* (1975) 146.

[40] Cēntaṉār, "Tiruppallāṇṭu." Project Madurai. January 18, 2008 <http://www.projectmadurai.org>

[41] Zvelebil, *Tamil Literature* (1975), 146, n.109.

[42] The term *tirumoḻi* is used to refer to a definable subset of the Tamil *patikam* 'decade' as further described in this discussion and in keeping with Hardy's usage in *Viraha-bhakti* 270-71.

[43] Schrader, F. Otto, *Introduction to the Pānchrātra and the Ahirbudnya Samhita* (Madras: Adyar Library and Research Center, 1973) 48.

[44] I discussed the structure of the *Tirumoḻi* in more detail in my thesis, Ate, Lynn M., "Periyāḻvār's Tirumoḻi – A Bāla Kṛṣṇa Text from the Devotional Period in Tamil Literature," Diss. University of Wisconsin, 1978.

[45] Ate 45.

[46] Monier-Williams s.v. "prabandha."

[47] For a full discussion of classical Tamil anthologies, see Zvelebil, Kamil, *Tamil Literature.* A History of Indian Literature X. 1. Ed. Jan Gonda. (Wiesbaden: Otto Harrassowitz, 1974) 7-51.

[48] Hardy, *Viraha-bhakti* 325.

[49] Hardy, *Viraha-bhakti* 372.

[50] While the *Nācciyār Tirumoḻi* of Āṇṭāḷ, Periyāḻvār's daughter, does not exhibit dramatic continuity from one *tirumoḻi* to the next, her *Tiruppāvai* maintains a recognizable storyline, but not with the same structure.

[51] Hardy, *Viraha-bhakti* 407.

[52] For discussions of dating the Āḻvārs, see Zvelebil, *Tamil Literature* (1974) 101-8; Hardy, *Viraha-bhakti* 261-8; Dasgupta,

Surendranath, *A History of Indian Philosophy,* Vol. 3 (Delhi: Motilal Banarsidass, 1975) 63-9; and Nilakanta Sastri 426-7.

[53] Hart, George L. III, *The Poems of Ancient Tamil* (Delhi: Oxford University, 1999) 148.

[54] For a discussion of the influence of classical literature on Āl̲vār texts, see A. K. Ramanujan and Norman Cutler, "From Classicism to Bhakti," *Essays on Gupta Culture*, ed. Bardwell L. Smith. (Delhi: Motilal Benarsidass, 1983) 177-214; and for influences on Nammāl̲vār's works, see Carmen and Narayanan 21-33.

[55] For translations and overviews, see A. K. Ramanujan, *The Interior Landscape* (Bloomington: Indiana University, 1975); A. K. Ramanujan, *Poems of Love and War* (New York: Columbia University, 1985); George L. Hart III, *Poets of the Tamil Anthologies* (Princeton: Princeton University, 1979); V. Murugan, *Kalittokai in English* (Chennai: Institute of Asian Studies, 1999); Eva Wilden, *Nar̲r̲iṇai, A Critical Edition and an Annotated Translation of the Nar̲r̲iṇai* (Pondicherry: École Française d'Extréme-Orient: 2008); and Martha Ann Selby, *Tamil Love Poetry, The Five Hundred Short Poems of the 'Ainkur̲unūr̲u'* (New York: Columbia University Press, 2011). For a more in depth discussion of features of classical literature, see Zvelebil, *Smile,* chap. I – IX.

[56] Cutler, Norman, *Songs of Experience: the Poetics of Tamil Devotion (*Bloomington: Indiana University Press, 1987) 82.

[57] For dates of early devotional texts, see Zvelebil, *Tamil Literature* (1974) 50. For a discussion of the influence of heroic poetry on the Āl̲vārs in general, see Ramanujan and Cutler 181.

[58] See Hart, *Poems* 38-40 for a discussion of the glorification of war in classical Tamil heroic poetry.

[59] Clooney, Francis X, "Nammalvar's Glorious Tiruvallaval." *Journal of the American Oriental Society* 111. 2 (1991) 261 <http://www.jstor.org>

[60] For discussions of temple pilgrimage as a feature of Āl̲vār poetry, see Karen Pechilis Prentiss, *The Embodiment of Bhakti* (New York: Oxford University, 1999), as well as Indira V. Peterson, "Singing of Place: Pilgrimage as Metaphor and Motif in the Tevaram Songs of

the Tamil Saivite Saints." *Journal of the American Oriental Society* 102.1 (1982) 69-90. <http://www.jstor.org>

[61] Zvelebil, *Smile* 56.

[62] Zvelebil, *Tamil Literature* (1974) 49.

[63] Peterson 81.

[64] Prentiss 51.

[65] See "Temple sites" in the concordance appended to this text for references to sacred sites in Periyāḻvār's works.

[66] For information on dating the Āḻvārs, see note 48 above.

[67] Carmen and Narayana 31.

[68] Aṇṇankarācāriyar, *Nālāyira* 482

[69] For a thorough discussion of rhetorical structures in Tamil devotional poetry and personal experience of god, see Cutler's *Songs of Experience*, Part I.

[70] Hardy, Friedhelm, "Mādhavendra Purī: A Link between Bengal Vaiṣṇavism and South Indian 'Bhakti.'" *Journal of the Royal Asiatic Society of Great Britain and Ireland* 1 (1974) 40. <http://www.jstor.org> See also David L. Haberman, *Acting as a Way of Salvation* (Delhi: Motilal Benarsidass, 1988) for an in-depth discussion of this religious approach.

[71] Ramanujan and Cutler 200.

[72] For perspectives on Periyāḻvār's role in the development of *piḷḷaitamiḻ,* see Zvelebil, *Tamil Literature* (1974) 213 and Paula Richman, *Extraordinary Child* (Honolulu: University of Hawai'i, 1997) 239, n. 6.

[73] Richman 53.

[74] Richman 12

[75] Richman 65.

[76] Narayanan, *Way* 16.

[77] Narayanan, "The Goddess Śrī" 224

[78] *Bhagavad Gīta*. Trans. Annie Besant. (Adyar: Theosophical Publishing, 1970) 64.

[79] Hawley, John Stratton, *Krishna, the Butter Thief* (Princeton: Princeton University, 1983) 95.

[80] *Bhagavad Gīta* 253

[81] Narayanan, *Way 111.*

[82] *Bhagavad Gīta* 175.

[83] Haberman 47.

[84] Haberman's text provides a complete study of ritual role-playing as a means of salvation.

[85] Hawley, *Krishna* 21-95.

[86] Hardy, *Viraha-bhakti* 481-552. Refer to header notes to *Tirumoḻi* III.6 for more details of this text's influence on the *Bhāgavata Purāṇa.*

[87] *Śrīmad Bhāgavata Mahāpurāṇa,* Trans. C.L. Goswami. (Gorakhpur: Gita Press, 1971) 1094.

[88] *Bhāgavata Mahāpurāṇa* 1073.

[89] Kingsley, David R., *The Divine Player: a Study of Kṛṣṇa Līlā* (Delhi: Motilal Banarsidass, 1979) 67.

[90] Kingsley 67.

[91] Kingsley 1.

[92] Monier-Williams s.v. "krīdā"

[93] Narayanan, *Way* 2.

[94] Smart, Ninian, *Doctrine and Argument in Indian Philosophy* (London: George Allen & Unwin, 1969) 110.

[95] Mumme, Patricia Y., "Grace and Karma in Nammalvar's Salvation." *Journal of the American Oriental Society* 107. 2 (1987): 258. <http://www.jstor.org>

[96] Mumme 266.

[97] Hardy, *Viraha-bhakti* 414.

[98] Hardy provides studies of the dates of the major Vaiṣṇava texts with the date of the *Harivamśa* on 70 and of the *Viṣṇu Purāṇa* on 90.

[99] For additional information on mythology in India, see Wendy Doniger, *Hindu Myths* (London: Penguin Books, 1975). R.K. Narayan presents enjoyable retellings of the epics in his *Mahabharata* and *Ramayana*. Hardy's *Viraha-bhakti* is an in depth study of the milkmaid episodes in the Kṛṣṇa myth, and Hawley's *Krishna, the Butter Thief*, includes a detailed review of Kṛṣṇa myths in literature and sculpture.

[100] Aṇṇankarācāriyar, *Nālāyira* 344. Translations in this section are my own.

[101] Aṇṇankarācāriyar, *Nālāyira* 420-1.

[102] Aṇṇankarācāriyar, *Nālāyira* 326.

[103] Zvelebil, *Smile* 125.

[104] Kāsivicunātan̲, Mu., *Cilappatikāra Mūlamum Na. Mu. Vēnkaṭacāmi Nāṭṭār avarkaḷ Uraiyum.* (Tirunelvēli: Caiva Cittānta, 1968) 152.

[105] Kāsivicunātan̲ 152.

[106] *Bhāgavata Mahāpurāṇa* 1083-4.

[107] Hardy, *Viraha-bhakti* 445.

[108] Kāsivicunātan̲ 152-3.

[109] The ten verses of Āṇṭāḷ's *Nācciyar Tirumoḻi III* present this episode, as does one verse of Mankaiyāḻvār's *Periya Tirumoḻi* (X.7.11), both contempory with or slightly later than Periyāḻvār's *Tirumoḻi.*

[110] Kāsivicunātan̲ 150-2.

[111] See Hardy, *Viraha-bhakti* 77 n. 95 for a short discussion of this relationship as found in the Southern Recension of the *Harivamśa.*

[112] For a discussion of winning Pin̲n̲ai by conquering bulls, see Erik Af Edholm and Carl Suneson's "The Seven Bulls and Kṛṣṇa's Marriage to Nīlā/NappiNNai in Sanskrit and Tamil Literature." *Temenos* 8 (1972). Also, Kamil Zvelebil provides a study of bull-fighting practices in classical Tamil literature and modern South India in his "Bull-Baiting Festivals in Tamil India." *Annals of the Náprstek Museum* 1 (1962).

[113] *Bhāgavata Mahāpurāṇa* 160, 1322-23, and 1434.

[114] Hardy, *Viraha-bhakti* 184-193.

[115] Hardy, *Viraha-bhakti* 407.

[116] *Prose translation of the Harivamsha,* Trans. Manmatha Nath Dutt. (Calcutta: Elysium Press, 1897) 733-4.

[117] Narayanan, *Way* 162.

[118] Monier-Williams s.v. "mahābhārata."

[119] Schrader, *Pāncharātra* 48.

[120] Aṇṇankarācāriyar, *Nālāyira* 350.

[121] Aṇṇankarācāriyar, *Nālāyira* 377.

[122] *The Mahābhārata.* Trans. Kisari Mohan Ganguli. 1883-1896. Internet Sacred Text Archive. Chap. 188. <http://www.sacred-texts.com>

[123] Aṇṇankarācāriyar, *Katāmrutam 64-5.*

[124] Aṇṇankarācāriyar, *Nālāyira.*

[125] Farquhar 86.

[126] *Bhagavad Gīta* 64.

[127] Cōmacuntaraṉār, Po. Vē., *Paripāṭal Mūlamum Uraiyum* (Tirunelvēli: Caiva Cittānta, 1975) *pāṭal* III, 16-21.

[128] Desai, Kalpana S. *Iconography of Viṣṇu* (New Delhi: Abhinav Publications, 1973) 97.

[129] Desai 110.

[130] Cōmacuntaraṉār, *pāṭal* XII, 24-37.

[131] Cōmacuntaraṉār, *pāṭal* III, 25-26.

Notes to Translations

[132] The text used for this translation is P. B. Aṇṇankarācāriyar's *Tiruppallāṇṭum Periyāḻvār Tirumoḻiyum* (Kancheepuram: Granthamala Office, 1962).

[133] Transliteration follows Kamil Zvelebil, *The Smile of Murugan on Tamil Literature of South India* (Leiden: E. J. Brill, 1973) xv.

[134] On the importance of *tulasī* to Vaiṣṇava worship, I offer Nammāḻvār's *Tiruviruttam* 53, simply because it is just too wonderful to ignore:

She's just a girl with newly-risen breasts, but this divine disease
Is due to that heavenly boy. Revive her
With a garland of cool *tulasī*, or one leaf, or even a twig,
Or with just the roots. Bring her some dirt where it grew!

[135] Fabricius, J.P., *Tamil and English Dictionary,* 4th ed. (Tranquebar: Evangelical Lutheran Mission, 1972) s.v. "celvam."

[136] Ramanujam, B. V. *History of Vaishnavism in South India upto Ramanuja* (Annamalai Nagar: Annamalai University, 1973) 206.

[137] For a discussion of this descriptive device, see Steven Paul Hopkins, *Singing the Body of God: the Hymns of Vedāntadeśika in their South Indian Tradition* (New York: Oxford University Press, 2002), 135-165.

[138] *Prose Translation of the Harivamsha,* Trans. Manmatha Nath Dutt (Calcutta: Elysium Press, 1897) 22-4.

[139] Burrows, T and M. B. Emeneau, *Dravidian Etymological Dictionary,* 2nd ed. (Oxford: Clarendon, 1984) s.v. "kīrai" which glosses *spinach* as *Amaranthus gangeticus.* Dr. Harold Corke of the Cereal Science Laboratory at the University of Hong Kong describes the red pigment of *Amaranthus* and mentions the traditional and modern agricultural uses of both its leaves and seeds. November 21, 2005 <www.hku.hk/ ~harold/ harold.htm>

[140] Aṇṇankarācāriyar, P.B., *Tiruppallāṇṭum Periyāḻvār Tirumoḻiyum* (Kancheepuram: Granthamala Office, 1962) 73.

[141] Fabricius s.v. "pūcci"

[142] Schrader, F. Otto, *Introduction to the Pānchrātra and the Ahirbudnya Samhita* (Madras: Adyar Library and Research Center, 1973) 48.

[143] "University of Madras Tamil Lexicon," Digital Dictionaries of South Asia. <http://dsal.uchicago.edu/dictionaries/tamil-lex> s.v. "naṟṟāy."

[144] Aṇṇankarācāriyar, *Tiruppallāṇṭum* 128-9.

[145] Monier-Williams, Monier, *Sanskrit-English Dictionary* (Oxford: Clarendon, 1970) s.v. "kautuhalam."

[146] Fabricius s.v. "kōtukam," and "kautukam."

[147] Fabricius s.v. "nāḻikai."

[148] *Harivamśa,* chapter 73, and *A Prose translation of the Vishnu Purana.* Trans. Manmatha Nath Dutt (Varanasi: Chowkhamba Sanskrit Series, 1972) Book 5, chapter 11.

[149] For a discussion of Āḻvār influence on the *Bhāgavata Purāṇa,* see Friedhelm Hardy, *Viraha-bhakti: The early history of Kṛṣṇa devotion in South India* (New Delhi: Oxford University, 1983), part 5, and 516-18 for a specific discussion of the Gopi's Song.

[150] *Madras Tamil Lexicon* s.v. "māl."

[151] For the date of the *Tolkāppiyam*, see Kamil Zvelebil, *Tamil Literature,* A History of Indian Literature X. 1. Ed. Jan Gonda. (Wiesbaden: Otto Harrassowitz, 1974) 34, n. 67.

[152] Ilakkuvanār, S., *Tholkāppiyam (in English) with Critical Studies* (Madurai: Kural Neri, 1963) 157.

[153] For the date of the *Tiruvācakam,* see Zvelebil, *Tamil Literature* (1974) 98.

[154] Pope, G. U., *Tiruvācagam* (Madras: Ceṉṉai Palkalai Kaḻakam, 1970) 175-82.

[155] Aṇṇankarācāriyar, *Tiruppallāṇṭum* 251.

[156] Narayanan, Vasudha, *The Way and the Goal: Expressions of Devotion in the Early Sri Vaiṣṇava Tradition* (Washington, D.C.: Institute for Vaishnava Studies, 1987) 13.

[157] Narayanan, *Way* 12.

[158] Thera, Soma. “The Way of Mindfulness: the Satipatthāna Sutta and its Commentary,” *The Theravada Library,* Access to Insight. 2005. <http://www.accesstoinsight.org/ lib/authors/ soma /wayof.html>

[159] Fabricius s.v. “eccam” and “poli,”.

[160] For a further discussion of this and related phrases, see Narayanan, *Way* 196, n.23.

[161] Aṇṇankarācāriyar, *Tiruppallāṇṭum* 289.

[162] Narayanan, *Way* 34.

[163] *Harivamsha 725-8*

[164] Jaiswal, Suvira, *The Origin and Development of Vaiṣṇavism* (Delhi: Munshiram Manoharlal

[165] Carmen, John, and Vasudha Narayanan, *The Tamil Veda: Piḷḷān's Interpretation of the Tiruvāymoḻi.* (Chicago: University of Chicago, 1989) xii.

[166] Aṇṇankarācāriyar, *Tiruppallāṇṭum* 322.

[167] Narayanan, *Way* 34-5.

[168] Schrader 57.

Appendix 1 - Concordance of Vaiṣṇava references

from *Tiruppallāṇṭu* (#) and *Tirumoḻi* (ex: I.1.1)

Arjuna	Pārtha: II.1.2, II.6.5, II.6.6; Vijaya: I.8.6, I.9.4
Ass demon	I.5.4, II.10.4, III.6.4
Bakāsura	II.5.4, II.6.3, II.7.5
Baladeva, Balarāma	I.7.5, IV.9.9
Bāṇāsura	#7, IV.2.2, IV.3.4, V.3.9
Banyan-leaf baby	I.2.13, I.2.18, I.4.7, I.5.1, II.6.6, II.7.2, II.7.9, III.7.11, IV.1.4
Bird demon	II.5.4, II.6.3, II.7.5
Bow	Kṛṣṇa broke: #10, II.3.7, IV.7.7; Rāma broke: III.10.1, III.10.9, IV.1.2; Śārnga: I.4.6, I.6.7, I.7.1, I.7.7, IV.1.2, V.2.9, V.4.4
Brahmin's children	I.5.7, IV.8.2
Bridge to Śrī Lanka	I.6.8, III.9.10, IV.1.3
Bulls, controlled	I.5.3, I.5.7, II.7.6, IV.1.4, IV.3.2
Butter theft	I.2.4, I.4.9, I.5.5, I.6.5, I.9.7, II.1.5, II.1.6, II.2.2, II.3.9, II.4.7, II.5.2, II.7.5, II.9.1, II.9.3, II.9.5, II.10.5, III.1.3, III.1.5, III.2.6
Calf demon	I.5.4, II.3.10, II.4.8, II.5.5, III.1.6, III.3.7
Charioteer	I.6.6, I.8.6, I.9.4, II.1.2, II.6.5, IV.1.7, IV.2.7
Churning the ocean	I.6.10, V.1.9
Conch	#2, I.7.6, I.8.2, II.1.1, II.8.9, III.3.9, IV.1.2, IV.1.7, IV.4.4, IV.7.5, IV.10.2, V.1.2, V.2.9
Crow attacks Sītā	II.6.7, III.10.6,
Curse on Rāma	II.1.8, III.9.4, III.9.8, III.10.3, IV.8.4
Dances	kuravai: II.3.5; pot: II.7.7, II.9.6
Demoness	Kṛṣṇa sucked life of: I.2.5, I.3.8, I.5.4, I.6.9, II.3.1, II.3.12, II.4.3, II.4.4, II.5.2, II.5.4, II.8.6, II.8.7, II.10.6, III.1.1, III.5.9, IV.1.6; Rāma cut nose of: II.7.5, III.9.6, III.10.5, IV.7.1; Tāḍakā: III.9.2

Devakī's children	V.3.1
Dhenuka	I.5.4, II.10.4, III.6.4
Discus	#2, #7, I.4.4, I.4.6, I.7.6, I.8.2, IV.1.2, IV.1.7, IV.10.2, V.1.2, V.4.4
Divya deśam	See "Temple sites"
Draupadī	IV.3.6, IV.9.6
Eating dirt	II.3.8
Elephant	Kṛṣṇa broke tusk of: I.2.7, I.5.3, I.5.6, II.7.5, II.8.7, IV.1.3, IV.3.2, IV.7.7, IV.9.3, V.4.7; salvation of: II.1.9, II.10.8, IV.2.5, IV.9.11, IV.10.1, V.1.9.
Exile of Rāma	II.1.8, III.9.4, III.9.8, III.10.3, IV.10.4
Gajendra Mokṣa	II.1.9, II.10.8, IV.2.5, IV.9.11, IV.10.1, V.1.9
Gambling match	II.1.1
Govardhana Mountain	I.1.8, I.5.2, II.3.7, II.9.6, II.10.4, III.3.8, III.4.4, III.5.1-10, IV.2.4, IV.7.6, IV.10.9
Guha	III.10.4
Guru, Kṛṣṇa's	IV.8.1
Haṃsa	I.5.11, I.8.10
Hanumaṉ	III.5.7, III.10.1-10,
Horse demon	IV.9.3
Horse, Arjuna's	IV.2.7
Hump backed girl	I.8.4
Incarnations	fish: I.5.11, III.3.7, IV.9.9; tortoise: I.5.11, III.3.7, IV.9.5, IV.9.9; boar: II.10.9, III.3.7, III.5.5, IV.1.9, IV.3.9, IV.8.8, IV.9.9; man-lion: I.2.5, I.5.2, I.6.9, II.7.7, III.6.5, IV.1.1, IV.4.6, IV.4.10, IV.8.8, IV.9.8, IV.9.9, V.1.9; dwarf: I.3.1, I.4.8, I.5.3, I.5.11, I.6.1, I.7.9, I.8.7, I.8.8, I.9.5, I.9.6, II.3.7, II.3.8, II.5.9, II.9.2, II.10.7, III.7.10, III.8.9, IV.3.9, IV.4.9, IV.7.2, IV.9.7, IV.9.8, IV.9.9, IV.9.10, V.2.5, V.3.10;

Incarnations (con't)	Paraśurāma: IV.9.9, V.4.6; Balarāma: I.7.5, IV.9.9; Kalki: IV.9.9. For Rāma and Kṛṣṇa, see specific references.
Indra	I.3.3, II.8.1, III.3.8, III.4.8, IV.3.8, V.3.6; his tree: I.9.9, III.9.1
Kāliya	#10, I.5.6, I.8.3, II.1.3, II.4.8, II.10.3, III.3.6, III.5.11, III.6.4, III.9.5, III.9.7, IV.3.2
Kalki	IV.9.9
Kaṃsa	II.1.4, II.2.4, II.6.3, II.7.6, II.8.7, III.2.1, IV.3.2, IV.7.7,V.1.4
Keśi	IV.9.3
Kuravai dance	II.3.5
Kūrmāvatara	I.5.11, III.3.7, IV.9.5, IV.9.9
Kuvalayāpīḍa	I.2.7, I.5.3, I.5.6, II.7.5, II.8.7, IV.1.3, IV.3.2, IV.7.7, IV.9.3, V.1.4
Laurel trees	I.2.10, II.5.2, III.1.3, III.9.9, IV.3.2, IV.9.3
Lime tree	IV.4.7
Matsyāvatāra	I.5.11, III.3.7, IV.9.9
Messenger, Kṛṣṇa as	I.8.3, I.8.5, II.1.1, II.6.4, II.6.5, III.9.5, V.3.4
Mountain umbrella	I.1.8, I.5.2, II.3.7, II.9.6, II.10.4, III.3.8, III.4.4, III.5.1-10, IV.2.4, IV.7.6, IV.10.9
Naraka	IV.3.3
Narasimhāvatāra	I.2.5, I.5.2, I.6.9, II.7.7, III.6.5, IV.1.1, IV.4.6, IV.4.10, IV.8.8, IV.9.8, IV.9.9, V.1.9
Ōṇam	#6, #9, I.1.3, II.4.2, II.2.7, II.9.7, III.3.9,
Paraśurāma	IV.9.9, V.4.6; Rāma conquered: III.9.2, III.10.1
Pārijāta tree	I.9.9, III.9.1
Parikṣit	IV.8.3, IV.9.6
Pot dance	II.7.7, II.9.6
Pralamba	III.6.4, IV.9.3
Pūtanā	I.2.5, I.3.8, I.5.4, I.6.9, II.3.1, II.3.12, II.4.3, II.4.4, II.5.2, II.5.4, II.8.6, II.8.7, II.10.6, III.1.1, III.5.9, IV.1.6

Rāma	III.10.6, IV.1.1, IV.1.2, IV.3.7, IV.9.9; built bridge: I.6.8, III.9.10, IV.1.3; conquered Rāvaṇa: II.6.8, II.6.9, II.7.5, III.9.10, IV.2.2, IV.7.1, IV.7.3, IV.8.5, IV.8.10; crossed Ganges: III.10.4; crowned Vibhīṣaṇa: II.6.9, III.9.10; crow's attack on Sītā: II.6.7, III.10.6, curse on: II.1.8, III.9.4, III.9.8, III.10.3, IV.8.4; cut nose of demoness: II.7.5, III.9.6, III.10.5, IV.7.1; destroyed Lanka: I.6.8, II.1.10, II.6.8, III.9.10, IV.3.7, IV.3.8; exile of: II.1.8, III.9.4, III.9.8, III.10.3, IV.10.4; Tāḍakā: III.9.2; threatened the ocean: I.6.7
Rāvaṇa	II.6.8, II.6.9, II.7.5, III.9.10, IV.2.2, IV.7.1, IV.7.3, IV.8.5, IV.8.10
Rukmiṇī's elopment	III.9.3, IV.1.5, IV.3.1
Śakaṭāsura	I.2.11, I.5.4, II.1.5, II.2.4, II.4.4, II.4.11, II.4.12, II.5.2, II.8.7, III.1.2, III.9.9, IV.6.6, IV.9.3
Sāndīpani	IV.8.1
Serpent demon	I.5.6, I.8.3, II.1.3, II.4.8, II.10.3, III.3.6, III.5.11, III.6.4, III.9.5, III.9.7, IV.3.2
Śiśupāla	IV.3.5
Śiva's curse:	I.8.9
Śrī Lanka destroyed	I.6.8, II.1.10, II.6.8, III.9.10, IV.3.7, IV.3.8
Stole from milkmaids	II.1.4, II.7.3, II.9.10, II.10.1, II.10.2, III.1.4
Sun hidden by discus	IV.1.8
Śūrpanakhā	II.7.5, III.9.6, III.10.5, IV.7.1
Swan	I.5.11, I.8.10
Tāḍakā	III.9.2

Temple sites	Ayodhya: III.9.6, III.9.10, III.10.9, IV.7.9; Badarī: IV.7.9; Cōlaimalai: I.5.8; Dvāraka: IV.7.9, IV.9.4, V.4.10; Kaṇṇapuram: I.5.8; Konku: II.6.2; Kurunkuṭi: I.5.8; Kuṭantai (Kumbhakonam): I.3.7, I.6.4, II.6.2, II.6.6, II.7.7; Mathurā: #10, III.6.3, IV.7.6, IV.7.9, IV.10.8; Śālagrāma: IV.7.9; Śrīrangam: I.3.9, II.7.2, II.7.9, II.9.10, III.3.2, IV.8.1-10, IV.9.1-11, IV.10.1-10; Tirukaṇṭankaṭinakar: IV.7.1-11; Tirukkoṭṭiyūr:#11, I.1.1, I.1.10, II.6.2, IV.4.1-10; Tirumāliruncōlai: III.4.5, IV.2.1-11, IV.3.1-11, V.3.1-10; Tirupēr: II.5.1, II.6.2, II.9.4; Vaikuṇṭa: I.2.1, II.1.10, III.5.11, III.10.10, IV.6.10, IV.7.9, V.4.10; Veḷḷaṟai: I.5.8, II.8.1-10; Vēnkaṭam (Tirupati): I.4.7, II.6.9, II.7.3, II.9.6, III.3.4, V.4.1, V.4.10
Tiru (Śrī Lakṣmi)	I.2.17, I.3.7, I.7.4, IV.1.10, IV.9.1, V.3.2
Trees	Indra's: I.9.9, III.9.1; Kṛṣṇa knocked over two: I.2.10, II.5.2, III.1.3, III.9.9, IV.3.2, IV.9.3; wild lime: IV.4.7; Rāma shot: II.4.2, IV.1.3
Vāmanāvatāra.	I.3.1, I.4.8, I.5.3, I.5.11, I.6.1, I.7.9, I.8.7, I.8.8, I.9.5, I.9.6, II.3.7, II.3.8, II.5.9, II.9.2, II.10.7, III.7.10, III.8.9, IV.3.9, IV.4.9, IV.7.2, IV.9.7, IV.9.8, IV.9.9, IV.9.10, V.2.5, V.3.10
Varāhāvatāra	II.10.9, III.3.7, III.5.5, IV.1.9, IV.3.9, IV.8.8, IV.9.9
Vatsāsura	I.5.4, II.3.10, II.4.8, II.5.5, III.1.6, III.3.7
Vibhīṣaṇa	II.6.9, III.9.10
Wheel demon	I.2.11, I.5.4, II.1.5, II.2.4, II.4.4, II.4.11, II.4.12, II.5.2, II.8.7, III.1.2, III.9.9, IV.6.6, IV.9.3
Wrestlers	#1, I.5.6, II.2.8, II.7.6, III.8.1, IV.2.6, IV.7.7, IV.9.3, V.4.7

Appendix 2 - Sanskrit Vaiṣṇava terms

Instances of Sanskrit terms do not account for the total number of references to a subject as Tamil descriptive terms are often used. For instance, "Vāmana" is only mentioned four times, but Tamil references to the dwarf incarnation are frequent. Some names are so common that they are found throughout the text; therefore, only the first occurrence has been cited. Effort has been made to be thorough; however, no guarantee of inclusivity is made.

Term	**Tamil transliteration and citations** from *Tiruppallāṇṭu* (#) and *Tirumoḻi* (ex: I.1.1)
Acyuta	Accutaṉ: I.2.6, I.3.8, II.3.13, IV.10.10
Airāvata	Airāvatam: IV.7.7
Ananta	Aṉantaṉ: V.4.8
Anantaśayana	Aṉantacayaṉaṉ: I.7.2, IV.3.10
asura	acurar:#5, I.2.16, III.3.7
Ayodhya	Ayōttiya: III.9.6, III.9.10, III.10.9, IV.7.9
Baladeva	Palatēvaṉ: I.7.5
Bāṇa	Vāṇaṉ:#7, IV.3.4, V.3.9
bhagava	pakavar: IV.9.6
bhaktas	pattar: II.8.10, III.4.10, III.5.11, IV.1.10, IV.4.7, IV.5.10, IV.9.6, V.2.2
Bharata	Parataṉ: II.1.8, III.9.6, III.10.5
Bhārata (War)	Pāratam: I.1.2, III.9.5, IV.1.7
Bhaṭṭa	Paṭṭar: I.2.21, etc.
Brahma	Piramaṉ: I.3.1, II.8.1, V.3.6
cakra	cakkaram: I.4.4, I.4.6, I.7.6, I.8.2, IV.1.2, IV.1.7, IV.10.2, V.1.2, V.4.4
caturbhuja	catuppuyaṉ: IV.7.3
Citragupta	Cittirakuttaṉ: V.2.2
Citrakūṭa	Cittirakūṭam: II.6.7, III.10.5, III.10.6

Dāmodara	Tāmōtaraṉ: II.3.12, II.5.8, II.9.8, III.2.9, III.3.3, III.5.7, III.5.9, III.8.3, IV.6.6, V.4.1
daṇḍa	taṇṭam: I.4.6, I.8.2, IV.1.2, V.2.9
Daṇḍaka (forest)	Taṇṭakam: III.9.8
Dāśarathi	Tācarati:III.9.2, IV.7.1
Deva	teyvam: I.1.7, II.6.3; tēvaṉ: IV.1.3, IV.10.7
Devakī	Tēvakī: I.2.1, I.2.6, I.2.17, I.3.4,I.6.6, II.1.6, III.6.6, III.9.3, IV.1.8
Dhananjaya	Taṉancayaṉ: I.9.4
Dhenuka	Tēṉukaṉ: I.5.4, II.10.4, III.6.4
Duryodhana	Tuccōtaṉaṉ: I.8.5; Turiyōtaṉaṉ: II.6.4, II.6.5
Dvāraka	Tuvarai: IV.1.6, IV.7.8, IV.7.9, Tuvarāvati: V.4.10
Garuḍa	Karuḷaṉ: V.1.1, Karuṭaṉ V.4.8
Gopāla	kōvalaṉ: I.2.13, III.6.1, III.8.7, IV.3.4, V.4.11; kōpāla: II.3.4, III.8.5
Govardhana	Kōvarttaṉam: III.5.1-11, IV.2.4
Govinda	Kōvintaṉ: I.9.1, II.2.7, II.3.4, II.5.6, II.9.11, III.3.10, III.4.1, III.6.2, III.6.3, III.6.7, III.6.8, III.6.11, III.7.3, IV.3.4, IV.4.8, IV.4.9, IV.5.8, IV.6.4, IV.6.5
Hanuman	Aṉumāṉ: III.5.7, III.10.9, III.10.10
Hari	Ari: IV.7.8
Hiraṇya	Iraṇiyaṉ: I.2.5, II.7.7, IV.1.1, IV.9.8
Hṛṣīkeśa	Iruṭīkēcaṉ: #6, II.2.6, II.3.10, III.1.11, IV.4.11, IV.5.5, V.4.5
Indra	Intiraṉ: I.3.3, II.8.1, III.3.8, III.4.8, IV.3.8, V.3.6
Īśa (Śiva)	Īcaṉ: I.3.2, I.8.9, II.8.1
Īśa (Viṣṇu)	Īcaṉ: III.5.5, IV.10.8
Janaka	Caṉakaṉ: III.10.1, IV.1.2
Jayadratha	Cayattirataṉ: IV.1.8
Kaikeyī	Kaikēci: III.10.3
Kākutstha	Kākuttaṉ: III.9.2, III.9.11
Kāla	Kālaṉ: IV.10.5
Kāliya	Kāḷiyaṉ: I.5.6, II.1.3, III.6.4, III.9.7, IV.3.2

Kalki	Kaṟki: IV.9.9
kalpaka	kaṟpakam: I.3.7, I.9.9, IV.2.4, IV.3.11
Kaṃsa	Kancaṉ: II.1.4, II.2.4, II.2.5, II.3.1, II.4.4, II.6.3, II.7.6, II.8.6, III.2.1, III.3.6, IV.2.5, IV.3.2, V.1.4
kāpāli	kāpāli: I.3.2, II.8.8
kāraṇa	kāraṇa: V.1.1, V.1.6, V.1.9
karma	karumam: #9
kaustubha	kauttuvam: IV.5.8
Keśava	Kēcavaṉ: I.1.1, I.7.10, II.3.1, II.3.3, II.9.8, III.3.8, III.7.5, III.7.7, IV.4.10, IV.5.1, IV.6.1
krīḍā	kirīṭai: II.9.1
Kṛṣṇa	Kaṇṇaṉ: I.1.1, etc.
Kuru	Kuru: V.3.4
Lakṣmaṇa	Ilakkumaṇaṉ: III.10.3, III.10.7
Mādhava	Mātavaṉ: II.2.11, II.5.1, IV.5.3, IV.6.4, IV.10.10, V.1.1, V.1.10
Madhusūdana	Matucūtaṉ: II.3.6, II.9.3, III.5.2, III.6.5, IV.5.6, IV.5.7, IV.10.10, V.1.8, V.1.10
Mahābali	Māvali: I.4.8, I.6.1,I.8.7, II.10.7, IV.3.4, IV.9.7
makara	makaram: I.2.18, I.5.1, II.3.13
Mathurā	Maturai: #10, III.6.3, III.8.1, IV.7.6, IV.7.9, IV.10.8
Mount Mandara	Mantaram: I.6.10
Mura	Muraṉ: I.5.4
mūrtti	mūrtti: IV.3.11
nāga	nākam: #8, #9
nāmam	nāmam: III.4.8
Namo Nārāyaṇa	Namō Nārāyaṇā: #4, 11, 12, IV.5.2, V.1.3
Namuci	Namuci: I.8.8
Nanda	Nantaṉ: I.2.8, II.1.5, II.2.3, III.1.8, III.6.3, III.8.5, III.8.8, III.9.11
Nandaka	Nantakam: I.9.4, IV.1.2, IV.7.4, IV.9.10, V.2.9
Naraka	Narakaṉ: I.5.4, IV.3.3

Narasimha	Naracinkaṉ: IV.4.6, IV.4.9, V.1.9
Nārāyaṇa	Nārāyaṇaṉ/Nāraṇaṉ: I.1.10, etc.
Nātha	Nātaṉ: IV 4.6, V.1.9
Nīlakaṇṭha (Śiva)	Nīlakaṇṭaṉ: IV.1.5
Nirmala	Niṉmala: V.1.4
Padmanābha	Paṟpanāvu: II.3.11
pāncajanya	pāncacaṉṉiyam: #2, III.3.5
Pāncāli (Draupadī)	Pāncāli: IV.3.6
Pāṇḍavas	Pāṇṭavar: IV.3.6, V.3.4
Paramamūrtti	Paramamūrtti: IV.10.5
Paramapuruṣa	Paramapuruṭa: V.4.2
Paramātman	Paramātmaṉ: #12
Parameṣṭhina	Paramēṭṭi: #12
Parampara	Paramparaṉ: I.5.1
Pārtha (Arjuna)	Pārttaṉ: II.1.2, II.6.5, II.6.6
Pavitrin	Pavittiraṉ: #12
Pralamba	Pilampaṉ: III.6.4, IV.9.3
Puruṣottama	Puruṭōttamaṉ: IV.4.10, IV.5.1, IV.7.1-11
rakṣasa	irākkatar: #3, #5, IV.2.1, IV.3.7
Rāma	Irāmaṉ: III.10.6, IV.1.1, IV.1.2, IV.3.7, IV.9.9, V.4.6
Rāvaṇa	Irāvaṇai: IV.8.5
Ṛg (Veda)	Irukku: II.8.9, V.1.6
Rukmin	Uruppaṉ: IV.3.1
Rukmiṇī	Uruppiṇi: III.9.3, IV.1.5, IV.3.1
śakaṭa	cakaṭam: I.2.11,I.5.4, II.4.4, II.8.7
Śālagrāma	Cāḷakkirāmam: II.9.5, IV.7.9
Sāma (Veda)	Cāma: V.1.6
Śankara (Śiva)	Cankaraṉ: IV.7.3
śankha	cankam: I.7.6, I.8.2, II.1.1, II.8.9, III.3.9, IV.1.2, IV.1.7, IV.4.4, IV.7.5, IV.10.2, V.1.2, V.2.9

Śārnga	cārnkam: #12, I.4.6, I.6.7, I.7.1, I.7.7, IV.1.2,V.2.9, V.4.4
Śiśupāla	Cicupālan̲: IV.3.5
Sītā	Cītai: II.6.8, III.3.5, III.9.4, III.10.9, IV.1.2, IV.3.7
Śrīdara	Cirītaran̲: I.4.5, II.3.9, IV.6.2
Śrīmālika	Cīmālikan̲: II.7.8
Śukra	Cukkiran̲: I.8.7
Śūrpaṇakhā	Cūrppaṇakā: III.9.8
Tapas	tavam: V.3.3
Trīvikrama	Tirivikkiraman̲: I.7.9, II.3.7
Tulasī	tul̲āy: #9, I.3.7, III.7.5, IV.7.2
Uttamā	Uttamā: II.2.10
Uttarā	Uttarai: IV.9.6
Vaidehī	Vaitēvī: III.10.4, III.10.5, III.10.8, III.10.10
Vaikuṇṭha	Vaikuntam: I.2.1, II.1.10, III.5.11, III.10.10, IV.6.10, IV.7.9, V.4.10
Vaiṣṇava	Vaiṭṭaṇavan̲: V.1.2
Vaiśravaṇa	Vayicciravaṇan̲: I.3.5
valampuri	valampuri: I.3.4
Vāmana	Vāman̲an̲: I.9.5, II.3.8, II.9.2, V.1.10
Varuṇa	Varuṇan̲: I.3.6
Vasudeva	Vacutēvar: I.2.6, I.2.16
Vāsudeva	Vācutēvan̲: I.7.3, I.7.8, II.2.3, II.2.5, III.3.8, III.6.3
Vāsuki	Vācuki: I.6.10
Veda	Vētam: II.8.10, II.9.6, IV.3.11, IV.4.1, V.1.6, V.2.1
Vedānta	Vētānta: IV.3.11
Vibhīṣaṇa	Vipīṭaṇan̲: II.6.9, IV.9.2
Vijaya (Arjuna)	Vicayan̲: I.8.6, I.9.4
Viṣṇu	Viṭṭu: II.3.5
Yajur (Veda)	Ecu: V.1.6
Yama	Naman̲: IV.10.2-4, IV.10.6-9
Yaśodā	Acōtai: I.2.1, etc.

Bibliography

Aṇṇankarācāriyar, P.B. *Tivyaprapanta Pakavat Katāmrutam.* Kanci: V.N. Tēvanātaṉ, 1971.

---. *Nālāyira Tivviyap Pirapantam.* Kanci: V.N. Tēvanātaṉ, 1971.

---. *Tiruppallāṇṭum Periyāḻvār Tirumoḻiyum.* Kancheepuram: Granthamala Office, 1962.

Ate, Lynn M. "Periyāḻvār's Tirumoḻi – A Bāla Kṛṣṇa Text from the Devotional Period in Tamil Literature." Diss. University of Wisconsin, 1978.

Bhagavad Gīta. Trans. Annie Besant. Adyar: Theosophical Publishing, 1970.

Carmen, John, and Vasudha Narayanan. *The Tamil Veda: Piḷḷān's Interpretation of the Tiruvāymoḻi.* Chicago: University of Chicago, 1989.

Cēntaṉār, *Tiruppallāṇṭu.* Project Madurai. Web. January 18, 2008. <http://www.projectmadurai.org> .

Cīṉivācaṉ, Ma. Pe. *Periyāḻvār.* New Delhi: Sahitya Akademi, 1999.

Clooney, Francis X. "Nammalvar's Glorious Tiruvallaval." *Journal of the American Oriental Society* 111. 2 (1991): 260-276. <http://www.jstor.org>.

Cōmacuntaraṉār, Po. Vē. *Paripāṭal Mūlamum Uraiyum.*Tirunelvēli: Caiva Cittānta Nūṟpatippu, 1975.

Cutler, Norman. *Songs of Experience: the Poetics of Tamil Devotion.* Bloomington: Indiana University Press, 1987.

Dasgupta, Surendranath. *A History of Indian Philosophy.* Vol. 3. Delhi: Motilal Banarsidass, 1975.

Dehejia, Vidya. *Āṇṭāḷ and Her Path of Love.* Albany: State University of New York, 1990.

---. *Slaves of the Lord: the Path of the Tamil Saints.* New Delhi: Munshiram Manoharlal, 1988.

Desai, Kalpana S. *Iconography of Viṣṇu.* New Delhi: Abhinav Publications, 1973.

Doniger, Wendy. *Hindu Myths.* London: Penguin Books, 1975.

Edholm, Erik Af and Carl Suneson. "The Seven Bulls and Kṛṣṇa's Marriage to Nīlā/NappiNNai in Sanskrit and Tamil Literature." *Temenos* 8 (1972).

Farquhar, J. N. *An Outline of the Religious Literature of India.* Delhi: Motilal Benarsidass, 1967.

Gonda, Jan. *Aspects of Early Viṣṇuism.* Delhi: Motilal Benarsidass, 1969.

Haberman, David L. *Acting as a Way of Salvation.* Delhi: Motilal Benarsidass, 1988.

Hardy, Friedhelm. "Mādhavendra Purī: A Link between Bengal Vaiṣṇavism and South Indian 'Bhakti.'" *Journal of the Royal Asiatic Society of Great Britain and Ireland* 1 (1974): 23-41. <http://www.jstor.org>

---. *Viraha-bhakti: The early history of Kṛṣṇa devotion in South India.* New Delhi: Oxford University, 1983.

Hart, George L. III. *The Poems of Ancient Tamil.* Delhi: Oxford University, 1999.

---. *Poets of the Tamil Anthologies.* Princeton: Princeton University, 1979.

Hawley, John Stratton. *Krishna, the Butter Thief.* Princeton: Princeton University, 1983.

---. *Sūr Dās: Poet, Singer, Saint.* Seattle: University of Washington, 1984.

Hawley, John Stratton, and Mark Juergensmeyer. *Songs of the Saints of India.* New York: Oxford University, 1988.

Ilakkuvanār, S. *Tholkāppiyam (in English) with Critical Studies.* Madurai: Kural Neri, 1963.

Hopkins, Steven Paul. *Singing the Body of God: the Hymns of Vedāntadeśika in their South Indian Tradition.* New York: Oxford University Press, 2002.

Jaiswal, Suvira. *The Origin and Development of Vaiṣṇavism.* Delhi: Munshiram Manoharlal, 1967.

Kaliyanam, G. *Guide and History of Sri Andal Temple.* Srivilliputtur: Sri Nachiar Devastanam, 1971.

Kāsivicuvanātan̲, Mu. *Cilappatikāra Mūlamum Na. Mu. Vēnkaṭacāmi Nāṭṭār avarkaḷ Uraiyum.* Tirunelvēli: Caiva Cittānta, 1968.

Kinsley, David R. *The Divine Player: a Study of Kṛṣṇa Līlā.* Delhi: Motilal Banarsidass, 1979.

Lawall, Sarah, ed. *The Norton Anthology of World Literature.* Vol. A, *Beginnings to A.D. 100.* 2nd ed. New York: W.W. Norton, 2002.

The Mahābhārata. Trans. Kisari Mohan Ganguli. 1883-1896. Internet Sacred Text Archive. <http://www.sacred-texts.com>.

Majumdar, A. K. *Bhakti Renaissance.* Bombay: Bharatiya Vidya Bhavan, 1965.

---. *Caitanya: his life and doctrine.* Bombay: Bharatiya Vidya Bhavan, 1969.

Mumme, Patricia Y. "Grace and Karma in Nammalvar's Salvation." *Journal of the American Oriental Society* 107. 2 (1987): 257-266. <http://www.jstor.org>.

Narasimhan, Chakravarthi V. *The Mahābhārata: an English Version based on Selected Verses.* New York: Columbia University, 1965.

Narayan, R. K. *The Mahabharata.* New Delhi: Vision Books, 1992.

---. *The Ramayana.* Mysore: Indian Thought Publications, 1973.

Narayanan, Vasudha. "The Goddess Śrī: The Blossoming Lotus and Breast Jewel of Viṣṇu." *The Divine Consort: Rādhā and the goddesses of India.* Ed. John Stratton Hawley and Donna Marie Wulff. Berkeley: Graduate Theological Union, 1982. 224-237.

---. *The Way and the Goal: Expressions of Devotion in the Early Sri Vaiṣṇava Tradition.* Washington, D.C.: Institute for Vaishnava Studies, 1987.

---. *The Vernacular Veda.* Columbia: University of South Carolina, 1994.

Nilakanta Sastri, K. A. *History of South India*, 3rd ed. Madras: Oxford University, 1966.

Peterson, Indira V. "Singing of Place: Pilgrimage as Metaphor and Motif in the Tevaram Songs of the Tamil Saivite Saints."

Journal of the American Oriental Society 102.1 (1982): 69-90. <http://www.jstor.org>

Pope, G. U. *Tiruvācagam.* Madras: Ceṉṉai Palkalai Kaḻakam, 1970.

Prentiss, Karen Pechilis. *The Embodiment of Bhakti.* New York: Oxford University, 1999.

A Prose translation of the Harivamsha. Trans. Manmatha Nath Dutt. Calcutta: Elysium Press, 1897.

A Prose translation of the Vishnu Purana. Trans. Manmatha Nath Dutt. Varanasi: Chowkhamba Sanskrit Series, 1972.

Raghava Iyengar, M. "Date of Periyāḻvār." *Journal of Oriental Research* 2 (1928): 57-61.

---. "The Date of Śri Āṇṭāḷ." *Journal of Oriental Research* 1 (1927): 157-169.

Ramanujam, B. V. *History of Vaishnavism in South India upto Ramanuja.* Annamalai Nagar: Annamalai University, 1973.

Ramanujan, A. K. *Hymns for the Drowning.* Princeton: Princeton University, 1981.

---. *The Interior Landscape.* Bloomington: Indiana University, 1975.

---. *Poems of Love and War.* New York: Columbia University, 1985.

Ramanujan, A. K. and Norman Cutler. "From Classicism to Bhakti." *Essays on Gupta Culture.* Ed. Bardwell L. Smith. Delhi: Motilal Benarsidass., 1983. 177-214.

Raychaudhuri, Hemchandra. *Materials for the study of the Early History of the Vaishnava Sect.* New Delhi: Oriental Book Reprint Corporation, 1975.

Richman, Paula. *Extraordinary Child.* Honolulu: University of Hawai'i, 1997.

Rosen, Steven J., ed. *Vaiṣṇavism: Contemporary Scholars Discus the Gauḍiya Tradition.* New York: FOLK Books, 1992.

Sankar, K.G. "The Contemporaries of Periyāḻvār." *Journal of Oriental Research* 1 (1927): 336-349.

Schrader, F. Otto. *Introduction to the Pānchrātra and the Ahirbudnya Samhita.* Madras: Adyar Library and Research Center, 1973.

Smart, Ninian. *Doctrine and Argument in Indian Philosophy.* London: George Allen & Unwin, 1969.

Śrīmad Bhāgavata Mahāpurāṇa. Trans. C.L. Goswami. Gorakhpur: Gita Press, 1971.

Thera, Soma. "The Way of Mindfulness: the Satipatthāna Sutta and its Commentary." *The Theravada Library.* Access to Insight. 2005. <http://www.accesstoinsight.org/ lib/authors/ soma / wayof.html>

Vēnkaṭacāmi Nāṭṭār, Na. Mu. *Cilappatikāram mūlamum uraiyum.* Tirunelvēli: Caiva Cittānta,1968.

Vēnkaṭakiruṣṇan, Ma. A. *Periyavāccā<u>n</u> Piḷḷai aruḷiceyta Tiruppallāṇṭu Viyākkiyā<u>n</u>am.* Cennai: Cennaip Palkalaik Ka<u>l</u>akam, 2006.

Venkatesananda, Swami. *The Concise Rāmāyaṇa of Vālmīki.* Albany: State University of New York, 1988.

Zvelebil, Kamil. "Bull-Baiting Festivals in Tamil India." *Annals of the Náprstek Museum* 1 (1962).

---. *Tamil Literature.* Handbuch der Orientalistick 2.1. Leiden: E.J. Brill, 1975.

---. *Tamil Literature.* A History of Indian Literature X. 1. Ed. Jan Gonda. Wiesbaden: Otto Harrassowitz, 1974.

---. *The Smile of Murugan on Tamil Literature of South India.* Leiden: E. J. Brill, 1973.

Index

(Note: For an index of references and terms within
the translations, see citations listed in the appendices.)

āḻvār, 154
Āḻvārs, 4, 7, 8, 10, 11, 15, 16, 32, 39, 44, 51, 53, 193
Aṇṇankarācāriyar, P. B., 6, 11, 52, 118, 174, 193
Āṇṭāḷ, 8, 15, 18, 21, 157
antaryāmin, 212
antāti, 3, 15, 104
Arjuna, 30, 47, 48
āṟṟuppaṭai, 20
avatāras. *See* incarnations
Baladeva, 39, 42, 45, 55, 88, 189
Bāṇa, 47
Bhagavadgīta, 28, 29, 30, 53
bhagavas, xi
Bhāgavata Purāṇa, xi, 4, 29, 31, 32, 33, 39, 42, 45, 128
  Periyāḻvār's influence on, 32, 149
bhaktas, 4, 178
bhakti, 4, 24, 67
Bharata, 49
Bhaṭṭa Pirāṉ, 5, 8
Buddhism, 3, 10, 182
celvaṉ, 63
Cēntaṉār, 12
Cilappatikāram, 41, 44, 45
Cīṉivācaṉ, Ma. Pe., 9
Ciṟiya Tirumaṭal, 40
Clooney, Francis X., 20
Cutler, Norman, 19
darśana, 70, 85
Desai, Kalpana, 55
Devakī, 39, 70

devotion, 138
  accessibility, 14, 29, 30, 95, 124
  bewilderment, 34
  infatuation, 141, 149, 153
  joyful union, 22, 30, 35, 37, 212
  longing, 21, 30, 31, 44, 135
  maternal love, 4, 25, 27, 31, 33, 101
  unconditional love, x, 4, 34, 124, 203
  unworthiness, 135, 149
devotional movement, 3
Divine Works, 3, 9, 11, 13, 29, 40, 41, 42, 45, 53, 54, 189
Draupadī, 47
Duryodhana, 47, 48
Dvāraka, 46
goddess, 27, 50, 196
Govardhana Mountain, 43
grace, 7, 29, 36, 37, 43, 52, 200, 209
Guha, 49
Hanumaṉ, 49
Hardy, Friedhelm, 6, 7, 9, 24, 32, 44
Harivamśa, 7, 16, 34, 39, 43, 47, 70, 145, 196
Hart, George, 19
Hawley, John Stratton, 29
heaven, 27, 35, 196
hell, 28, 55, 182, 186, 200
Hiraṇya, 54
illusion, 17, 28, 88, 138

incarnations, 28, 29, 42, 53, 168, 196, 212
Jainism, 3, 10
Jayadratha, 48
Kaikeyī, 49
Kalittokai, 46
kāma, 23
Kāma, 47
Kaṃsa, 39, 46
Kaṇṇaṉ, 4, 50
kāppu, 11, 25, 121
karma, 36, 37
Kauravas, 47
Kingsley, David R., 34
Kṛṣṇa, 48
  personality, 16, 17, 31, 48, 98
  unconditioned nature, 34, 109, 124, 128, 131
  uncontrolled behavior, 17, 34, 44, 45
Kṛṣṇa mythology, 15, 28, 30, 32, 39
  ass demon, 42
  bow festival, 46
  butter theft, 40
  calf demon, 42
  conquored wrestlers, 46
  controlled bulls, 45
  cross cousin marriage, 45, 109, 157
  demon cart, 40
  Devakī's children slain, 39
  eloped with Rukmiṇī, 46
  fell woodapple fruit, 42
  freed Vasudeva, 46
  Govardhana Mountain, 43
  heron demon, 42
  horse demon, 42
  in Yādava community, 46
  Kāliya, 43
  Kṛṣṇa eats dirt, 42
  Kṛṣṇa tied to a mortar, 40
  Kṛṣṇa's birth, 39
  Kṛṣṇa's dances, 45
  married 16,100 maidens, 47
  Pralamba, 42
  Pūtanā, 40
  returned four children to life, 47
  severed Bāṇa's arms, 47
  shaved Rukmin's head, 46
  slayed an elephant, 46
  stole from milkmaids, 44
  stole *kaṟpaka* tree, 47
  toppled laurel trees, 41
  toppled wild lime tree, 41
Kulacēkaraṉ, 15, 18, 31
Kūrattāḻvāṉ, 30
kuravai dance, 45
kuṟinci, 22, 174
Lakṣmaṇa, 49
līlā, 34, 98, 124
Mahābhārata, 16, 47, 51
  gambling match, 47
  Kṛṣṇa as a charioteer, 48
  Kṛṣṇa as a messenger, 48
  Kṛṣṇa hid the sun, 48
  Pāṇḍavas exiled, 47
  water for Arjuna's horses, 48
Maḻicaipirāṉ, 10, 53
Māṇikkavācakar, 161
Mankaiyāḻvār, 15, 18, 40, 47, 70
Markaṇḍeya, 51
māyā. *See* illusion
Māyaṉ, 67
Mumme, Patricia, 36
Mūṉṟān Tiruvantāti, 51
Murukaṉ, 20, 24
Mutal Tiruvantāti, 40, 51
Nācciyār Tirumoḻi, 8
nakha śikha, 70
Nālāyira Divyaprabandham. *See Divine Works*

namāvali, 186
Nammāḻvār, 15, 21, 30, 37, 47
Namo Nārāyaṇa, 11, 36, 50, 186
Namuci, 55
Nanda, 40
Nāṉmukaṉ Tiruvantāti, 10
Nappiṉṉai. *See* Piṉṉai
Nārada, 196
Naraka, 47
Nāraṇa. *See* Nārāyaṇa
Nārāyaṇa, 3, 6, 27, 37, 39, 50, 53, 54, 63, 67
  twelve names, 13, 104
Narayanan, Vasudha, 11, 174, 178
Nāthamuni, 3, 9
Neṭumāṟaṉ, 5, 171
Nilakantha Sastri, K.A., 10
Pakaḻikkuttar, 24
pallāṇṭu, 7, 12, 25
Pancajana, 46
Pāncajanya, 46
Pāncarātra, 174, 178
Pāṇḍavas, 47
Parikṣit, 48
Paripāṭal, 20, 53, 54, 55, 56
paruvam, 24
Periya Tirumoḻi, 18, 41, 47, 52, 70
Periyāḻvār
  'Great Āḻvār', 9, 12
  date, 6, 18, 171
  innovations, 5, 11, 15, 16, 18, 24, 27, 31, 98, 189
  life of, 5, 6, 8
Periyavāccāṉ Piḷḷai, 11
personal god, 4, 17, 23, 28, 30, 31, 34, 209
Perumāḷ Tirumoḻi, 31
Peterson, Indira, 21
pilgrimage, 21
piḷḷaittamiḻ, 5, 24
Piṉṉai, 45, 109, 158
plant names, 61
poetic voice, 9, 13, 16, 23, 24, 30, 32, 44, 104
Pope, G. W., 161
Poykai, 40
prapatti, 36, 200
Pūtanā, 40
Rāma, 3, 20
Rāma mythology
  attacked the ocean, 50
  conquored Lanka, 50
  demon deer, 49
  epithets, 49
  Hanumaṉ's speech to Sītā, 49
  Rāma's exile, 49
  Rāvaṇa, 49
  severed Rāvaṇa's heads, 50
  shot seven trees, 49
  Śūrpanakhā, 49
  Vibhīṣaṇa, 196
religious acts, 36, 37, 200, 209
rhyme, Tamil, 59, 85, 149
Richman, Paula, 24
Rukmiṇī, 46
salvation, 36, 37, 52, 63, 196, 200, 209
Sāndīpani, 46
Satipatthāna Sutta, 182
Satyabhāmā, 46
sectarianism, 10, 53, 75
Śiśupāla, 46
Sītā, 49
Śrīvilliputtūr, 9
  (also Putuvai, Villiputtūr, Puttūr), 5
Śūrpanakhā, 49
Tamil classical poetry, 19, 24
  heroic poetry, 20, 21
  love poetry, 19, 21, 23, 44, 157
temples, 20, 21

Tiruccantaviruttam, 53
Tiruccentūr Piḷḷaittamiḻ, 24
Tirukkuṟantāṇṭakam, 52
tirumoḻi, 12, 59
fourth line, 17, 25, 75, 92, 98, 128
structure, 13, 15, 17, 24
Tirumoḻi, 3, 12, 13, 19
dramatic continuity, 15, 25
folk roots, 9, 13, 16, 19
Tirumurukāṟṟupaṭai, 21, 24
Tiruppallāṇṭu, 9, 63
Tiruppāvai, 8
Tiruvācakam, 161
Tiruvāymoḻi, 15, 22, 47
Tiruviruttam, 52
Tolkāppiyam, 157
transliteration, 61
tulasī, 61
untipaṟa, 161
Vaikuṇṭha, 27
Vaiṣṇava mythology, 39
babe on a banyon leaf, 51
Baladeva, 55
boar incarnation, 54
churned ambrosia, 52
dwarf incarnation, 54
ended Śiva's curse, 52
epithets, 51
fish incarnation, 53
five weapons, 75
Kalki, 55
man-lion incarnation, 54
Paraśurāma, 55
plough and pestle, 189
saved the elephant, 52
swan incarnation, 56
tortoise incarnation, 54
Vasudeva, 39, 70
Vāsuki, 52
Vedas, 7, 61
Vēyar, 5
Vibhīṣaṇa, 50
Vijayavenugopalan, G., 161
Viṣṇu, 3
Viṣṇu Purāṇa, 32, 39, 43, 47, 145
Viṭṭucittaṉ, 5, 6, 7, 8, 12
vyūha, 174
Yaśodā, 23, 29, 30, 32, 34, 37, 40, 45, 61, 70
yoga, 36
Zvelebil, Kamil, 3, 20, 24

SASA Books is a project of the South Asian Studies Association, a recognized 501(c)3 non-profit, public benefit corporation of scholars and others interested in South Asia.

Using a *pro bono* model, SASA Books is dedicated to publishing high quality, fully vetted scholarly material. The SASA website is www.sasia.org. SASA Books can be found at www.sasabooks.org.

www.ingramcontent.com/pod-product-compliance
Lightning Source LLC
Chambersburg PA
CBHW062012220426
43662CB00010B/1292
* 9 7 8 0 9 8 3 4 4 7 2 1 4 *